HIDDEN BATTLES ON UNSEEN FRONTS

HIDDEN BATTLES ON UNSEEN FRONTS

Stories of American Soldiers with Traumatic Brain Injury and PTSD

BY
PATRICIA P. DRISCOLL AND CELIA STRAUS
FOR THE
ARMED FORCES FOUNDATION

CASEMATE
Philadelphia & Newbury

Published in the United States of America and Great Britain in 2010 by
CASEMATE
908 Darby Road, Havertown, PA 19083
and
17 Cheap Street, Newbury, Berkshire, RG14 5DD

Copyright 2009 © The Armed Forces Foundation
Reprinted November 2010

Paperback Edition: ISBN 978-1-935149-40-8
Digital Edition: ISBN 978-1-61200-0251

Cataloging-in-publication data is available from the Library of Congress
and the British Library.

Printed and bound in the United States of America.

For a complete list of Casemate titles please contact:

CASEMATE PUBLISHERS (US)
Telephone (610) 853-9131, Fax (610) 853-9146
E-mail: casemate@casematepublishing.com

CASEMATE PUBLISHERS (UK)
Telephone (01635) 231091, Fax (01635) 41619
E-mail: casemate-uk@casematepublishing.co.uk

Mixed Sources
Product group from well-managed
forests and other controlled sources
www.fsc.org   Cert no. SW-COC-002283
© 1996 Forest Stewardship Council
FSC

CONTENTS

*For the
men and women who have
sacrificed so much to
serve us so well.
We honor you.*

FOREWORD

By Brigadier General Loree K. Sutton, MD

For many of our warriors, "coming home" is not the end of war—far from it.

Leaving the battlefield far behind, the battle often continues—in hearts and minds, relationships and communities after deployment. Families and loved ones often find themselves fighting a battle, too, striving to understand and support the person they care for after a life-changing experience that they may not want to remember, let alone talk about. Warriors may feel isolated in a frightening and unfamiliar struggle to cope with memories of war, one of the most intense experiences a human being can endure.

The intensely personal stories in this book place a human face on the adversity of war that frequently remains hidden from public attention: the challenge of post-traumatic stress, concussion (also known as mild traumatic brain injury), and other psychological health issues among our returning warriors. Despite the struggles, those who have shouldered the adversity of war may also seize this opportunity to experience post-traumatic growth—deepening one's faith, cherishing relationships, reordering life priorities, and extending compassion and empathy for others.

Many will adapt to their "new normal" in a few weeks or months; some will take additional time to come to terms with their experience. Killing in combat, witnessing or participating in atrocities, losing beloved buddies, coming home to a strained or even fractured marriage, experiencing "survivor's guilt," witnessing the death of innocent civilians, craving the adrenalin surge of living in the shadow of death —such are the timeless challenges known to warriors of all ages—past, present and future.

Reintegration with home, work, family and community can be arduous—as one sergeant put it, "It's tough to move from being a target to shopping at Target!" Some find that memories can be even more disturbing than the actual experience, because what they once believed could touch them only on the battlefield has now "followed me home." Where sleep was once a rejuvenating respite, slumber may now be punctuated with nightly replays of combat's peril. Further, the routine of family life may be overwhelmed by demands unseen but remembered, compounded by the frustration of loved ones who are attempting to understand what their warrior is experiencing.

The challenges are real. Celia Straus' and Patricia Driscoll's timely book—a story of stories—is ultimately a story of hope, strength, love, courage, forgiveness and redemption.

In these pages, you will witness the accounts of real warriors and learn of their battles at home and at war, as well as the strengths they have claimed along the way. These gripping stories harness the power and the promise of recovery in the most poignant manner possible— by seeing through the eyes of those who have actually lived it.

Successful recovery and reintegration call for resilience—the human capacity to adapt and grow in the face of stress, adversity, trauma and tragedy. Realizing this capacity requires the sometimes painful work of finding meaning, purpose and value in life's harshest experiences, marked by breakthroughs, heartaches, lapses, triumphs and, at times, despair. Hope must prevail—we are NOT alone.

It is especially fitting that this book includes essays from caring professionals now in the field supporting our warriors. These first-person accounts describe the practical mechanisms of resilience and recovery—a holistic union of mind, body and spirit. Many are informed by their own experiences with war and trauma, and know firsthand the vital imperative of keeping hope on the horizon. These stories provide a real-world view of how warriors and their families interact with psychologists, social workers, chaplains and other "fellow travelers" on this journey from trauma to transformation. Troops wage war; healers wage hope.

In many ways, this book answers the call to a sacred duty as old as the family of man: to tell the story of the wounded warrior. Repeated throughout history and literature, this call marks the human need for meaning, purpose and a sense of belonging beyond one's self. Consider Hamlet on his deathbed, making his final request to Horatio, his dearest and most trusted friend: "If thou didst ever hold me in thy heart, absent thee from felicity awhile and enter my harsh world and draw my breath in pain to tell my story."

Withdraw yourself from your comforts to see through my eyes, says Hamlet. Tell the world my story.

The warriors whose stories are collected in this book demand to be heard. The extraordinary candor of these men and women reflects a courageous willingness to make their most intimate fears—and enduring hopes—part of the public record of our fellow Americans at war. This gift of service and sacrifice symbolizes the trust and love that, in our best moments, enables humans to act selflessly on the battlefields of war and peace. These lessons, gained through time, courage, patience, prayer and fellowship, will lead the way home for warriors throughout the ages. We are privileged to stand on the shoulders of such giants.

Someone once said: "Be kinder than necessary, for everyone we meet is fighting some sort of battle." Believe it. Psychological injuries —leading to unseen battles on hidden fronts—are real, urgent and potentially lethal. We are NOT alone . . . seeking support IS an act of strength and courage. We are all in this journey of life together. Perhaps that is the greatest blessing of all.

Army Brigadier General Loree K. Sutton, MD
January 2009

Note: The views expressed herein are those of BG Loree K. Sutton and not necessarily those of the U.S. government.

"Every war has its signature wound. In World War I it was poison gas-damaged lungs. In World War II it was radiation that caused cancer. In Vietnam it was Agent Orange that caused neurological damage and skin disorders; and for the Iraq and Afghanistan conflicts it is TBI. Since August 2007, when screening for TBI, 83% of wounded troops were diagnosed with TBI, the largest group being 21-year-olds."

—"The Hidden War: American Soldiers vs TBI," Tracy Williams, *New Orleans Picayune*, May 5, 2008

INTRODUCTION

By Patricia P. Driscoll,
President, The Armed Forces Foundation

For almost three years we at the Armed Forces Foundation (AFF) have labored to bring *Hidden Battles on Unseen Fronts* to publication. I am honored to have led our effort and am grateful to the wounded warriors who offered their stories as well as to the military and civilian healthcare providers that graciously provided their insight. I hope readers everywhere will find these stories of courage inspirational, and the essays by the caregivers and advocates illuminating.

The nature of our work at AFF is defined by the changing needs of those we serve, particularly as the war in Iraq enters its seventh year. AFF designs programs to address new issues facing troops such as Traumatic Brain Injury (TBI) and Post-Traumatic Stress Disorder (PTSD). *Hidden Battles* is the result of our commitment to this goal, with all royalties from this work going directly to the front line of support for wounded warriors and their families.

The modesty of our warriors is extremely admirable. Many troops dismiss their sacrifice as "part of the job." But how many jobs demand the sacrifice of sanity? What other job requires infinite amounts of courage, caring, resourcefulness and resiliency to win against the odds? And how many jobs challenge the employee's family just as much? Only our nation's service members can answer that question.

Never in our history as a nation have we had a more talented, experienced, committed, and diverse armed forces. They are the clearest demonstration of our destiny as a nation and for that they deserve to be heard and helped; this is the goal of *Hidden Battles*.

1

One in six combat troops returning from Iraq suffers from some form of brain trauma. These troops are at a heightened risk for developing a host of physical and mental symptoms in both the short and long term. They may struggle for months or a lifetime with depression, memory loss, an inability to concentrate, irritability, sleep problems, flashbacks and much more. What makes TBI and PTSD so troublesome is that these mental health conditions are unseen and can be undiagnosed. Those who suffer from TBI and PTSD often feel stigmatized by their symptoms and hide their wounds instead of taking steps to heal them.

It is my sincere hope that the stories contained in this book will raise awareness of these unseen wounds and create a more open and helpful dialogue. Our troops and their families make valuable and honorable contributions to the welfare of our nation every day and every hour, and have much to teach us. We at AFF are still learning from them and I hope you will as well.

THE ARMED FORCES FOUNDATION

In 2001 the Armed Forces Foundation (AFF) was established under the U.S. Department of Defense's military support program. AFF offers vital assistance to active-duty and retired personnel, National Guard, Reserve Components and military families as they cope with difficult circumstances. The Armed Forces Foundation is dedicated to providing comfort and solace to members of the armed forces community through financial support, career counseling, housing assistance and recreational therapy programs. AFF has been recognized by the President of the United States, the Department of Defense, the Department of Veterans Affairs, the Department of Education and the Department of Energy for its dedication to America's service members. For more information on how you can help AFF carry out its mission visit www.armedforces foundation.org.

HIDDEN BATTLES
ON UNSEEN FRONTS

1

DEPLOYED, DECORATED AND LIVING IN A CAR

The Story of US Marine Corps Sergeant Christopher Horman

"I was about 50 meters away when it blew up. The blast knocked me off my feet and into the side of a Humvee. I must have blacked out for a minute or two, but when I came to there was nothing left of the vehicle. No remnants; just char and a crater."

When 28-year-old Christopher Harmon was discharged on May 26, 2006, after eight years in the Marine Corps, he had a chestful of decorations and a pile of honorable citations.

During his deployment to Iraq in 2005 Chris led an elite bomb squad patrolling the neighborhoods and alleyways of Baghdad and smaller towns like Kandari, site of Abu Ghraib Prison. During the siege of the prison on April 5, 2005, Chris and his 15-man team were the only ground troops outside the walls during the precision-timed offensive. "We were on a foot patrol at the rear of the insurgents. They didn't know how many of us there were but we knew there were over 100 of them, so I told everyone to spread out."

Chris sprinted from man to man during the 54-minute firefight, encouraging them to be aggressive. "My machine gunner shot 850 rounds. It was like nothing I've ever experienced." Afterward, US military officers would call the siege the most sophisticated and concerted insurgent attack up to that point in the war, and would single out Chris' leadership as critical to the attackers' defeat. The next day, while securing a deserted car suspected of containing an IED, the vehicle exploded. "I was about 50 meters away when it blew up. The blast knocked me off my feet and into the side of a Humvee. I must have

5

blacked out for a minute or two, but when I came to there was nothing left of the vehicle. No remnants; just char and a crater. It scared the living shit out of me."

While his discharge papers described compression injuries to his back, knees and ankles, and a chronically dislocated shoulder from repeatedly jumping out of vehicles while carrying heavy backpacks and equipment, as well as his two-year struggle with PTSD, Chris was not tested for Traumatic Brain Injury.

Chris returned to Seattle with his wife, Kathy, and their three boys, Austin, 9 (from a previous marriage), Zachary, 5, and Xandar, 2. Kathy was from North Carolina and she'd never been out of the state. "Except for worrying about Chris' safety, the boys and I had been comfortable at Camp LeJeune. I didn't see the logic of moving to Seattle but I was willing to try it if that was what Chris wanted to do. The hardest part was getting out there a month before he was discharged." She had met his parents once. Chris and Kathy moved in with Chris' father and stepmother, and almost immediately the situation soured. "Before I went to Iraq I was open and happy; but after I got back I started getting depressed. I was scared of going out in crowds. When Kathy and I would go to the grocery store, I'd break out in a cold sweat if I couldn't find her. The smallest things like a pop or a bang made me jump."

Chris' VA benefits hadn't kicked in yet, and he had to find a way to support his family. He started job hunting. Personable and, at the time, highly motivated, Chris overcame his lack of a college degree and mental problems and found a job at the Union Pacific Railroad as a conductor in training. During his time in Iraq Chris had been given 80mm of Proszac a day for his PTSD, an amount that shocked the physicians at the Seattle Veterans' hospital where he went for treatment. "Why the hell are you on a major anxiety drug?" one doctor said. "I wouldn't give this to anyone in your condition, particularly in combat." The doctors experimented with various cocktails of medications: Zoloft, Paxil, Efferex, Cymbalta and others, singly and in combinations. Each prescription had side effects and none really worked.

Then, after just six weeks, the Union Pacific training program was suddenly dismantled and Chris was let go. He became depressed and anxious and withdrew into himself. "I tuned out. I'd stare at the television all day and see nothing. I had headaches and ringing in my ears, but most of all I was drowning in a black hole." His father, an Army veteran of 32 years, couldn't understand why his son, the youngest of four brothers, two of whom were deceased, could not get his act together. They fought. "He yelled at me, 'The way you're acting, you're spitting on all your dead brothers.' I took Kathy and the kids and left the house." Chris moved his family to Spokane to live with his birth mother, whom he had not seen since he was two, but he was unable to find work and returned to Seattle, this time moving in with his brother's family.

He was accepted into "Hard Hats," a program training military veterans to become sheet metal workers. "The problem was, I was out of shape and had gained weight and my body couldn't take it. I'd try to lift or carry those heavy sheets of metal, and my back would just give out." Two weeks into the job Chris told the foreman he couldn't physically handle the work. A few weeks later he found another job, this time as a security guard at $6.00 an hour. But his depression was worsening along with disturbing new symptoms such as loss of memory. He was unable to concentrate on the simplest of tasks.

"I got so paranoid. I was in a state of panic most of the time. I don't think people understand the pain of what goes on in your head. You've lost yourself and it's scary as shit. No one sympathized. I mean it wasn't as though I'd lost a leg or gotten shot up. It was all in my head." After ten minutes on the security guard job, Chris' back, knees and legs would seize up, putting him in excruciating pain. He had to quit. "I had no money for gas so I spent a lot of time on the Internet trying to find a job. My brother didn't understand what was going on. His wife got fed up with us and had the cable disconnected. We had a big argument and I said, 'Okay, I guess we're uninvited.'" Chris and his family were homeless.

Kathy sent her oldest son, Austin, back to North Carolina to live with his father. "It was the hardest thing I've ever done in my life," she says. "I'd raised him by myself, and it broke my heart to have to send him where I knew he wasn't wanted, but we weren't getting by and I didn't know what else to do." To make ends meet, Chris and Kathy sold their belongings and pawned their wedding rings. Yet a few days later they and their two sons were living out of their car. Someone told a radio station about their plight and it broadcast their story, which raised enough money to pay for a cheap motel and food for the two boys.

"I wanted to give up so many times," Kathy recalls, "but even at his most depressed, Chris believed we could do it." At the end of their rope, they were rescued by the Marine Corps in the form of a final check for moving expenses for transitioning out of the military. They got their rings out of the pawnshop, packed up their few belongings and drove across country back to Raleigh, North Carolina where Kathy's older sister lived. However, instead of improving, their lives went downhill.

"We got Austin back and moved in with Patty. But her husband was a drunk and a month after we got there he threatened me with a shotgun. That night we packed up our bags and left. It was the worst of the worst. We'd sold all our furniture, and the souvenirs I'd brought back from my deployments. Everything we owned was in three Rubber Maid tubs. By 3 a.m. we'd been driving around Raleigh for hours." The next morning Chris called "Marine 4 Life" asking for help. Within 24 hours the Marine 4 Life team had moved the family into a motel.

It was then that Chris and his family first came to the attention of the Armed Forces Foundation. The Marine 4 Life team contacted the Foundation requesting financial assistance for Chris and his family while they helped him look for a job. The foundation immediately paid for the family's lodging and food for the week. Chris interviewed with Norfolk Southern Railroad and there was a good possibility of employment. At the end of the week the Marines moved the family into the Warrior homes at Camp LeJeune, fully furnished on-base housing designated for injured veterans and their families. Better yet, during their two and a half months stay there Chris was able to get regular treatment for his PTSD symptoms. A number of organizations, including the AFF and the Semper Fi Fund, covered the family's expenses. Chris's paranoia and depression lessened, and the night-mares that awakened him three and four times each night began to dissipate. The worst was over.

The position with Norfolk Southern was still iffy, so in August when Chris was offered a job as a manager trainee with the Kangaroo

Pantry in Greenville he took it, even though the starting salary was miniscule and there was no health coverage until he spent a year with the company. The Semper Fi Fund helped move the family and paid their first and last month's rent so that they could get settled into an apartment. Austin and Zachary needed to begin school. The Armed Forces Foundation contacted Aaron's Furniture to see if they would donate furniture since the family still owned nothing but a few bundles of clothing. Aarons donated a living room suite, bunk beds and a toddler bed for the boys' room, a bed and chest for Chris and Kathy, and a washer and a dryer. By now Chris was receiving $1,100.00 a month in Veteran's benefits but he still couldn't feed his family, get treatment for his PTSD, and pay the rent.

In early October, Norfolk Southern accepted him into their conductor training program, and Chris decided to take their offer as a second chance to find the security he and his family so desperately needed. The railroad job came with medical benefits after two weeks of work, as well as higher pay. "His optimism always won me over," Kathy says. "I remember times when we had to drop everything and leave, but I always trusted him because he never gave up. He said 'My boys deserve better and I promise I'm going to get it for them.'" The family moved into an apartment in Norfolk, enrolled the two older boys in school, and Chris started training. They had to pawn their wedding rings a second time in February 2008 to pay their electrical and heating bills, but by the end of March Chris completed his training and became a conductor for Norfolk Southern. He had made good on his promise.

MEDALS

Combat Action Ribbon (Iraq), 2 Marine Corps Good Conduct Medals, Humanitarian Service Medal, 6 Sea Service Deployment Ribbon, Armed Forces Expeditionary Medal (Haiti), Iraq Campaign Medal, Global War on Terrorism Service Medal, National Defense Service Medal, 2 Navy Unit Commendations.

"The story of Mr. Woodruff's recovery is nothing short of a miracle. He considers himself lucky to have received incredible care. Not only did he have to go through surgery and grafts to repair the physical damage to his face and head, but needed rehabilitative for the unseen damage to his memory, thought processes and speech. In addition to his initial treatment upon returning from Iraq, he needed constant follow-up therapy to recuperate his cognitive abilities."

—"Brain Injured Newspaperman Speaks Out For Returning Iraq War Veterans," Fern Cohen, www.ezinearticles.com

2

DECIDING WHO IS SANE ENOUGH TO FIGHT
The Ethics of Military Medicine in a Time of War

By Alice Psirakis, LCSW

Specialist D, a young 20-year-old soldier, walked out of the psychiatrist's office and sat in the waiting room until we could get his paperwork ready. He was a mobilizing soldier, having just arrived on post one short day ago. His unit was being processed through the medical stations when a red flag popped up, sending him over to our department for an evaluation.

The soldier had informed the medical provider that he was on Depakote, a medicine used for bipolar disorder or, sometimes, as an overall mood stabilizer. Anytime a soldier revealed that he was on any psychotropic medication, an instant referral to Behavioral Health was generated for clearance to continue mobilizing. In this soldier's case, the psychiatrist did not feel comfortable clearing him because he would most likely be unable to get blood work done in theater (Iraq) to monitor his Depakote levels. It was dangerous to deploy someone who was on Depakote or Lithium because of the extreme heat, so those medications were automatic disqualifiers.

But when I handed the soldier the paperwork containing the information that would generate the process to return him back home, I felt a piercing inside me. The soldier looked at me, about to break down. He was heartbroken as though we had just crushed his dream. Whenever I used to tell my dad about grandiose plans I had and he would ask me a thousand logistical questions, I'd always say to him in an exasperated tone, "Dad, you're such a dream-squasher."

11

In that moment, I felt like a dream-squasher. He looked at me with such a look of devastation that I felt sorry for him almost as if we were responsible for doing something cruel to him. Imagine that—I felt guilty for not sending someone to war. What had my world come to? The existence of that type of guilt itself seemed warped.

And yet, I felt it.

Sergeant K was a tall, husky, 49-year-old Army Reservist who was mobilizing for the third time to a combat zone—one tour in Afghanistan and one in Iraq had earned him the diagnosis of Post Traumatic Stress Disorder (PTSD). He suffered from nightmares, intrusive memories and emotional numbing. Yet here he was, having volunteered to deploy once again—a phenomenon all too common. He came through our doors as a self-referral, with a primary complaint of insomnia. After an extensive psychosocial history it was clear that SGT K was suffering from PTSD. During a session in which I encouraged him to discuss his intrusive memories, he told me about a young Afghan girl who was killed. SGT K broke down, sobbing as he remembered this, feeling that he was somehow responsible for her death. But SGT K was insistent on being redeployed. He had not come to Behavioral Health to get sent back home—he just needed to sleep. He told me, "If I could just sleep I'll feel better. My guys need me." I couldn't argue with him about that.

But I also remember telling him that I thought this third deployment was going to be the psychological death of him. SGT K agreed.

Yet Sergeant K had been training effectively with his unit over the past few months. He was mission-oriented, taking care of his lower-enlisted soldiers the way an NCO (Non-Commissioned Officer) is supposed to. He had a vast supply of knowledge and experience to contribute that only a seasoned combat veteran could have. He hadn't frozen or panicked at all during any simulated fire and training exercises. Other than his insomnia, none of his other PTSD symptoms seemed to be affecting his training at this current time—*this current time* being the operative phrase. He wanted to deploy. He felt a responsibility toward his younger, less experienced soldiers who were counting on him during this deployment.

And the truth was, no concerning training or behavioral issues had been observed or reported by his leadership thus far. Considering the circumstances, SGT K was functioning extremely well.

After a short-term treatment regimen combining brief psychotherapy and medication management, we decided to deploy SGT K on antidepressants, with instructions to follow up at Combat Stress Control once he got to Iraq.

While I served as the Chief of Behavioral Health Services at one of the largest Army deployment installations from 2004 to 2007, that was my entire life. Day in and day out, my staff and I were tasked with deciding who went to war, who returned home, who would deploy at a later date to the combat zone, who could redeploy and who couldn't. The military refers to this as Fitness for Duty Evaluations. Thousands of soldiers walked through our doors awaiting a disposition that, no doubt, would alter the course of their lives.

I was a New York State-licensed clinical social worker; a member of the National Association of Social Workers, whose code of ethics highlights values such as client self-determination (the client is ultimately responsible for his own course of action and decision-making). I had spent years working as a community-based public health social worker. But I was also a Captain in the United States Army. I was a medical officer whose corps motto was "To Conserve the Fighting Strength." Years ago, I had sworn to protect my country and serve as a personal reflection of the Army's core values. My warrior ethos talked about things like, "I will always place the mission first." And so here I was—a social worker plucked out of the civilian world and now mobilized to carry out the Army's mission.

And I was responsible for placing the mission first.

Very few people understand the cognitive dissonance that begins to take place here, and the potential ethical conflict that starts brewing between what I may think a soldier needs and what the Army needs. As a military social worker serving in a time of war, sometimes it was unclear to me who I worked for. In my civilian life the answer was easy—the client of course! In the military the answer was much more blurred. Who was I responsible to? Where did my clinical loyalties lie? Did I work for the individual soldier? Or did I work for the collective Army as a whole?

The reality, I discovered, was that I worked for both simultaneously—a balancing act which would prove to be a huge challenge over the course of my tenure at Fort Dix. I knew in my heart that client-self determination was a paramount part of my professional ethos, but that was not a value to be emphasized in the Army. It didn't matter if someone *wanted* to go to war; they just *had* to. And we had to figure out if they could. However, I need to make something clear here: neither I, nor the team that I supervised, ever operated in any unethical ways. When my team and I made a decision whether or not to deploy a soldier, we struggled and struggled to make the *right* one. While I understand that civilians who read this may judge the clinical decisions I made as compromising, my hope is to offer an insider's perspective and expose them to the intricacies of the military mental health system during a time of war.

When we deployed SGT K we were not saying that he did not have Post Traumatic Stress Disorder—quite the contrary. We were deploying him with PTSD. To many, that is simply disturbing, and I can understand and respect that. But allow me to explain how that is even possible in the world of military medicine. The secret is this: It all came down to *level of functioning.*

The last criterion in the DSM IV-TR diagnostic guide for almost all psychological disorders asks: how severely do these symptoms impact the person's current social and psychological level of functioning? In other words, how distressing is this condition/illness to the person in their interpersonal relationships, in their place of work, at school, in how they interact with the world in general? Taking this into consideration, we recognized how two people with a diagnosis of PTSD may have very different symptom manifestations of it. Some are completely incapacitated, while others exhibit fewer symptoms, causing them lesser distress.

There were so many other factors that guided my decision-making: where was this soldier deploying? Would he be "outside the wire" and thus potentially exposed to violence if not combat most of the time? What was his MOS (Military Occupation Specialty); in other words, what was his job? Was he a computer technician who would be inside the wire fixing computers most of the day or was he a gunner going on several patrols a week, probably engaging in live fire exchanges? Was he an administrative clerk who was helping out the Executive Officer all day or was he a truck driver, going back and forth to different bases in Iraq? How savvy was his command about mental health issues, and could we trust him to take care of his soldiers if he observed behavior that concerned him?

Was there a combat stress team deploying with his unit? Could the soldier receive his psychotropic medication while in theater (the combat zone)? What was the soldier's previous level of traumatic exposure? What would his potential level of traumatic exposure be in the combat zone this time around? How was he reacting during training here in the States? Was he freezing up during the simulated mortar attacks? Was he withdrawing and isolating himself from his comrades? Was he unable to work as a team player? Did he run for cover every time the cannon went off at 1700hours daily on post? How disruptive was his hypervigilance to his everyday functioning? The list goes on and on . . .

It is very difficult to predict human behavior and psychological deterioration in general, much less in a combat zone. And on some level, that is what I was being asked to do. The reality is, not everyone is built and wired the same way. We don't really know why some people will break down while others don't. We don't really know why some people will get PTSD when others, having endured similar trauma, won't. We have some ideas, but we don't truly know. And the truth of the matter is, on some level, as clinicians, we took a risk answering these questions and hoped that our clinical expertise, coupled with a prayer here and there, would prove to be the right answer.

The front cover of the June 16, 2008 issue of Time magazine was titled, "America's Medicated Army, bringing to light the controversy of deploying soldiers on medication or giving them meds to assist them with symptoms while in combat. I never saw that as unethical—I saw it as practical, a necessary evil almost. In a rose-colored glasses world, that would not be the case. But the reality of war dictates otherwise.

About 45 million Americans are on antidepressants—all living, working and functioning on very different levels. The military is a microcosm of American society. Being on an antidepressant does not automatically mean that you are not functioning. We tried to look at each soldier individually, and never use a cookie-cutter approach while ultimately trying to *conserve the fighting strength*.

I found out over a year later that SGT K had come by Behavioral Health to say hello to us after he returned from his third tour in Iraq. I was no longer working there when he came in, but I often wonder how he is doing now.

3

LANDMINE BLAST TO A SOUL
The Story of Army SPC Walter Blackston

"She asked me if I couldn't move back with my parents until this was all straightened out. I said, 'Ma'am, I'm 47 years old. I can't move back in with my parents. I need to get my life back.'"

During the spring of 2003 Walter Blackston was working around the clock, responsible for far more than his formal assignment as Chief of Communications for Task Force 44 out of Afghanistan. He headed up communications for Med-Com, XVIIIth Airborne Corps, gave multiple briefings a day to Medevac crews, and ran convoys that crisscrossed the countryside outside of Kabul.

At 42, divorced with two grown sons, Walter was one of the older reservists called up after September 11. Moreover he had fully recovered from injuries to his face and eyes when a simulator hand grenade had blown up during a training accident right before his deployment with the 48th Combat Support Hospital, Fort Meade, Maryland. His work was earning him a number of medals and citations.

While deployed out of Bagram, Afghanistan, he'd even been featured in the newspaper *Freedom Watch* for inventing a 24-hour paging system that enabled doctors and nurses to respond to an emergency at the field hospital far faster than before. So with only a week left before returning home, while he was keen to get back to his family, he felt that he'd contributed to the war effort.

May 24, 2003 started out busy as usual. "Ever since the invasion of Iraq we'd been shorthanded so I was doing a little bit of everything. Around 1800 I got the word that command was sending me and three medics to retrieve some soldiers 'who were down.' That's about all they told us. Not how it happened or if they were alive or dead. The location coordinates they gave us were bad so it took us a while to find the site, and when we got there we saw the smoke in the distance. A Black Hawk had crashed. Between us and the helicopter was a field. We didn't know for sure but we had to figure it was mined. The Russians mined neighborhood alleys in Kabul, so sure as hell they'd mined an open field. We moved slowly. When we got to the crash site it was a nightmare. The smoke. The bodies. Two solders were dead and the third was bleeding out. If we had gotten there fifteen minutes earlier we could have saved him. I remember standing there looking down at his face while the medics did what they could and thinking, 'Just fifteen minutes sooner and he would have lived.'"

Walter and his companions loaded the bodies on two gurneys and started making their way back across the minefield to safety. "We couldn't follow our footprints. It was too dark. One of the guys, a good friend, was walking ahead of me and I was praying that he'd know where to step. Suddenly there was a huge explosion. I threw my hands up to protect my head and that's all I remember. The next thing I was struggling to get up and someone was holding me down, and then I felt the pain." Walter's friend had stepped on a land mine, killing himself and injuring the other three. The blast knocked Walter unconscious, injured his spine and embedded shrapnel in his armpits and face. No one had been wearing body armor. "That was a bad night. A bad . . . bad night."

With one week left before he was to be sent home, Walter was stitched up and kept on the job with orders to report to Walter Reed Medical Center when he returned stateside. By the time he got to Walter Reed an infection had spread throughout both his arms. The doctors would have to cut out the infected flesh again and again, unable to prevent nerve damage in the process. He would spend the next three years undergoing spinal surgery, multiple surgeries to each arm, and skin grafts. Haunted by nightmares, memory problems and paralyzed with depression, he started treatment with a hospital psychologist for Post-Traumatic Stress Disorder.

On January 31, 2004, while he and his roommate watched the Super Bowl on television, he took a turn for the worse. "They had cut more flesh out from under my arm and packed it with sponge, but they hadn't gotten all the infection out. You could smell it soon as you came near me." Feeling progressively worse minute by minute, Walter rang for help. "They finally got a doctor to take a look. To clean the wound he had to pull out the staples and he snagged an artery. Then his pager went off and he left the room." Walter began to bleed out. "The guy in the bed next to me was a double amputee so it was hard for him to go for help, but when he saw what was happening he started hollering. Finally a nurse came in."

When the nurse saw what had happened, she called for backup. They repacked the wound with dressing, changed the sheets and put Walter back in bed. Then they left. "I lay there feeling warmth seeping down my back and onto the mattress. We kept buzzing for the nurses but no one came." He called his mother in Baltimore.

"I picked up the phone and I heard Walter on the line saying, 'Mom, I'm not going to make it. You got to get here. I love you,'" recalls Luvinia Blackston, who lives in Baltimore and is a retired surgical nurse. "It took me and Walter's step dad close to two hours to get to the hospital. Route 29 from Baltimore to Silver Spring was bumper to bumper traffic so I drove on the shoulder the whole way. I called Walter's sister and said call him and keep him on the phone talking until I get there. She asked what was wrong and I said, 'Just call him!' I was praying that the police would pull me over so I could tell them I needed an escort to the hospital, but no one stopped me." When Luvinia got to her son's hospital room she froze. Walter lay unconscious on his bed surrounded by a pool of his own blood.

His roommate had pulled himself into his wheel chair and gone out to the nurses' station for help but no one had responded. "I wrapped a towel around my hand and pushed on the artery. The whole time I was screaming for help. My husband couldn't take it. He went into the bathroom and threw up." Once Luvinia got the attention of the medical staff, they went into overdrive. Walter's bed was unplugged and he was rushed to the operating room, where he underwent surgery and received transfusions. "I pushed on the artery all the way to the OR. It was the only way to keep him from bleeding to death. While they were operating on him I waited outside, and a nurse came up to me and saw my arm covered in blood past the elbow. She said, 'You should have worn a glove,' and I said, 'He's my son. His blood is my blood.'" For the next 48 hours Walter remained in intensive care until he was stabilized enough to return to the unit. Luvinia stayed the entire time. "When he came around, he said, 'Oh, Mom, I'm so glad you're here.' He had tears in his eyes."

By 2005 Walter was quartered outside Walter Reed at Summit Hills apartments in Silver Spring where he lived with another soldier, a young sergeant who coped with his PTSD by going AWOL every chance he got. Three months later they were moved to Building 18, the hospital's former student barracks, doubling up in a single room. "It was so small that the only way to get any privacy was to separate our bunks with the wall locker. The paint was peeling off the walls in strips. There was mold on the ceiling, mice, cockroaches. The bathroom was disgusting. You couldn't go out alone at night because it was too dangerous. In the short time I was there two soldiers were robbed and beaten. Coming from Baltimore, I knew how to watch my back so I would sit in the lobby and talk to the guys, give them advice on how to protect themselves."

Walter wrote a letter to the House Committee on Oversight and Government Reform about the state of the building but never heard back from them. "After two months I couldn't take it any longer. I demanded that they find me another place to live." He was relocated to an efficiency at Knob Hill Apartments, another complex near Walter Reed. Two weeks after he moved in he attempted suicide. "I wanted to take myself out. I was emotionally drained. I felt that there was nothing left for me. I struggled for days but I couldn't find a reason to keep on living. I took a bunch of medications and washed them down with alcohol, but I vomited everything up almost immediately." After a second botched attempt, he gave up trying to kill himself.

In May of 2006 he was given three days to sign his Medical Evaluation form, but he hesitated. "I sought out a guy named Danny Sotto from the Disabled Veterans of America to explain the paperwork to me. Danny was a saint. At that time there must have been 600 soldiers at Walter Reed, all disabled and all being discharged, and we were clueless about what it all meant. Danny helped each and every one of us." Ultimately Walter was discharged from Walter Reed and declared fit for duty, although he had been under almost daily treatment for his PTSD for over a year and a half, and had severely limited range of motion in his upper body. "The scarring was so terrible.

The skin had healed like a web under both my arms but they only rated me 20 percent disability." Once he was out on his own, the undiagnosed Traumatic Brain Injury (TBI) he received during the land mine explosion worsened precipitously.

"There were days I couldn't remember who I was, where I lived or where I worked. I didn't remember things I used to do or what I used to like to eat. When I was in Afghanistan I invented a 24-hour pager and got written up in a newspaper, and I have no memory of doing that at all. I'd wake up in the morning and feel like someone was holding me down just like after the explosion when I came to." There was no job waiting for him as promised when he was called up, so he returned to Jessup, Maryland and lived on savings for as long as he could while waiting for his Veterans Disabilities to kick in, but he heard nothing for almost a year. "After that I borrowed from my family and friends. I lost my job, my house, my fiancée, my cars, my credit—but worst of all, I lost my mind." There was a silver lining, however. While he waited, Walter was finally screened for TBI.

Feeling desperate, Walter went to the Veterans Administration in Baltimore for help, bringing photocopies of all his records with him. The benefits associate who saw him was not sympathetic. "She asked me if I couldn't move back with my parents until this was all straightened out. I said, 'Ma'am, I'm 47 years old. I can't move back in with my parents. I need to get my life back.'" Walter demanded to see her boss. After hours of waiting he was ushered into another office where the Baltimore Director of the VA waited to see him. "I took off my shirt and said, 'This is what I look at every day.' She said, 'I'm so sorry.' And I said, 'Do not be sorry. Help me.'" Two days later Walter received a 90 percent disability rating and a 100 percent unemployable rating which translated into $2,500 a month disability.

Arthritis in his back made staying in a cold climate impossible. Walter moved to Atlanta near a VA hospital and started carving out a new life for himself. Finances were bleak for a time, which was when The Armed Forces Foundation gave him money for his car payment. It's still a battle. "I have blackouts. I don't drive a car often. I forget everything. The VA gave me a Palm Pilot to record everything I need to remember, and I use it all the time. This life takes its toll; there are frustrations every day. I miss my family, but Maryland was too cold and too expensive to keep living there. I've lost it a couple times. I've thought about suicide. But I have my boys. I raised my oldest, Anthony by myself, and even though Corey has graduated high school and is now in college, I need to be here for him. When I first came back from Afghanistan and he came to see me at the hospital, I didn't know who he was, my own son. I can't let him down."

Walter continues to take an increasingly proactive role in his mental health care. He sits on the Advisory Committee of a veteran's hospital in Atlanta as an advocate for better care of veterans with PTSD and TBI. He is partnering with his church to start a "Veterans for Christ" program with a web site and the motto: "Veterans connecting and protecting." He is also participating in the hospital's pilot "Life Coach" program, a weekly one-on-one session with a social worker that addresses a wide range of issues. "We've talked about my problems with going out in public and fear of crowded places; about paperwork pending within the VA system; about managing my finances; about anything and everything. Sometimes we meet at the mall. It's that informal."

Walter's attitude is hopeful, and he is determined to continue his recovery. "I just want to lead a fruitful life. To know how I used to be and to not be able to be that person again, ever, is frustrating. But I have to start from where I am now. It's all on me. I used to sit for days and just look out the window, and I thought that withdrawing from people and breaking off relationships was normal considering what I had been through. Now I know it's not. If I had one thing to say to vets like myself it would be, 'We earned the right to be proud of who we are. Be the squeaky wheel. Dig down in your heart and get the help you need.'"

MEDALS
The Army Commendation Medal, Army Achievement Medal, 3 Army Reserve Components Achievement Medals, 2 National Defense Service Medals, Armed Forces Reserve Medal, 2 Non-Commissioned Officer Professional Development Ribbon, Armed Service Ribbon, Overseas Service Ribbon.

4

AMERICA KEEPS ITS PROMISE
The Truth about Military Care of Warriors
with Traumatic Brain Injury

By Christopher S. Williams, USAF, MC

Although the popular press and several recent reports suggest that the Department of Defense and Department of Veterans Affairs are falling short in the care of our warriors with invisible wounds such as Traumatic Brain Injury (TBI) and Post-Traumatic Stress Disorder (PTSD), nothing could be farther from the truth—America is keeping its promise. Just as important, never has Congress, the Department of Defense (DoD), and the Department of Veterans Affairs mobilized itself more briskly, delivered personnel, and appropriated resources to such a degree to deliver improved access to care for these "signature wounds" of the War on Terror. I will share a story with you that I believe illustrates the level of commitment.

On September 13, 2007, I deployed to a northern Iraq air base to command a small Air Force combat hospital caring for thousands of US Army, Air Force and contractor personnel. It was an honor to command this unit of splendid Air Force medics, but also a daunting task given the casualties we were seeing during the four-plus months we were there. Unfortunately, we witnessed firsthand the horrific injuries sustained from Improvised Explosive Device (IED) blasts. For most of us, the sights and sounds are etched indelibly in our memories forever; but for the wounded, they are not only etched in their memories but in the scars they bare. While I cared for over sixty traumas, there is one that remains most vivid.

In late October, a US Air Force member working with an Explosive Ordnance Disposal (EOD) team was critically injured with a "booby-trapped" IED device that was being disarmed. The explosion traumatically severed and destroyed his left arm at the mid-upper arm level. It caused severe injuries of a fractured face, destroying his left eye and injuring his right one. As you can imagine, he also suffered a Traumatic Brain Injury. He lived only because of the prompt and expert field care of a 19-year old Army medic who applied a tourniquet to his severed arm and was able to initiate administration of fluids in the field while awaiting helicopter medical evacuation.

Upon arrival at our hospital, it was obvious that there was no way to save his left arm, so after emergency resuscitation he was taken to surgery to complete the amputation of the arm and possible surgical exploration of his abdomen and chest. Once he was stable, he was promptly transferred to the Air Force theater hospital in central Iraq where otorhinolaryngologic (ENT) surgeons stabilized his multiple fractured facial bones, ophthalmologists attempted repair of his severely injured right eye (his left was beyond repair), and neurosurgeons could provide neurosurgical intervention if it became necessary. Unfortunately, despite multiple eye surgeries in the theater hospital, in Germany, and back in the United States, his right eye could not be salvaged and he was left not only with an amputated left arm but totally blind as well. Fortunately, he recovered from the TBI without permanent effects.

In the ensuing time since being in Iraq and commanding the hospital where he was initially cared for, I was reassigned to my current position (I am a neurologist) as Senior Executive Director for Traumatic Brain Injury at the Defense Centers of Excellence for Psychological Health and Traumatic Brain Injury (DCoE) in Washington, DC. However, I never forgot about this airman. During a trip to the University of Pittsburgh in September of 2008, I met retired Major General Gale S. Pollack, who served as interim USA Surgeon General in 2007. General Pollack is now the Executive Director of the Center for Ocular Regeneration and Vision Restoration at the University of Pittsburgh Medical Center, and shares with me a passion for caring for our wounded warriors. In our meeting she told me about a revolutionary vision device that I had only read about in a book, "The Brain That Changes Itself." I did not realize that it was actually being developed by a company in Madison,

Wisconsin. The device takes advantage of the innate neuroplasticity of the brain while utilizing a camera, small computer, and sensory portals applied to the tongue. The first person I thought about benefiting from this device was the young airman we had cared for.

The device works and is under careful evaluation and further development with the hope of obtaining FDA medical device approval in the next year or two. However, I immediately wondered if we could connect the airman to the company and provide DoD funding so he could utilize the technology while being a part of the evaluative process for the FDA request. With the help of the Air Force Reserve Surgeon, Colonel Dominec DeFrancis, I was able to track the airman down to Brooke Army Medical Center in San Antonio, talk with his case manager and connect with the technology company, Wicab, Inc., in Madison that is developing the BrainPort® vision device. As I write and relate this story, we are exploring ways to get this technology to him for evaluation and use. Although we have not completed the task, my experience to date is that DoD will do whatever is necessary to help wounded warriors, one by one, wherever, whenever. I believe that in the next several weeks, he will be evaluated and be using this technology.

Today we see an unprecedented partnership between DoD and the Veterans Administration to improve access and care for our warriors. That partnership reports frequently to Congress on the progress of improved care of soldiers with trauma, TBI and psychological health problems. This applies even to those cases which are still under investigation. Research funds allocation and America's superior resources on important healthcare issues allows America to keep its promise to its warrior veterans. Every day we are committed to meeting the healthcare needs of those who have sacrificed for our country, and I am proud to be involved with this collaborative and cohesive effort.

"Treatment is most effective when the patient is in charge and the ultimate expert in his or her recovery. Treatment works best when the doctor or therapist acts as a kind of expert consultant. As Home Depot puts it: 'You can do it, we can help.'"

—"Healing the Troubled Mind Takes More Than a Pill," *The Washington Post*, February 10, 2008

BRINGING THE WAR HOME
The Story of Army Chief Warrant Officer
Richard Gutteridge

*"Reliving the horrors of evacuating fallen soldiers' and Marines'
remains, searching through body bags for dog tags and watching
soldiers die was too much. I became more withdrawn and distant
from my family. I was having what I was later told were 'suicidal
ideations.' I also began to increase my use of alcohol to cope. I am
not proud of this, and it is difficult to admit."*

Richard Gutteridge almost ended his life on Christmas Day 2007. "I
no longer had a desire to continue. I felt as though my condition
would never change. I just wanted it to be 'like before,' and quite honestly I couldn't fathom staying like this." Late that evening he phoned
the nurse practitioner who had been seeing him at the military clinic
in Ansbach, Germany and told her what was going on.

"I felt relieved calling her, but knew that as soon as I placed the
call my career would be over. After I told her that I was 'safe,' she told
me to come see her the next morning in her office. When we met she
told me that I needed more help with my PTSD than she could give.
She told me that I could go to Landstuhl Medical Center on my own,
or else I would be taken there by force. I couldn't see a way out so I
gave in." Richard opened the office door to see his wife standing there
with his suitcase. She was accompanied by his brigade commander
and a chaplain. "Reality kicked in. I only had time for a quick goodbye and I was on my way to Landstuhl in a van. I never felt more alone
in my life."

Earlier that year he had returned home from Iraq to Germany
where his wife and two young sons waited to greet him. The homecoming was sweet. "I was required to complete a Post-Deployment

Health Assessment after returning. At that point, I didn't feel like I had any problems that needed immediate attention. Completing the required forms was a ticket to begin leave and I didn't want to be delayed.

"I began to clear my unit in Friedberg, Germany—the 1st Brigade of the 1st Armored Division was casing its colors and returning to the States. Friedberg was closing." Since Richard wanted to stay in Germany, he executed a Consecutive Overseas Tour (COT) and moved to Ansbach. While he was in-processing to his new unit, he was told that he had failed to complete the 90-day Post Deployment Health Reassessment (PDHR).

"I had been back from Iraq for about four months when I started to have the nightmares. Gradually more and more things reminded me of what it was like being over there. Besides the constant reminders I started having these intrusive horrible thoughts about what had happened, specific moments. I found myself becoming easily angry at the littlest of things—the kids being too loud or a car pulling out in front of me. I was also having trouble sleeping and I'd begun to withdraw from my family. So for whatever combination of reasons this time I answered the PDHR more "honestly." After a doctor in Ansbach reviewed the assessment he told me that I had chronic PTSD and combat stress." He was referred to the Behavioral Health clinic in Ansbach. Facing a mental health issue was not how he envisioned his return from combat.

The second oldest of seven children of a loving, "very Catholic" family, Richard was living in Greensboro, North Carolina when he graduated high school in June of 1982. Although his father had a well paying job, college wasn't an immediate option. "The Army was a way for me to get money for a college education. I joined for the VEAP money [Veteran's Education Assistance Program] which was a recruitment tool used for a short time between the G.I. Bill and the 'new' G.I. Bill."

Richard spent his first tour in the Army at Fort Bragg as a paratrooper in the 82nd Airborne Division, and then spent the next eight years in Germany followed by another tour in the 82nd as a Sergeant First Class, and then four years at Fort Hood, Texas. During the next sixteen years he would deploy for Operation Desert Storm (Saudi

Arabia to Kuwait and Iraq and then back to Saudi Arabia), Bosnia, Kosovo, Turkey, Romania, and twice more to Iraq as part of Operation Iraqi Freedom. While based in Germany he was assigned to the 1st Armored Division and deployed to Baghdad in 2003 for thirteen months. He returned to Germany in July 2004 and then redeployed to Iraq in December of 2005, serving in Al Anbar Province fourteen months until February 2007.

"During my last deployment I was the Battalion Motor Officer for the 1-36th Infantry Regiment of the 1st Armored Division. I was in charge of a combat outpost in the city of Hit [pronounced "Heat"] which housed my maintenance operation as well as the Battalion Aid Station. During this time I was also in charge of day-to-day operations of a combat outpost with 57 soldiers. My outpost also contained our detainee center where we processed over 2,000 detainees during my stay. I was also in charge of day and night Medevac missions, receiving casualties, coordinating with the air crews, relaying information between the battalion surgeon and his team of medics to the air crews, setting up the landing zone, organizing litter teams, helping with providing triage, and loading the aircraft in a timely manner due to the frequency of mortar attacks, sniper and small arms fire."

During Richard's fourteen months in Hit, over 100 US soldiers and countless other combatants as well as civilians were Medevac'd out. His task was to remove the human remains from destroyed vehicles and search through body bags for dog tags to help positively identify fallen US troops. "I was involved in handling the remains of more than a dozen dead soldiers, Marines and combatants. We didn't have any mortuary affairs personnel, so three of us handled the task: Dr. (Major) John Rumbaugh, our Battalion Surgeon, Specialist First Class Gregory Wilson and myself." Because they didn't want to expose any young soldiers to what they were doing, they did it all themselves. "We took this task as seriously as defending our outpost, so we did it slowly with dignity and respect."

On a September day in 2006, Richard was checking serial numbers on destroyed vehicles that were to be taken out of service. As he opened the door of a blown-up Humvee his arm was suddenly smashed up against the vehicle. It was a sniper. "I was taking my chances walking out to check the vehicle. It was located within the boundary of our outpost, but in direct view of the city only 100 meters away. I didn't hear the shot. I felt like an idiot because I had been so careless." After controlling the bleeding, he called the battalion aid station on his hand-held radio and told them what had happened. "The medics cleaned my wound and prepared me to be Medevac'd but I refused because I wasn't leaving my men—I was in charge." Two days later he drove to Al Asad Airbase and had his forearm x-rayed. Sure enough the image showed four slivers of bullet fragments.

It was the body bags, not the near brush with death that Richard would talk about to the nurse practitioner psychiatrist throughout the fall of 2007. "I began therapy sessions on August 2, 2007 and thought the first ones went pretty well. As a result of one of my earliest sessions she recommended that I adjust my Cytalopram [Celexa] medication and told me to call the clinic if I needed to."

But his condition worsened. "I continued to have nightmares and I felt as though I was losing control. I called the clinic in Ansbach a week later to see the nurse again but she was on leave and her next appointment was not for twenty days. I inquired about seeing a doctor and was told that the next available appointment was twenty-one days from then. I told the receptionist that I would drive to Landstuhl Hospital to see a doctor (two and a half hours away). But she told me that was not possible. Instead she told me that she would place a telephonic referral for me to speak to a doctor who was "deploying soon" from Vilseck, Germany and that he had 72 hours to contact me." Richard was asked if he was "suicidal" because being suicidal was the only way to get immediate help. "But I didn't feel suicidal at that moment; I just felt panicky, and that's what I told her."

He felt frustrated and angry. "I e-mailed the Wounded Warrior Hotline and told them that I needed help now. I said that I was a senior Warrant Officer with 24 years of active duty and that I had served in Iraq during Desert Storm and that I had two extended Iraqi Freedom tours. If this is how I was being treated, how would a young infantry soldier be treated?"

It wasn't long before he received a phone call from the Wounded Warrior Hotline, and shortly after that a phone call from the doctor who had been given his telephone referral. "We discussed my condition, and he made recommendations concerning my medication. I began to feel better." Weeks later he resumed his one-on-one care with the nurse practitioner. But as the fall progressed his memories became particularly disturbing. "I was reliving the horrors of evacuating fallen soldiers' and Marines' remains, searching through body bags for dog tags and watching soldiers die, and it was too much. I became more withdrawn and distant from my family. I was having what I was later told to be 'suicidal ideations.' I also began to increase my use of alcohol to cope. I am not proud of this, and it is difficult to admit."

Once he got to Landstuhl, Richard was admitted to the in-patient psychiatry ward. He was issued a hospital gown and socks with tread woven into the soles. "When they snapped on the hospital bracelet, reality really set in. Having to be observed 24 hours a day, shuffling around in socks behind locked doors marked 'elopement risk' was humbling."

"I was observed twice daily for the next seven days for signs of alcohol withdrawal. I had to answer simple questions and was instructed to hold my hands out and steady to see if I was shaking. Even more humiliating, I was watched when I shaved or ate (with plastic utensils). My only reprieves were the 'fresh air' breaks—two cigarettes in quick succession while standing out in the cold winter air wearing a hospital gown under the constant supervision of one of the staff. Eventually I realized that the purpose of my being in a lockdown ward was for my own safety. It was tremendously difficult for me, but ultimately I have nothing but great respect and admiration for all the personnel who worked on that ward."

As New Year's Day 2008 approached, one of his psychiatrists told Richard that he was recommending medical retirement. He was to be sent to Walter Reed Medical Center to out-process from the Army via the Warrior Transition Brigade. He was told that he would receive PTSD care at a Veteran's Administration facility after he was separated. "I cried for the first time since returning from Iraq. I was heartbroken. I didn't want to retire." He said goodbye to his wife and two sons and then flew to Walter Reed on New Year's Day.

After landing at Andrews Air Force Base in Virginia, Richard was taken by bus to Walter Reed. He was allowed one quick smoke before being escorted into the hospital and taken to Ward 54, the in-patient psychiatry ward. "I had never been to Walter Reed, but I had heard the stories and was very apprehensive. Once I got to the ward I realized that having been through the initial 'drill' at Landstuhl I wasn't as apprehensive of the in-processing procedures. A short while later I was back in a hospital gown with a 'new' bracelet. But I was now able to wear shoes without laces instead of those socks."

On Ward 54 Richard soon reacquainted himself with a few of the soldiers he had met at Landstuhl. They assured him that the ward was "cool." "I felt much better then. I began talking with psychiatrists and psychologists who were very kind and understanding. I immediately expressed my desire to not be medically retired, and they told me that I would be my own best advocate so I made the decision to make the best of it. I participated in group therapy and followed orders; I made friends with my fellow patients. But even so the smoke breaks continued to be all that I looked forward to—those and phone calls to my wife."

Once Richard heard of the Specialized Care Program at Walter Reed specifically geared toward PTSD he made up his mind that being admitted into that program would be key to fulfilling his goal of recovery and staying in the Army. He had hope for the first time in weeks. Even so there was one group of patients who "got to" him.

"I quickly became disgruntled with the Initial Entry Soldiers who were also on Ward 54. These trainees were still learning to be "soldiers," and I'd sit in group therapy listening to them, people less than half my age, complaining that they could not adapt to the Army, could not get along with their Drill Sergeants and so on. Our experiences had nothing in common." Richard's disdain of the entry soldiers was shared by other combat veterans who had PTSD issues. They soon branched off into their own group and shared their own stories about combat stress and how to deal with it on the battlefield and at home.

"My whole being was focused on getting moved to Ward 53—the outpatient psychiatry ward. After almost two weeks on Ward 54, I was released to Ward 53 and moved into Abrams Hall. This time I almost cried tears of joy." The new environment was "a breath of fresh air." The staff was friendly and accommodating. The atmosphere was refreshing and hopeful. Richard had made his intentions clear early on about wanting to be admitted to the Specialized Care Program specifically geared toward the treatment of PTSD. He began a series of interviews with psychiatrists, psychologists and social workers from the Deployment Health Clinical Center at the hospital. "Initially I was discouraged because I felt that I had not made the cut during the final phase of the process, but I began the program on February 4, 2008."

"The Specialized Care Program was awesome. From the very first day I knew I was in the right place. I looked at the other seven soldiers in the program and I saw the same worn, haggard, distant look that I became accustomed to seeing in the mirror each morning." The intense, three-week PTSD program provided an overall health care assessment as well as an understanding and recognition of symptoms of PTSD.

Richard learned to normalize his reactions to combat experiences. Coping skills such as breathing techniques and yoga were coupled with one-on-one therapy with doctors and nurses to help him reduce his hyper-arousal and vigilance. And then there was telling his story to others who had had similar experiences.

"To me it was the group therapy with my fellow PTSD sufferers that made the biggest difference because we were all providing each other with mutual support. The program saved me. I can now manage my depression and grief associated with PTSD. I am now aware of self-care and available resources. I feel like a husband and a father again. I owe the staff of the Specialized Care Program my life." Today Richard continues to serve his country as the Brigade Motor Officer for the 12th Combat Aviation Brigade in Ansbach, Germany.

MEDALS

Two Bronze Stars, Purple Heart, 3 Meritorious Service Medals, 12 Army Commendation Medals, 10 Army Achievement Medals, 4 Army Good Conduct Medals, 2 National Defense Service Medals, Armed Forces Expeditionary Medal, Southwest Asia Service Medal with 3 campaign stars, Iraqi Campaign Medal with 3 campaign stars, Global War on Terror Expeditionary Medal, Global War on Terror Service Medal, Armed Forces Service Medal, Military Outstanding Volunteer Service Medal, Non-Commissioned Officer Professional Development Ribbon with number 3 device, Army Service Ribbon, Overseas Service Ribbon, NATO Medal, Saudi Arabia Kuwaiti Liberation Medal, Kuwait Kuwaiti Liberation Medal, The Combat Action Badge, Parachutist Badge.

"There is a lag between the time someone experiences trauma and the time he or she reports symptoms of post-traumatic stress. This can range from days to many years, and it is typically much longer while people are still in the military."

—"Counting the Walking Wounded," Professor Lawrence Wein, *The New York Times*, January 26, 2009

6

HEALING THE HUMAN SPIRIT, HOUR BY HOUR

By Barbara V. Romberg, PhD

In the spring of 2005 I heard a story about a young man who had returned home from Iraq. He was clearly experiencing severe repercussions from his experience in combat. Unfortunately, he had no idea what was happening to him. He lost his job, his wife and kids, and was living out of his car.

At about the same time I was driving with my two daughters through Bethesda Maryland, a suburb of Washington, DC. As we often do, we saw a homeless veteran on the street corner. He was wearing fatigues and holding up a sign that said, "Homeless Vietnam Vet. Please help. God bless." My oldest daughter, who was nine at the time, turned to me and asked, "Mom, if that man fought for our country how come he's homeless?" Soon after that I founded Give an Hour.

My father was a veteran of World War II. He served in the Navy and was injured during a battle in the Pacific. He never talked about the war, but my brothers and I saw the consequences of his combat experience. Growing up in a rural community in California during the 1960s and '70s, I saw many young men head off to Vietnam. Some never returned; some returned but were never the same. They became the homeless men that we whispered about and crossed the street to avoid.

Give an Hour is a nonprofit organization that consists of a national network of mental health professionals who provide free mental health services to US troops and their families. Our plan is to continue recruiting mental health providers so that anyone affected by the current war who is in need of mental health support or care will be able to access it easily. Currently we have providers in every state, with the network growing daily. In addition to providing direct service to returning troops and family members, we assist with phone support, public education and consultation to veterans' organizations, private employers, schools and other state and local agencies.

According to a Rand Report released in April 2008, approximately 320,000 of the men and women who had returned from combat at that time indicated that they had experienced a Traumatic Brain Injury, or TBI. Only a small percentage of these individuals suffered TBI as a result of a penetrating wound. The vast majority of these men and women suffered potentially disabling neurological wounds from the blast waves of IEDs (improvised explosive devices), mortar shells or other explosive weapons—all without so much as a scratch of physical evidence.

Since founding Give an Hour, I've spoken with a number of veterans and family members. One family member I talked to was a physician in Texas who reported what has become a very typical story. His son was deployed to Iraq and spent several months riding around in one of the Army's Bradley fighting vehicles. Although he wasn't wounded in the traditional sense of the word, he was in the immediate vicinity of multiple blasts. This father told me that upon his return his son had chronic headaches, difficulty sleeping and hearing loss. Despite these concerning symptoms of possible Traumatic Brain Injury, this young soldier shipped out for another deployment to Iraq soon after I talked with his father.

I have also met many people in the military who are trying to stay in front of these issues. Indeed, they are working tirelessly to address the psychological and neurological needs of the troops through a variety of excellent programs within the military culture. In addition, they are reaching out to organizations like Give an Hour to partner in this critical effort.

Fortunately we have the knowledge and the human resources to attend to these deserving men and women and their families. In fact, we have over 400,000 mental health professionals in our country—many of them eager to help. Through collaborative efforts with the

Department of Veterans Affairs, the Department of Defense, state and local governments and other nonprofit organizations, I believe that we can create a comprehensive support system that ensures proper care for our military community.

In order to reach those in need, however, we need to educate the public and the entire military community. Most people—both civilian and military—do not understand how a strapping young man or woman, courageous and full of life, can return from a deployment so psychologically damaged. The soldiers themselves don't understand what is happening to them. Those suffering symptoms of combat stress often feel ashamed; they are afraid they are losing their minds, and are also afraid of losing their families and careers. They don't talk about it—they try to go on.

Those suffering from traumatic brain injuries often feel confused; frequently, their conditions are not accurately diagnosed. They return home to find that they have trouble concentrating, focusing and carrying out the tasks of daily life. They may also experience frequent headaches and difficulty controlling their moods.

Sadly, it is not uncommon for this new generation of veterans to have multiple physical, psychological and neurological injuries with which they must cope. As a nation, we must prepare for the return of these men and women. We must assist in their recovery and—when needed—plan for their long-term care.

"The number of troops with new cases of post-traumatic disorder jumped by roughly 50 percent in 2007 amid the military buildup in Iraq, increased violence there and in Afghanistan. Records show roughly 40,000 troops have been diagnosed with the illness, also known as PTSD, since 2003. Officials believe that many more are likely keeping their illness a secret."

—"Wartime PTSD Cases Jumped Roughly 50 Percent in 200,"
Pauline Jelinek, AP, January 2008

7

DEEPER THAN WAR
The Story of Marine Corps Captain Tyler Boudreau

"Their trauma, it seems, was not all based strictly on those moments of powerlessness when they'd been shot at, mortared or IED'd. There were clear incidents of moral distress, too. As many Marines as I dealt with who were agitated by the dangers they encountered, there were as many more agitated by their own actions. Most often, I suspect, veterans contend with some varying blend of the two."

In 2004 Tyler Boudreau was a rifle company commander in the US Marine Corps. "Our battalion had just returned from Iraq and would be heading back exactly nine months later. In Iraq our area of operations had been dubbed by the media "The Triangle of Death." Many of our men were wounded or killed. The violence was heavy on all sides. Those who returned home had much to consider. We weren't stateside for long before Marines started trickling into my office to talk about the turbulence brewing inside them." This was his introduction to the world of post-traumatic stress.

At the time, Tyler had been in the Marine Corps for about eleven years. "I knew of post-traumatic stress, of course. I'd read about it in the books. I'd even seen it portrayed in the movies. But I'd never been confronted with it face to face, especially not as an officer. What those outside the military must appreciate most is the predicament this creates for a commander. In the military the mission always comes first; troop welfare comes after. It doesn't mean a commander doesn't care about his troops or that he can't love them—he can and he should—but he must love the mission more. It's doctrine, it's written, and quite frankly it's common sense; the mission—that is, the greater good—must always take precedence over the individual."

39

Within the doctrinal texts and the stuffy tomes of military history, that sounds reasonable enough. Even on the battlefield, as one imagines a line of soldiers assaulting an enemy strongpoint, the notion of "the unit" and "the mission" being a life-or-death priority makes sense. But to Tyler, in the context of soldiers coming home from war with post-traumatic stress, it began to sound a little bit less sensible.

"With no enemy bearing down, it was certainly difficult for me not to give my full compassion to every Marine who experienced the slightest distress. But as a commander, I needed to always bear in mind that my unit would soon be back in the combat zone and, further, that manpower was not an inexhaustible spigot. There is an expectation that a commander preserve his force to every possible extent. There will come a point when the spigot runs dry and the deployment date arrives; when it does, you go. Whether you're ready or not, whether you're full strength or shorthanded, when D-Day arrives, you go. Of course, going to war shorthanded or mentally ill-prepared is not only dangerous for the unit; it is inherently detrimental to the mission." And therein lay Tyler's predicament.

He had nine short months to prepare 150 Marines for battle. "I had to process out the departing Marines and train from scratch the arriving ones. I had to inventory weapons and equipment, plan training, draft orders, conduct inspections, and continually petition for all those things in short supply. Some Marines have specialized skills; they're hard to find, and the good ones are even harder. The best ones often go to the most effective advocates." A commander's business is as much about scrounging, bargaining and downright fighting for the best personnel and equipment he can find as it is about leading his men in battle.

"These were the issues that occupied the bulk of my time and thoughts during the months before our second deployment. So when my armory custodian (an essential figure) showed up in my office with the Company Gunnery Sergeant to explain that he wanted an appointment with the Division Psychiatrist, I'll admit I was dismayed. When one of my best machine-gunners came in with the same request, I was concerned." When nearly a dozen more Marines poured in, all looking to "get out," Tyler was downright alarmed. "It struck me almost instantly as a negative trend—a method to avoid our deployment, and I grew worried that this trend would catch on."

A rash of men suffering from post-traumatic stress can bear a striking resemblance to general low morale within the unit. "I suspect this is hard for those outside the ranks to really understand. This is one of the primary struggles for a commander—to maintain the esprit de corps of his men so that they perform well together on the battlefield. Breakouts of "malcontent" can be devastating to a unit, and furthermore extremely contagious. While rampant instances of discernible apathy or melancholy, or even flagging discipline among the troops may very well be symptoms of a post-traumatic stress epidemic, they may occur to a commander instead as fatigue or buckling will. Unfortunately, the remedy for one is quite contrary to the remedy for the other."

Tyler had to ask himself, how he could balance the needs of the Corps and country with the needs of an individual Marine in pain? How could he prevent himself from slipping into the habit of viewing all such men as shirkers or malingers?

"I can say from my own encounters with this dilemma, it is difficult. What I found even more difficult to fathom at the time was the non-uniform nature of their reports. Their trauma, it seems, was not all based strictly on those moments of powerlessness when they'd been shot at, mortared or IED'd. There were clear incidents of moral distress, too. As many Marines as I dealt with who were agitated by the dangers they encountered, there were as many more agitated by their own actions. Most often, I suspect, veterans contend with some varying blend of the two."

"Collateral damage" is a term used in the military to describe the unfortunate, unintentional and often unavoidable destruction that occurs on the battlefield in the execution of a mission. "In Iraq, collateral damage was not uncommon, particularly because, in most cases, those who we fought were indistinguishable from those who we meant to protect. Mistaken identities were simply inevitable, and when they resulted in death, it was truly heartbreaking for all of us, especially for the unlucky Marines who'd pulled the trigger. What I discovered about their anxiety was that it did not include any context whatsoever. In other words, justifications were never permitted by their conscience. "

"I made more speeches that I can count defending Marines to themselves—those who had fired their weapons in self-defense, but because the situation had been unclear (as so many situations in Iraq tended to be), they'd inadvertently killed non-combatants. Occasionally those non-combatants were very young indeed, and that made their memories all that much more tenacious. I argued to them that the circumstances had compelled them to fire. Their lives and the lives of their fellow Marines depended very much on them having done what they did.

"But all my reasoning had little effect. Their moral consternation existed in a vacuum beyond the scope of reason. The killing of people, combatant or non-combatant, can for many men be a trying event, and sometimes an utterly devastating one. All the justifications in the world, legitimate or not, cannot sever them from their pain. This was a reality I found hard to accept. I must admit, once I'd explained the situation to these Marines, I rather arrogantly expected them to just "snap out of it." But they didn't snap out of it. I couldn't understand why such cogent logic, presented by me, their own commander, was not enough to get them back on track. Thinking on it now, I tend to believe that my very position as commander induced a certain myopia within me, which I could not shed until I shed my uniform and relinquished my command."

The greatest irony of his resistance to truly understanding their condition was that, at the very same time, Tyler was experiencing his own share of post-traumatic stress. "I too was agitated. I wasn't sleeping. When I did sleep, I was prone to some incredibly violent dreams. I was jumpy, excitable, downright volatile. I could flip to rage at the slightest provocation, and the rage was difficult to subdue. On top of it all, I did bear an undeniable regret for the violence that I'd inflicted in Iraq. All of this festered inside my body and mind until those crucial preparations for our deployment were utterly edged out of my consciousness. After a while, the stress owned virtually all of my thoughts. I would arrive at work at one or two o'clock every morning and I'd sit alone in a darkened building and just stew until dawn. Throughout our training exercises, I had trouble concentrating on the tasks at hand. My duties as a commander became an afterthought. Finally, after months of deterioration, after I'd really begun to lose confidence in myself as a leader of Marines, I made the most difficult decision of my life—to relinquish my command and resign my commission."

After Tyler left the Marine Corps he began to see the inherent conflict presented to a commander who must care for his men suffering from post-traumatic stress while simultaneously preparing his unit for combat. "It was not until I ceased to function optimally as a Marine myself that I started to really acknowledge that those Marines in my company who'd come to me seeking help were not, in fact, malingerers, but just men in pain."

Tyler Boudreau served 12 years in the Marine Corps infantry. He enlisted in 1989, was commissioned a 2nd Lieutenant in 1997, and was deployed to Iraq as a Captain in 2004 with 2nd Battalion, 2nd Marines. Boudreau resigned his commission in 2005 and is the author of *Packing Inferno: The Unmaking of a Marine*. He currently lives with his family in western Massachusetts.

"If you put enough stress on your back, 10,000 pounds on your back, it doesn't matter how strong your back is. It's going to break. The brain is the same way. It can only take so much stress. A broken back may not seem like a reassuring analogy, but at least it addresses the shame that my patients so often feel. 'The brain can't just change the channel, like a TV remote,' I tell them. Why do people expect their brains to be endlessly pliable, to be able to heal rapidly and perfectly after such trauma? Perhaps it's because a mental injury is invisible. For my patients, the trauma isn't something that happens to you. It is you."

—"Treating Wounds You Can't See," Linda Blum, *Washington Post*, June 29, 2008

8

THE VA'S SUICIDE PREVENTION HOTLINE
Saving the Lives of Veterans

By Janet Kemp, VA National Suicide Coordinator

The VA program for suicide prevention is based on a public health approach utilizing universal, selective, indicated strategies. The VA recognizes that suicide prevention requires ready access to high quality Mental Health Services, supplemented by programs that address the risk of suicide directly. For veterans this means that the VA understands the need to make the right care and support available for those who need it, when they need it and for as long as they need it. To accomplish this goal a vital resource has been made available to Veterans: the VA National Suicide Hotline—1-800-273-TALK—with the option to push "1" if the caller is "a veteran or someone who cares about a veteran."

The VA National Suicide Hotline is located in a large room inside an older brick building on the campus of the VA Medical Center in Canandaigua, New York. The room is simply furnished with workstations that contain phones, headsets and computers. The walls are decorated with clocks that give the time in various time zones across the country and posters that state the VA Suicide Prevention message: "It takes the courage and strength of a warrior to ask for help."

There are pictures of the workers' families on the desks and the requisite bowls of snacks and candy. The workers are calm, quietly answering the phone twenty-four hours a day, seven days a week. Health technicians are busily calling for local rescue people to help, or searching medical records, or following up on callers to make sure that they have been seen at their local VA as promised.

The hotline is unique and differs from community-based "Crisis Lines" in several ways. It is staffed with VA Mental Health professionals who have the ability to make immediate referrals to local Suicide Prevention Coordinators and also do checks to determine that the callers get the care and follow-up that they need. Utilizing all aspects of the VA system, the responder is able to provide the caller with far more than just an answer to a phone call. The staff is trained in both crisis response and VA issues. They understand that it is equally as important to help those who are not yet in crisis as it is to help those who are already in dire trouble. Their work is critical because calls come in to staff at the center where action can be taken immediately. The follow-ups are done at the local levels afterward. When it comes to suicide prevention, these call center workers are unique within the military in providing veteran-specific care.

A few individual cases may illustrate the complexity of the task, as well as the capability of these dedicated workers.

"A female veteran called the hotline in extreme distress. She stated she had pills and was going to walk into the woods and take them all. She stated that no one believed her and she couldn't go on. She just wanted to talk to someone while she did it. I could hear her park her car and start walking through the words. She refused to give any identifying information other than her first name. We were able to determine the area code she was calling from on her cell phone and called the VA in that area code. The Suicide Prevention Coordinator (SPC) quickly reviewed her high-risk list and was able to identify the person by her first name. The hotline stayed on the phone with her—repeatedly calling her back when she would end the call. Her husband was found by the SPC and he was able to identify the make and model of her car, and he and the local police began a road-by-road search in the area for the vehicle. Several hours later her car was located and the police found her deep in the woods sobbing and holding the bottle of pills and the phone. The local SPC stayed at the facility late into the evening until she was brought in. She is now receiving intensive therapy."

"Last evening at 10:18 a Desert Storm veteran called the hotline from a cell phone. I could hear traffic whizzing by while he stated that he was standing on a bridge intending to jump off. He was tearful, and spoke of being hopeless and helpless. He focused on all of the things that he has lost in his life and said he saw no way for his life to get better or a reason to go on. He did give me his name and the last four digits of his SSN but would not tell me his location because he said, "Then you will send the police and I will not die." I kept him on the phone as long as I could while another staff member called the police, but she was told that unless we knew which bridge he was on they could not dispatch officers. He finally hung up stating, "No one can help me." I tried to call him back but he hung up and then turned off his phone. I was able to identify him through the electronic medical record system through process of elimination. We called the police back, giving them his home address and asking them to dispatch officers to the closest bridge to his house, and with our insistence they did dispatch officers. I called back about 30 minutes later to hear the outcome and was told that additional officers responded to the scene, with four officers at that time. I called back about 30 minutes later and was told that now six officers were at the scene. Finally, at about 12:25 p.m., I spoke with the initial responding officer. He told me that after an hour's time, and six police officers and the crisis intervention team responding, they were able to talk him off the bridge and bring him for a mental health evaluation."

"At 2:55 am I got a call from a 21-year-old OEF/OIF (Operation Enduring Freedom/Operation Iraqi Freedom) veteran, who said that he no longer wanted to live. He reported that he was discharged from the army after he attempted to kill his roommate with a plan to then kill himself. He reported a history of self-injurious behaviors and the desire to kill other family members. He told the responder that his plan was to cut himself so deep that he would bleed to death. He reported drinking a half-gallon of Crown Royal that evening as well as taking drugs. He said he had several guns, loaded and not loaded, knives and a sword in the home. He made vague references about the safety of his father who was sleeping in his bedroom of the trailer they shared. He continuously said that he did not want to go on and that he will not go on. Approximately 30 minutes into the call, emergency services were initiated. The caller would not give us any identifying information, and using our tracking capabilities the Hotline came up with only limited information. However, the caller was using a cell phone that the police were able to trace to get an address. This took quite some time and I had to establish good rapport to keep the caller on the line. A team of police, firemen with equipment and ambulances surrounded the home, having been told to approach it with lights and sirens off. Another staff person got on the phone with the police department's hostage negotiator so the call center could coordinate communication with them. Working together with the hostage negotiator, I was able to facilitate a three-way call between the veteran, the call center and the hostage negotiator. Over the course of the next hour the veteran had extreme difficulty trusting the negotiator, but he remained on the line because he trusted me. Eventually, he put the phone down and went outside where he was apprehended. He was transferred to a community hospital for an evaluation and then to the VA Medical Center for a psychiatric admission. The veteran's father was confirmed to be safe."

"Late this morning a Vietnam Vet with PTSD called the hotline. He found out last night that his wife was leaving him, thought about it all night, and decided that he would kill himself rather than suffer any more pain. He was in extreme distress, having increased PTSD symptoms, and feeling hopeless. He called the hotline as a last resort. He had a gun and a plan. He refused 911 services but said he would leave the gun and drive to the VA where he was enrolled. He was apprehensive about telling people in admissions or the ER his story, and felt he really couldn't explain the situation to any more people. I made an immediate referral to the Suicide Prevention Coordinator who called the Veteran and made arrangements to meet him at the door. The patient was escorted through the system and admitted voluntarily to the inpatient unit where he is safe and doing well."

"Around 6:00 this evening a young man, crying and very depressed, called the hotline. He asked us if hotlines really worked, because if he didn't get help he had no other options. He was a Reservist recently back from deployment. He hadn't accessed VA services and had never really thought about it being a real option, but he decided to choose the veteran option on the hotline number when he called, on the chance that someone would understand his problems. After about 30 minutes of interaction on the call, he decided that he would accept VA help. We were able to connect with the Suicide Prevention Coordinator at the nearest VA medical center, who in turned called him and arranged for him to come in for an evaluation later that evening. When we called him back he was getting ready to go to the VA, his friend had agreed to take him, and he repeatedly expressed his gratitude and thanks for providing him with help. He said that just knowing we were ready to help him made him feel like he should keep trying."

The VA National Suicide Hotline is only one piece of the overall VA Suicide Prevention Strategy. All of the pieces are dependent on each other and are based on the premise that suicide prevention is effective when there is accelerated and easy access to high quality mental health care supplemented by enhanced care specifically aimed at reducing the risk for suicide. This strategy depends on the concept that "suicide is everybody's business." To that end, massive awareness and education efforts are being made within the VA to ensure that all VA staffmembers are aware of the risk factors and warning signs for suicide.

Suicide Prevention Coordinators and in some cases Suicide Prevention Teams have been placed at each VA Medical Center across the country. These individuals and teams are the conduit by which Veterans in need—even in crisis—get this enhanced level of care that they need. Various systemic programs have been put into place to assist the Suicide Prevention Coordinators provide this high level of preventative care.

For example, the VA has developed a high-risk notification system so that the patient's medical record alerts other providers when they are working with someone known to be at high risk for suicide. The system also provides health care staff with safety planning templates to guide discussion with the high-risk veteran about actions to take that can help prevent getting into a crisis situation or acting on suicidal thoughts when in a crisis. Evidence-based treatment programs are being piloted, and training in various psychotherapeutic approaches is being done. Community awareness programs are being conducted across the country. The media has been called upon to help the VA get the message out to veterans that help is available.

It's an incredibly awesome task and goal, reducing suicide in the veteran population. We are at war. The economy is struggling. Our older veterans are experiencing loss and physical illness. Our newer veterans are sometimes coming home to broken relationships, economic hardship or dealing with physical injury. Substance abuse and mental illness continue to affect some of our population. The numbers of veterans now diagnosed with Post Traumatic Stress Disorder and Traumatic Brain Injury are growing, and these both may be risk factors for suicide.

Over 35,000 veterans have called the hotline. The local Suicide Prevention Coordinators have received many more local referrals from staff and the community. The media campaign and outreach efforts have touched hundreds of thousands of people. The VA Suicide Prevention program is making a difference all day and every day, all across the country, one veteran at a time.

9

A SHARPSHOOTER FIRES BACK
The Story of Army PFC Robert Kislow

"I wish I could go back and make a movie of that day because I remember every detail. How the wind was blowing and the smell of the brush . . . how I slid down the rocks . . . how the man looked after he'd shot me and how he looked after I'd killed him. A Delta Force guy sent me a photo of his body. To be truthful, it helps me sleep knowing he is dead."

For Army Specialist Rob Kislow, the exotic game hunt at James Ryffel's Eagle Ranch outside of San Antonio on June 5, 2007 almost ended before it began. Rob, who had lost his right leg fighting with the 82nd Airborne in Afghanistan, was walking to get some ice from a cooler after his arrival when he tripped on some rocks, fell and broke his prosthesis. "I thought ah, man, I just got here and now I'll be on crutches. My hunt's over."

"I could see the frustration in his eyes," Eagle Ranch manager "RB" Parker said. "He looked like he was going to cry. So I went over and asked, 'What's that thing made of. I bet I can fix it.'" With a little Texas ingenuity, epoxy and duct tape, Rob was back in business. "For the next three days I shot at everything that moved. I went out with the ranch owner's two sons and we were walking through the wilderness and they said, 'We heard you were a sniper,' and I said 'Yup' and they said, 'What can you do?' A little while later we saw some deer running in a herd about 200 yards away. All I had was a .22 Hornet rifle with open sights and no scope but I took a shot and hit two deer just like that. One of the kids said, 'That was awesome!' That whole experience made me feel free again."

Rob grew up in Northampton, a rural town 10 miles outside of Bethlehem, Pennsylvania surrounded by an extended family of enthusiastic outdoorsmen. As soon as he was old enough to hold a rifle or a bow, he learned how to shoot them, trailing along with brothers, Ryan, Michael and Jason and his father. He hunted deer, turkey, dove, pheasant, groundhog and rabbit. "When I was around ten my brothers and I were messing around with .22s and a grouse flew out of the brush. It scared the crap out of me. My reaction was to blast it out of the air. My dad says that was when he realized I had the potential to be a good shot."

Rob and his brothers used to go "plinking." "We'd toss acorns into the air and try to hit them, or shoot European starlings which are nuisance birds around where I come from. They're the size of a parakeet and fly real fast. When they land you've got about two seconds before they're off again. The European starling—that's what made me a sharpshooter." Before he shipped out to Afghanistan, Rob's going away present from his father was a bear hunt. "Dad said I had to experience one just in case I didn't come back." He almost didn't.

It wasn't long after joining the Army straight out of high school that someone noticed Rob could shoot. While at the Ranger Indoctrination Program at Fort Benning Georgia, his training got accelerated until by Christmas 2004 he'd graduated infantry and airborne school and become a sharpshooter for the 82nd Airborne.

On April 3, 2005 he deployed to Afghanistan and was assigned to Forward Operation Base Salerno, located just north of Khost on the mountainous border between Afghanistan and Pakistan. At the time the facility was occupied by the 3rd Battalion, 505th Parachute Infantry Regiment, and was named for the Italian beachhead that the 505th parachuted onto on September 14, 1943. Because of its size and close proximity to the Pakistan border, a large contingent of engineers and supporting troops were stationed at the base, including Alpha and Bravo Companies of the 82nd Airborne's 3/505th. Bravo prowled around the jagged, mountainous terrain of the Afghan/Pakistan border "looking to kick ass and take names . . . ferret out the bad guys, Taliban, insurgents, you name it." Rob had just turned nineteen.

"Most of my team was older than me, but I'd spent my life hunting and fishing and blowing things up, so 'lock and load' was business as usual." Mountain warfare fit Rob to a tee. Fording rivers and scrambling through scrub oak on search and destroy missions wasn't so different from tracking down a deer in the Pennsylvania woods. The mountain villages were also fertile territory for weeding out insurgents, and Bravo Company was soon performing house-to-house "kick in the door," "search and question" missions. The adrenaline surge never let up: "There were always rocket attacks and mortar fire." Three months into his tour of duty Rob had what soldiers call their "Alive Day." Rob's was June 10th, 2005.

"There were three teams of us and we were engaging the enemy in a mountainous area right on the Pakistan border when we discovered another group of insurgents was flanking our position. They dropped in some Special Forces guys by helicopter to help us and we were channeling the enemy into a ravine, sort of like a bull run. My buddy Derrick, who was front man, was shot in the knee. They got him to cover and I took his place in the assault position. Suddenly everyone said 'Fuck it! We're going down after them!'"

Rob scrabbled down a steep ravine through the underbrush chasing some of the insurgents, when one popped up in front of him and shot him point blank in the leg, arm and head. "He was less than ten meters away. My right arm, my trigger hand, blew up in front of my eyes." Somehow Rob managed to crawl behind some rocks, pull himself together and take aim. His first round killed the man who had shot him. "I wish I could go back and make a movie of that day because I remember every detail. How the wind was blowing and the smell of the brush . . . how I slid down the rocks . . . how the man looked after I'd killed him. A Delta Force guy sent me a photo of his body. To be truthful, it helps me sleep knowing he is dead."

In a makeshift field hospital, while Navy surgeons reattached his arm and removed the bullet lodged behind his left ear, Rob stayed awake, insisting that he be the one to call home to tell the family he'd been injured. Twenty-four hours later he was at Landstuhl Medical Center in Germany, and then Walter Reed Medical Center in Silver Spring, Maryland, where he would spend the next two years.

Besides recovering from his arm and head injuries, he had to cope with severe TBI. "I used to talk real fast but now my speech was all screwed up. I talked like a drunken sailor. I couldn't pronounce vowel sounds. I had hearing loss and big time memory loss." Because the trauma was on the left side of his brain, it was his right arm that became numb, the one that was already injured, making physical therapy twice the challenge. "But I was never alone, and that can make or break you. I don't think there was a person I knew from before Afghanistan who didn't come and see me. My dad stayed a whole month straight. My mom, who is divorced from my dad, came from California."

But it wasn't the TBI or even the gradual onslaught of PTSD symptoms that caused him the most frustration. He was in a battle to keep his right arm while at the same time convincing doctors to amputate his left leg. The blast to Rob's elbow had almost severed his arm, and there were times throughout the 13 reconstructive surgeries he had to fight to keep the surgeons from amputating it. "Ultimately they did a great job of patching me up with rods and fake tendons to maximize what functions I had left, but it took a lot of arguing on my part."

Rob argued for the opposite solution for his leg injury. His ankle had been almost completely shot off. "My doctors tried replacing it with every substance known to medical science, from cadaver bone to coral to synthetic bone. Even my dad said I should try to save it, but I just wanted it gone. I wanted them to cut the damn thing off so I could get on with my life and out of Walter Reed. No amount of therapy was going to help me because just being there was more depressing than anything else." Seventeen operations and one year later, on June 12, 2006, Rob finally got his wish. By fall he received his 30 days of convalescent leave and went home with his first prosthesis.

"Even when I got home I was pretty depressed. I'd lost my memory and couldn't sleep. My buddies said, 'It's pheasant season. Let's go hunting.' So we did, and it was the best therapy I could possibly have had." He went hunting in the Pennsylvania woods with camouflaged crutches. "That was when I first broke my prosthesis, chasing a pheasant through some roughage and jumping over a fallen tree."

When he returned to Walter Reed he earned himself designation as the perfect patient to endurance-test prostheses. He went through twelve. "They tried all the new technologies, and found that the only thing I couldn't destroy was titanium with a carbon fiber socket. He would hop up and down the steps of the hospital doing impact tests. "The problem was "stump shrink." Your leg shrinks so they have to keep replacing the socket at $5,000 a pop. But once they got it right,

I could run, bike, fish, hunt. I won myself a little aluminum boat in a bass fishing contest. I even got myself a sponsorship on an amateur paintball team." Rob prided himself on creating his own physical therapy regime. "I never liked PT. I hated them telling me what I could and couldn't do. I tried it myself, and surprisingly ended up doing almost everything they said I'd never be able to do. From the beginning I did my own research by talking to other amputees."

Before Rob broke one of his later prosthesis at the exotic game ranch, he'd already made an impression on Armed Forces Foundation volunteers, all successful businessmen who had put the hunt together for four wounded warriors, including Rob and a wheelchair-ridden veteran named Andrew. The problem of transportation to Texas was solved by Ted Gateman, the president of Greenpak, who had offered his corporate jet. "It was my first hunt and it was one of the most rewarding experiences I've ever had," recalls Jeff Shaver, a Greenpak vice president who was part of the group. "I have this visual memory as we're boarding in Manassas," says Shaver, "of Andrew in a wheelchair and I'm wondering, 'How is he going to get on the plane?' and then Rob crouches down in front of him and says, 'Get on my back.' Rob carried Andrew onto the plane. That's how the trip started. Inspirational isn't the word for it."

At 22, Rob is taking courses at Northampton Community College in Bethlehem, Pennsylvania, where his family lives. His ability to walk was recently tested by scientists at the University of Delaware. "They wanted to see how it was possible for me to walk as well as I did. I impressed the hell out of them." He plans on opening a garage that services foreign cars, he just got a truck, and is in the midst of building a race car. Meanwhile, in the spring of 2008 he received an all expenses paid, four-day vacation to the Venetian Hotel in Las Vegas courtesy of the Armed Forces Foundation.

MEDALS

Purple Heart, 2 Army Commendation Medals, Global War on Terror, National Service Medal, Afghanistan Campaign Medal, Combat Infantry Badge, Airborne Tab and Wings, Combat Patch with the 82nd Airborne Division.

"It is a black box of injuries. It's is one of the most complicated injuries to one of the most complicated parts of the body."

—Dr. Alisa D. Gean, in "War Veterans' Concussions Are Often Overlooked," *The New York Times*, August 26, 2008

10

THE EXPERT CONSULTANTS: OUR PATIENTS

By Kelly Petska, PhD, and Donald MacLennan, PhD

Shortly after the invasion of Iraq in March of 2003, service members wounded in combat began to be referred to Department of Veterans Affairs (VA) hospitals for rehabilitation. The injuries sustained by these young men and women ranged from mild to severe, and were often complicated by cognitive impairments associated with brain injury and/or post-concussive syndrome, mental health disorders, or a combination of the two. This pattern of injuries to multiple body parts or systems has been termed Polytrauma. The VA responded to this challenge by rapidly developing a continuum of rehabilitation services called the Polytrauma System of Care (PSC).

Initial efforts of the PSC focused on acute rehabilitation. While VA's acute care facilities were providing comprehensive, state of the art rehabilitation, transitional rehabilitation services were extremely limited in the VA system. In 2006, a summit was held in Washington DC, gathering experts in brain injury rehabilitation from the VA, the Department of Defense (DoD), and the private sector. These experts outlined a plan for the development of transitional care within the VA system.

Transitional rehabilitation typically occurs between acute—the initial period of hospitalization after injury—and outpatient services, but these services can be helpful to those who are struggling in the community as well. The mission is to improve the transition from a medical environment back into the soldiers' own community. Programming emphasizes skills needed to independently manage daily living, resume social roles, and engage in the workforce, school system or a volunteer setting.

While many people with brain injury and/or post-concussive syndrome are able to successfully transition into their community, supported by outpatient services, others require additional services to successfully resume their former roles. Cognitive impairments—meaning problems in thinking skills such as memory, perception, problem-solving, conceptualization or attentional deficits—present more significant barriers to community participation than do physical impairments after a brain injury. For this reason, cognitive rehabilitation becomes the centerpiece of transitional rehabilitation programs.

To develop the Polytrauma Transitional Rehabilitation Program (PTRP) at the Minneapolis VA Medical Center, we turned to the 35–40 years of literature on cognitive rehabilitation to develop programming that was consistent with best practice in the treatment of cognitive impairments, social skills, independent living skills and vocational pursuits. As patients came into our program, it became clear that they reflected both ends of the spectrum: half the patients presented with moderate-severe Traumatic Brain Injury (TBI) and the other half presented with mild TBI and symptoms of Post-Traumatic Stress Disorder (mild TBI/PTSD). Review of outcomes revealed that those with moderate to severe TBI were clearly benefiting from the programming; however, those patients with mild TBI/PTSD were showing less benefit.

While there were similarities among patients with moderate-severe TBI and those with mild TBI/PTSD, there were also distinct differences. Both groups presented with impairments in attention and memory as well as difficulty in social situations. However, patients with mild TBI/PTSD were aware of their impaired abilities as opposed to those with moderate-severe TBI, who had greater struggles with insight. In fact, some of the mild TBI/ PTSD patients showed a hyper-awareness of symptoms. This presented itself when patients would have frequent physical complaints based on minor changes from their own personal baseline and spend considerable time focusing on these differences. For example, some patients focused on their physical symptoms; these complaints changed frequently, and even after being evaluated by proper medical staff were found to have no medical basis; thus the symptoms were likely psychological or emotional presenting as physical symptoms.

In addition, patients with mild TBI/PTSD showed an ability to learn readily, while patients with moderate-severe TBI often required extensive practice to develop skills. For example, when learning how to utilize an external memory aid, such as a palm pilot, the patients with mild TBI/ PTSD showed rapid learning and often required minimal instruction, while the moderate-severe patients required extensive practice and multiple cues. We also witnessed mild TBI patients who learned to use complex functions of the palm pilot, without staff instruction, over a single weekend and taught other patients in the program how to download audio and video files and to surf the internet with the palm. Given this faster rate of learning, patients with mild TBI/ PTSD appear better able to accelerate their participation in vocational programs than do patients with moderate-severe TBI. While this may seem like an obvious conclusion, it took increasing tension to make the point clear.

As the cohort of patients with mild TBI/PTSD grew, patients increasingly began to complain about particular aspects of PTRP. The complaints centered mainly on policy and procedural aspects of the program. For example, patients became agitated with locked cabinets that couldn't be accessed without staff assistance. This fell under hospital policy and was not specific PTRP policy. While this cohort was focusing on their displeasure on program policy and procedure, it became apparent to staff that the real issue may have been that the clinical programming being offered was not meeting their specific needs.

The literature on cognitive rehabilitation is overwhelmingly focused on people with moderate-severe TBI. While literature exists for treatment of mild TBI and treatment of PTSD individually, there is little to no literature on how to treat those with both mild TBI and PTSD. This raised the question: "What do we do now?"

We chose to use the patients as expert consultants to assist us in developing programming that would better meet the needs of patients with both mild TBI and PTSD. We held a focus group and asked these mild TBI/PTSD patients what they wanted to achieve and their barriers to achieving these goals. Three main responses came out of this focus group: 1) Their struggle with social anxiety and social issues due to symptoms of PTSD; 2) Their cognitive impairments, such as attention and memory; and 3) Their concerns about their ability to return to or attend college/additional training. This focus group allowed the multidisciplinary PTRP team to develop additional, more appropriate programming based on these expert opinions.

Based on the feedback from the focus group, we created additional programming for the mild TBI/PTSD patients focusing on their issues related to PTSD and other trauma-related symptoms such as depression or anxiety. For example, we started a group focusing on emotion regulation, with emphasis on healthy, appropriate expression of anger. This group included psychoeducation, processing of current stressors (not trauma), and learning new skills/strategies for expression. For example, some patients learned how to verbally communicate their emotions more effectively while others learned how to recognize their anger based on their physiological response (e.g. increased heart rate, sweaty palms, or clenched jaw). Recognizing their physiological responses allowed them to use relaxation strategies to calm themselves down, versus responding out of anger or succumbing to other emotions and thus increasing the escalation.

Other changes included mental health providers modifying current PTSD treatments to accommodate for the cognitive impairments that each patient experiences for one-on-one sessions. Some examples of modifications included shortening handouts to make them individualized and less complex, using more bullet points and less technical language, making handouts/homework specific to the patient's struggles, and offering shorter sessions with more repetition.

While both groups of patients endorsed, or were identified, as having difficulty with social situations, it was clear that the differences were significant. Mild TBI/PTSD patients noticed that their anxiety often involved specific social situations, which led to their avoidance. They also reported feeling over-stimulated or fatigued, likely due to a combination of attentional impairment, hyper-vigilance and social anxiety. For example, one patient reported having a party in his home with close friends with whom he knew and trusted. The over-stimulation of multiple conversations and music resulted in a feeling of increased anxiety. This increased anxiety, over time, caused the patient to avoid such social situations.

In addition, their insight into their deficits can cause increased social anxiety (e.g., "I know I can't follow this conversation, what if they ask me a question?") Finally, they also reported a reduced range of emotions, often with the exception of anger. This reduced range of emotions often led to statements such as, "I know I should be happy that I have a new healthy baby, but I just don't 'feel' anything."

This presentation is quite different from moderate-severe TBI patients, who often have difficulty with social situations due to impulsivity, the need to learn or re-learn social skills, and an inability to pick up on social or non-verbal cues. Thus it made sense that we have different groups of social skills for these two distinctly different populations. The mild TBI/PTSD patients participated in social skills groups. These groups included psychoeducation regarding relaxed breathing training (including sympathetic and parasympathetic nervous system education), PTSD and other mental health symptoms, biofeedback (technology that allows patients to immediately see their physiological response, such as heart rate or body temperature), and gradual exposure to uncomfortable emotions/feelings by going into perceived stressful situations or community settings. Sometimes the exposure can be as small as walking through the VA cafeteria during lunch time or as big as going to the Mall of America. The idea was that it would start with a small outing on the VA campus, and gradually increase to outings outside of the hospital with increasing stimulation (an increase in the number of people, crowds, noise, distractions).

One area in which patients with mild TBI/PTSD and moderate-severe TBI showed great similarity was the area of cognitive impairment. Patients with mild TBI/PTSD ranked memory difficulties as one of their greatest concerns, often on a par with PTSD/trauma-related symptoms (including depression). Patients with mild TBI/PTSD also endorsed difficulty with attention. Often, their complaints centered not so much on slowed cognitive processing but rather on distractibility. They shared with us that they could be engaged in conversation, smiling and nodding, but mentally they were distracted to the point of not following the conversation up to several times per minute.

Patients speculated that this might be related to the skilled vigilance they developed while in the combat theater. They reported being taught to develop a 360-degree sense of vigilance. They indicated that their ability to divide their attentional focus over a wide-area may have come at a cost of losing their ability to selectively focus their attention on one thing. Patients believed the consequence of this attentional impairment to be quite significant. Three of the patients with mild TBI/PTSD wanted to go to school but expressed concerns regarding their ability to listen to a lecture and take notes.

One treatment approach that worked well for attentional impairment was self-instructional training, or self-talk, which is a technique used successfully to improve attention with children with attention deficit disorder (ADD). Self instructional training involves periodic mental rehearsal of adaptive behaviors that may improve functional behavior, for these purposes, listening. Patients practiced thinking the phrase, "I will focus on the speaker, and try to echo each word in my head as it is said" at intervals as they engaged in conversation or school lectures. Over time this approach improved patients conversational listening skills. Two patients used this technique to improve concentration while watching videos of school lectures by actual college professors. Initially, both patients identified well over 40 episodes of distractibility while viewing a 30-minute lecture. After extensive practice, over a 3–4 week period, the moments of distractibility for each patient decreased by nearly two-thirds.

Three out of four of our expert patient consultants expressed an interest in going, or returning to, college to pursue a career. They all voiced concerns about their ability to return to school with cognitive impairments in attention and memory. Our consultants participated in a simulated college experience, including a series of lectures and tests that assessed their ability to learn college-level information. Lecture content focused on the nature and consequences of brain injury (e.g. cognitive impairments and treatment strategies) as well as on academic strategies (e.g. how to read and retain information from chapters and test-taking strategies). In between lectures and tests they were coached on study-techniques and compensatory cognitive strategies to improve cognitive skills.

All three of our consultants experienced considerable difficulty learning information as they began the college simulation. Two clearly showed improved performance as they progressed through the program (and they are currently taking college courses). Unfortunately, one of the patient's injuries aggravated his pre-existing ADD and dyslexia. Based on this experience, he came to the realization that he was unlikely to succeed in college. However, this realization has allowed him to pursue a vocational track, which he began working toward in our PTRP program and continued in his home community upon discharge.

Traumatic Brain Injury has been described as the "signature injury" of the wars in Afghanistan and Iraq; however, we suspect this perception may change given the significant number of combat veterans with symptoms of mild TBI and PTSD (and potentially other mental health symptoms) that are so prevalent in these conflicts. We believe it is this combination of mild TBI with PTSD that will ultimately come to be seen as the signature injury for returning OEF/OIF service members. Oddly, war has a way of advancing medical practice and forcing providers to make changes in health care delivery, as we described above. The Chinese word for crisis is "dangerous opportunity." The crises experienced by the heroic men and women coming home with a complex presentation of injuries may in fact be an opportunity to change the face of rehabilitation—to find a way to blend traditional rehabilitation practices with those of mental health treatments in order to provide the best treatment future to those we serve. Not only are these men and women changing the course of history with their military contributions; their contributions as expert consultants are helping to change the future of rehabilitation.

"Some soldiers who suffer from PTSD are reluctant to share their experiences in traditional psychiatric therapy, said Colonel Charles Engel, an Army psychiatric epidemiologist. He said those soldiers may be more willing to use acupuncture and other alternatives if they are effective."

—"Pentagon Researches Alternative Treatments," Gregg Zoroya, *USA Today*, October 9, 2008

11

WAR CHANT

The Story of Sergeant John "Medicine Bear" Radell

*"We knew not everyone was the enemy, but no one told us how to
tell the difference. I wound up killing a 12-year-old boy because I
thought he was an insurgent getting ready to throw a grenade.
I killed a man and his wife and the small child she was holding in
her arms when their car wouldn't stop at our roadblock. When
reality set in and I realized what I had done I tried to talk to my
superiors, but they basically said, 'Suck it up and drive on.' It's one
of those demons I'll always live with as a soldier."*

John "Bear" Radell deployed for war in Iraq with the California
National Guard's 1498th Transportation Company on May 15, 2003.
He was thirty-five. His mission was to supply, service, live in, drive
and provide protection for Heavy Equipment Transporter Systems
(HETS), recovering and hauling everything from M-1 battle tanks and
Humvees to Port-o-Johns across war-torn Iraq. He would be attacked,
ambushed, blinded in sandstorms, swelter in 130-degree heat and perform dangerous, two-week-long convoy missions without adequate
body armor, radios or supplies, including, at times, basic parts to his
truck such as cab doors that could open and shut. For John the roads
crisscrossing Iraq were like the endless rice paddies of Vietnam. By the
time he was injured on July 22, 2003, he had either experienced firsthand or observed enough violence, killing, torture and mayhem to sear
his psyche forever.

"Camp Liberty in Kuwait was a grim, hot, sandy tent-city. There
was a military mess tent and not much else. We lived in containers for
the first couple of weeks to acclimate, and then we were off and running. What we found out was that, despite what they told us at briefings, each time our supply convoy went out the action changed to

front line combat conditions. This was nothing remotely like simple supply runs. To make things more disorienting, our rules of engagement changed on a daily basis."

Most roads held the potential of ambush, and some, like the highway between Baghdad and its airport, guaranteed a drive fraught with danger. Bear got used to living out of the truck for fifteen days at a time and driving for days without sleep in dust so thick he could seldom see the truck in front of him. Since he was trained as a weapons specialist it wasn't long before he was moved from the driver's seat to the turret of a converted Humvee with a 50mm machine gun in hand instead of a steering wheel.

On his "Alive Day" the convoy was traveling north to Mosul to supply the 4th Infantry Division. Suddenly an IED hit the truck in front of the one Bear was protecting. It was the start of an ambush. For an instant he could neither see nor hear, the blast was so close. Moments later a bullet from an AK47 slammed into his right leg just below the knee. "At the time I was oblivious to my injury. We were in the midst of a firefight, and guys were going down all around me. Then I saw the corporal. He had grabbed his video camera and was taping the action while four of our personnel lay dying on the ground at his feet. I was so angry that when the firing stopped I went after him; and then his brother, who was also in our unit, went after me. Two days later I took after him again, but this time a battle buddy knocked the rifle out of my hands."

A medic treated his bullet wound and Bear went back to business until the convoy returned to its Forward Operating Base almost a week later. "There was a lot of frustration over the red tape during our missions. We lost fifteen guys in the time I was there. We'd be in the midst of an RPG attack and be taking twenty or thirty rounds, and then we'd have to call in for permission to engage the enemy: 'Would it be appropriate to return fire? We have two men down.' I felt like here we are, soldiers trained to fight, and all we can do is to watch our comrades fall by the wayside."

His frustration built up over the months as it became more and more difficult to tell who was friendly and who was not. "We knew not everyone was the enemy, but no one told us how to tell the difference. I wound up killing a twelve-year-old boy because I thought he was an insurgent getting ready to throw a grenade. I killed a man and his wife and the small child she was holding in her arms when their car wouldn't stop at our roadblock. When reality set in and I realized what I had done and was a part of I tried to talk to my superiors, but they basically said, 'Suck it up and drive on.' It's one of those demons I'll always live with as a soldier."

Iraq wasn't Bear's first experience with military service. After graduating from high school and attending a vocational school to study computer graphics, he joined the Army in 1987. By 1990 he was serving with a Special Forces unit. "I was searching for an identity. I was born Blackfoot and Cherokee but I was adopted into a white family and never came to terms with my ancestry. It took me ten years before I came to grips with being a Native American." In 1996 he met Aiyana ("Flowering Blossom") at a Native American drumming circle. A few years older, divorced with a daughter, Aiyana brought love and serenity into Bear's life. "She and I got to talking and learned that we were both interested in exploring more about our spiritual heritage." They stayed together for fourteen years.

"When the towers got hit, I was working in the Post Exchange at March Air Force Base. It wasn't long before I got a certified letter saying they were going to activate my old unit." In February 2003 he started 90 days of training at Camp Roberts, a 42,000-acre base in central California, and then shipped out to Iraq. Before leaving, he and Aiyana were married on the 14th of April. Six months earlier he had reunited with his biological mother, sister and brother through a birth registry in Nevada. "I left three families when I deployed to war: my adopted family, my biological family and Aiyana."

It would be August 20, almost a month after he was injured, before Bear was flown back from Iraq to the United States. "I was in crazy pain but they told me to perform my duties, so that's what I did. When I got back to Fort Lewis they fixed my leg and discovered damage to my eye and ears due to the blast. But my worst injury was Post-Traumatic Stress Syndrome and no one recognized that condition, not even me, not back in 2003." He would spend the next year fighting for his sanity.

"The year at Fort Lewis was bad. My first therapist was an Army Major who refused to believe I had PTSD. She thought that it all related back to being spanked as a child. I got so angry that I slapped her. She pressed charges for that and I almost got an Article 15. Instead they labeled me 'unstable' and didn't allow me off the base." At one point John was reviewed by a medical board to see if he was capable of being redeployed to Iraq, but was deemed "a threat to the military" and "suffering from a moral flexibility."

"I trained so long and so hard that I did what I was told, totally cut off from my emotions. But eventually it came back to haunt me. I had to pay for all that."

On February 1, 2004, Bear was retired from the Army with 100 percent disability, 70 percent PTSD. It would be years before his Traumatic Brain Injury from repeated exposure to IED blasts would show up in a CATScan prescribed only because he'd lost all feeling in his right arm. He returned to his family in Oceanside, California, changed.

"I couldn't relate to anyone when I first got home. I couldn't hold my wife or my fifteen-year-old daughter. I felt like I was stained. I saw blood on my hands. I had night terrors. I've been prescribed up to thirteen medications a day in various combinations, depending on my levels of anxiety and depression." Bear isolated himself in front of his computer for almost two years. "I became a hermit. It took me a year and a half just to spend twenty minutes inside of a WalMart. People thought I was crazy, but to me they were the ones not connecting the dots. Today it's the same. If I never left home again, I'd be happy."

Bear knew he was in for a long haul after an incident at a grocery store. "I was next to a lady pushing a cart and talking on her cell phone. Her little boy should have been in the booster seat but instead he was running around pulling things down from the shelves and dropping them. Finally the lady yelled and smacked him. I went up to her and said, 'Lady, if you hit him again I'll break your arm and shove it up your ass. You should spend less time on the phone and more time taking care of your kid.' She said, 'How dare you speak to me like that!' and I replied, 'Lady, I've earned the right. I bled on the battlefield for you.' When things like that happened, I just withdrew more."

John recognized low tolerance for things people said or did that, before he went to Iraq, would have "rolled right off my back." After four years of intense therapy, sometimes as often as three times a week, he is coping better with his level-four PTSD, but still grapples with "My evil twins: general anxiety and panic attacks."

Early on he also knew his PTSD was affecting his marriage. While he sat paralyzed with anxiety and depression Aiyana was left to run the household, from managing their finances to taking care of the pets, the children, the cooking and the cleaning. When Bear overdrew their bank account with his debit card, they decided she would give him a monthly allowance instead. By 2007 they were wise enough to get some marriage counseling. "There were only so many times that she could hear the same excuse: 'I've got PTSD.' We had to work through the issues. Now I have a weekly chore list I'm supposed to do but I still forget about it, and that causes trouble." In the fall of 2008 Bear and Aiyana separated. He now lives in an apartment near his biological family in Las Vegas, where he continues to recover from his PTSD.

MEDALS

Army DSC, Silver Star, DoD DSM, Bronze Star, Purple Heart, Joint SVC Commendation, Army Commendation, Army Good Conduct Medal, USA Reserve Achievement Medal, Army National Guard Achievement, Army Defense, Army NCO, Army Service, Army Overseas Ribbon, Army Presidential Unit, Joint Meritorious Unit, Combat Action Badge.

"The photo captures everything that Americans wanted to believe about the Iraq war in the earliest days of the invasion in 2003. PFC Joseph Dwyer, an Army medic whose unit was fighting its way up the Euphrates to Baghdad, cradles a wounded boy. The child is half-naked and helpless, but trusting. Private Dwyer's face is strained but calm."

—"Losing Private Dwyer," Lawrence Downes, *The New York Times*, July 15, 2008

12

THE WEAPON OF CHOICE—
PATIENCE

By Charles "Chip" West, PhD

As reported by the Rand Corporation in the spring of 2008, Post-Traumatic Stress Disorder (PTSD) is one of the top three most frequently occurring "hidden" conditions our soldiers are bringing back from deployment to Iraq or Afghanistan; the other two are major depression and Traumatic Brain Injury (TBI). Combat Stress Reaction, a term used inside the military, is generally a short-term condition that is not interchangeable with PTSD.

PTSD is classified as a psychiatric disorder, the symptoms of which can be treated. But it presents unique challenges. As a carryover of an intense, real-life experience, PTSD seems to lurk in the shadows, a part of you but not quite part of you. Most people with PTSD feel a troubling loss of self-control as a result. Post-traumatic symptoms defy the willpower war veterans repeatedly muster day after day as they try to move on with their lives. But why does PTSD so often trip up those who suffer from it even as they recognize and do their best to cope with this illness? What is it about psychological trauma that stands apart from other human experience?

Trauma is an intense experience that for many people is not processed by their nervous system like other episodes in their lives. It connects with a deep survival mode in the human mind that engages when we are participants in, or witness to, a scenario of real danger to life and limb. Penetrating our "safety zone," traumatic events expose our mortality and serve as a permanent reminder that feelings of per-

71

sonal safety from moment to moment are not guaranteed. You feel in the midst of the traumatic event or later recognize—through physical sensations perhaps rather than through clear feelings or thoughts—that the threat was powerful enough to shatter your faith in a continuous stream of safe moments. To have unusual personal reactions or "symptoms" in the wake of such an experience is quite normal. Reactions to trauma only move into the realm of PTSD when they endure over time and are consistently disruptive to your life as you now try to lead it.

No predictive model has yet been devised that can reliably distinguish the at-risk from the immune to PTSD. It can inflict anyone. Most notably, courage and bravery are separate attributes from susceptibility to PTSD. Soldiers can win the Purple Heart and have performed courageously in countless ways known only to the soldiers themselves, yet still can suffer from PTSD. What does that say? Character flaws are not the reason PTSD emerges. A prior history of traumatic experiences can count as a factor, as can certain life values related to the "shoulds and should-nots" of human behavior that you saw violated in the war zone, yet PTSD does not spare the courageous and inflict the weak-minded. There are few blacks and whites and many shades of gray.

Because your war zone experience went on for months, with daily exposure to danger for which you were trained with fellow soldiers, you lived the military culture of grinding on through life-threatening experience as routine. The routine threat, however, never invited complacency, and you were forever vigilant and ready to protect against it for the survival of your fellow soldiers and to accomplish your mission. Your PTSD was enmeshed in this culture, but you didn't have the luxury of down time to experience its symptoms. While in theatre, as we read in the experience of Sergeant John Radell in the previous chapter, you had to "suck it up and drive on." But now PTSD is like throwing gas on the fire of cultural differences you already feel with civilians upon your return from the war. Your own family and loved ones know you have changed, but you cannot bridge over to them from where you are because you cannot describe what happened to you "over there."

You risk suffering in isolation because of fear of being judged—a feeling that increases the sense of alienation from yourself and leads you to not feel at home in your own mind and body. You have changed as a function of your war zone experience. You feel different from other people and estranged from some aspects of American culture that used to have a comfortable familiarity. All those feelings that alienate you from others make it that much more challenging to trust anyone enough to let them help you.

Mustering the courage to allow others to help you even while you feel unsafe is one of your bigger challenges. As Second Lieutenant Sylvia Blackwood-Boutelle recommends in the next first-person account,

"You have to get 'Team You' together. You can't be afraid to ask for help." Patience is needed on the road to recovery. You cannot control how long it will take to free yourself of active symptoms—those day-to-day anxiety and panic attacks that paralyze—you can only keep supporting yourself and allow others in.

As you engage the next challenge in your life, you have to patiently respect your pace of recovery. If you return to civilian work, you will have limited control over what you are exposed to and get "triggered" into PTSD symptoms from time to time. Riding in a car in heavy traffic, you will have times of barely holding panic in check. But you are doing the work with yourself that you have to do—slowly building a new track record of safety in the world. You do so because there is no simply snapping out of the consequences of the traumatic experiences you have had. The key is not trying to avoid experiences that trigger symptoms, but having the resiliency to push past them.

You also need patience when it comes to accessing the right level of care. You have to be a relentless advocate for yourself. You are entitled to good care, but pursuing that care can be very frustrating if your sense of entitlement is not in sync with the resources of your local health care system. Managing this frustration will by itself test your capacity to champion your own recovery. Let other people partner with you in identifying what programs and services are accessible to you.

When you investigate treatment options, you will discover that there are so-called "evidence-based" treatments available that do not involve drugs. Evidence–based refers to the fact that these procedures have been through trials of scientific testing that support the claim that their use leads to positive outcomes. Underlying several of the treatment methods is the idea that repeated, controlled exposure to reminders of the original traumatic events while under the supervision of a trained mental health professional allows your nervous system (including the power plant of your nervous system, the brain) to settle down. A successful outcome is remembering clearly what happened while learning to dampen down the more extreme emotional and physical response to the event(s). You may still need to talk with a professional about the bigger picture of your experience—like the question of where to go from here—but you have unhooked yourself from the daily dread of being triggered into a gut-wrenching reliving of the trauma.

Above all, keep the faith that you can restore some balance to your life again as a civilian. Obtaining well-deserved benefits from the government does not fill the vacuum left when you have not yet found a new productive and meaningful use of your time. Not surprisingly, veterans who return to work in some capacity have an easier time with a host of adjustment issues, including the management of PTSD symptoms. Anchor efforts to help yourself around a new focus, occupation or mission, for the more you build from where you are now the more resilience you will find within yourself.

13

A WOMAN AT WAR
The Story of Army Second Lieutenant Sylvia Blackwood-Boutelle

"Death was all around you all the time. It was war, after all. People were being injured, killed; people I knew, friends. But no one talked about the gore. We denied it because if we didn't deny it we'd mess up our careers."

On the evening of March 29, 2007, Sylvia Blackwood-Boutelle was taking the subway to a reception. She was working in Crystal City as chief of media relations for the Special Inspector General for Iraq Reconstruction, and social events after work were ordinary occurrences. But as the train pulled up to Metro Center she blanked on where she was going or why, and she panicked. "At that moment my whole life came crashing down. I found my way home and cried the entire night." By 4 a.m. she had pulled out her Leatherman knife intending to slash her wrists. "Then I saw my son's face and I realized I just couldn't kill myself."

At sunrise she drove to a VA medical center, sobbing the entire way. "I got myself to the hospital in DC and begged them to admit me. I waited for hours before they finally let me talk to a doctor." Sylvia spent the next week in 3D East, the psychiatric ward. "I was locked down with twenty men and a couple other women," she remembers. "The place was empty. Barren. There was nothing to do but walk the corridors and pray that your meds would kick in long enough to make the panic attacks go away for a few hours. I spent a lot of time joking around with everyone about how crazy we all were."

She would talk to a number of psychologists during that week, but none of them offered any remedy for her mental anguish. "A friend of mine, who was a doctor in the Air Force, made some calls and found me a space at the Fort Thomas PTSD residential women's clinic in Kentucky." The clinic provides highly personal care to only a few veterans at a time with hours of group and individual therapy each week. It was there that Sylvia learned she had Post-Traumatic Stress Disorder. She was forty-two, a mother of a seven-year-old boy and a veteran of three deployments to Iraq.

Recognizing her PTSD didn't make it go away or any easier to cope with. "When I returned to the house in DC where I was renting a room from two women, one of whom was a veteran of the Iraq war, I discovered they had kicked me out. They'd packed up all my stuff in boxes and put the boxes in a storage unit. I went to live with friends fifty miles outside Washington and commuted to my job in Crystal City, until my car was stolen a couple of months later. Basically you could say that for the next year I was always on the verge of homelessness and always battling PTSD." This wasn't how her career path was supposed to unfold.

Sylvia grew up in a military family. Her father was a colonel in the Army, and her mother had been a staff sergeant in the Air Force. After graduating from high school Sylvia left for Los Angeles. "I wanted to be a rock star, and naturally the only place to do that was LA. Of course that didn't work out and eventually I came to my senses and decided to go to college." She graduated with a degree in English literature from San Francisco State, and by 1994 had joined a Civil Affairs unit out of Oakland Army Base, first as a reservist and then going active duty so she could make enough money to buy a car.

By 2000 she'd been married six years and was in the process of volunteering for Bosnia when she discovered she was pregnant. She went back to being a reservist, but then in September 2003 she was called up to serve with the 222th Broadcast Operations Detachment in Baghdad. "When I found out that I was going to Iraq I went numb all over. I had less than two months to prepare for leaving my two-year-old son, Holden." Sylvia trained at Fort Lewis, Washington for a month, and then on November 13 flew directly to Baghdad. "It was so cold there, especially on the convoys. We had Vietnam era vests, no heavy coats. I spent Thanksgiving at Logistics Support Area Anaconda, or 'Camp Anaconda' outside of Balad Airbase . . . we called it 'Mortaritaville'."

Although she spent her first two months "crying her eyes out," Sylvia soon realized that she had the opportunity of a lifetime. As a military reporter she could travel anywhere, write about anything, and the sooner she got involved in her job, the faster the time would pass. By January she was living in the Green Zone in Baghdad.

"They gave me a lot of freedom. I produced stories for the American Forces Television, and then later the Pentagon Channel. I'd grab my Sony 170, shoot and narrate my own stuff, then come back and edit it on the AVID. I must have done seventy to eighty pieces that year. It was awesome. I rubbed elbows with the best and the brightest of journalism and media—everyone from Jim Glanz from the *New York Times* to Brian Bennett from *Time* magazine."

There was only one caveat: "We were ordered to tell the good news about Iraq's reconstruction. They wanted evergreen feature stories that were happy, happy, happy." She got involved with the Association of Free Prisoners, a coalition that collected Saddam Hussein-era execution orders from throughout the country. She taped footage at the Baghdad Correctional Facility, otherwise known as Abu Ghraib Prison, once before and twice after "60 Minutes" broke the story about prisoner abuse. But there was a dark side to all the excitement.

"Since I went everywhere I saw, no, I experienced a lot of violence. In places like Mosul and Balad we were bombed every night. I remember one night I was dangling my feet in the swimming pool and a mortar shell dropped into the water three feet away. One morning I left my trailer only to find pools of blood on the ground and splattered waist high on the walls. I saw a severed arm, and went through an IED attack." She buried her emotions, refusing to admit that anything might be amiss in her psyche. "Death was all around you all the time. It was war, after all. People were being injured, killed; people I knew, friends. But no one talked about the gore. We denied it because if we didn't deny it we'd mess up our careers."

When she returned home in the fall of 2004 to California, she found herself ill at ease with civilian life, even though she delighted in being with her son. By then she and her husband were working out the terms of their divorce, but they remained good friends. Today it is her ex-husband who takes care of Holden. Meanwhile Sylvia started having nightmares and panic attacks in the midst of the most innocuous excursions. "I would freak out walking down the aisle of a grocery story and have to walk out right then and there and go home." At the end of the year during a medical exam she was given a test for PTSD.

"The first time I took it I came up with all the symptoms. I told doctors, 'No way: that cannot be. Let me take it again.' So they did, and I answered all the questions differently. I wasn't about to ruin my career. I'm a high-energy person. I figured I could deal with it myself." Sure enough, the second time around she passed the test. Three months later, in March of 2005, she was back in Iraq working for the State Department's press office at the US Embassy in Baghdad. She would spend another year and a half coping with her stress and anxiety by herself. "I was a Portfolio Press Officer. I handled the entire anti-corruption effor, plus economic issues and the diplomatic side of health. But my mental condition just deteriorated, and at the end I couldn't keep busy enough to stay in control. I was always on edge; always in fight or flight mode." She let it be known that she wanted to come home.

Once she was back in California she withdrew from the world, hiding in her apartment overcome with anxiety, paranoia and insomnia. Loud noises triggered panic attacks. She was irritable and jumpy. "When Holden threw a temper tantrum I broke one of his toys. I couldn't eat; I couldn't sleep. If the AC went on, I hit the floor. I knew I was losing it, but I still didn't trust anyone enough to tell them what I was going through." In late September she was hired by the Inspector General's Office for Iraq Reconstruction and moved back east. But just when she thought she might be able to get back on an even keel, she received orders for a third deployment to Iraq, this time as a public affairs officer for the Inspector General's office.

With trepidation she flew into Bagdad on November 25th, 2006, dreading another holiday season "in theater." But two days earlier, her job had ceased to exist. The official who had demanded she take the position had changed her mind and was herself leaving her job to report to the US Embassy in Baghdad as Director of Communications. "At first no one would tell me what was going on, and then when I found out, I blew up. I can't describe how angry I felt; how betrayed."

Luckily a good friend, the person at the Inspector General's Office who had hired her in the first place, came to her rescue. He had emergency orders written for her to go from Iraq to California to visit her mother, who was very ill and in the hospital. By January 14th of 2007 she was back at her old desk in Crystal City. Three months later was when she contemplated killing herself.

Sylvia is still in the Army. She is still being treated for her PTSD at various VA facilities. "I knew something was wrong for so long, but I didn't tell anyone soon enough. I was so afraid to admit that I needed help. The thing is, I'm proud I'm in the military and did my part for my country. I got to do something worthwhile. But urban warfare took a lot out of me." Now she is determined to get the treatment she needs to heal. "You have to get 'Team You' together. You can't be afraid to ask for help. You can't be afraid to be the big mess that you are because PTSD scatters your brain until your life becomes one constant state of anxiety. It's horrible. What's worse is that because it's a mental state, people don't see it. It's so easy to convince them that nothing's wrong with you, when everything is."

The Armed Forces Foundation helped Sylvia rework her resume and gave her career counseling as well as a four-day all expenses paid trip to the Venetian Hotel in Las Vegas in the spring of 2008. Sylvia is in the process of writing two books, one of which is a novel entitled *Bitch Chicks of Baghdad*.

MEDALS

National Defense Service Medal, Global War on Terrorism Expeditionary Medal, Global War on Terrorism Service Medal, Armed Forces Reserve Medal w/m Device, Army Service Ribbon, Army Good Conduct Medal, 2 Overseas Service Bars, Army Achievement Medal, Army Commendation Medal.

"The Army was unprepared for the high number of suicides and cases of post-traumatic stress disorder among its troops, as the wars in Iraq and Afghanistan have continued far longer than anticipated. Many Army posts still do not offer enough individual counseling and some soldiers suffering psychological problems complain that they are stigmatized by commanders."

—"Soldier Suicides at Record Levels," Dana Priest, *Washington Post*, January 31, 2008

14

I JUST WANT TO BE BACK IN IRAQ

By Alice Psirakis, LCSW

"I wish I was back in Iraq—things were so much easier there." I can't tell you how many times I used to hear that statement from soldiers who had returned from combat in Iraq. The statement itself seems like an oxymoron. I remember the first couple of times I heard it, I thought it was completely bizarre. At what point does a combat zone begin to feel safer, more predictable; easier than life back home in the United States?

Over time, however, it began to make perfect sense to me.

I was a captain in the US Army Reserve for eight years, serving as a licensed clinical social worker. From 2004 to 2007 I ran the mental health clinic at Fort Dix, New Jersey. I probably saw a thousand soldiers during my tenure. The clinic provided mental health services to soldiers getting ready to deploy to Iraq and Afghanistan, as well as to the injured combat veterans who returned.

What broke my heart and surprised me the most was how isolated in their symptoms were the combat veterans I treated. As a clinician, I heard the same symptoms being described to me over and over again by the soldiers who came in. I just assumed the veterans talked with one another and knew what they were all going through. I couldn't have been more wrong: most of the time they had no idea that other veterans were experiencing the same symptoms, and they suffered in isolation.

Soldiers told me how they slept with box cutters under their pillow because it made them feel safer, but how their wives refused to sleep in the same bed with them out of fear they might use the weapon in their sleep. Soldiers told me about getting up in the middle of the night and conducting surveillance around their house because they could feel the Iraqis lurking.

Soldiers told me about never calling back a girl they took to dinner because they were horribly embarrassed after jumping in their seat when they heard the door slam, a sound reminiscent of gunfire, mortars or IEDs. Soldiers told me about knocking themselves out with alcohol every night because it was the only thing that made them fall asleep and kept them asleep, giving them momentary relief from their intrusive nightmares.

Soldiers told me about trying to navigate an impenetrably bureaucratic medical system and wondering how they were going to support their families once they got back home with, say, their sprained vertebrae—one of the most common injuries I saw. Soldiers told me about avoiding going to sleep with their spouses, preferring to stay up and watch TV in an effort to avoid sexual intimacy, not understanding why they just didn't feel like being close to their wife in that way.

Soldiers told me about going home to visit their family in Brooklyn on weekends and hearing the neighborhood mosque call its Muslim community to prayer and having a flashback. Soldiers told me about the increasing agitation and rage they felt riding on a New York City subway when someone happened to accidentally bump into them during rush hour. Soldiers told me about the paralyzing fear they felt driving under a highway overpass, afraid something would be dropped down and explode in front of them.

Soldiers told me about coming home to a factory job in Tennessee, after they had spent twelve months in Iraq serving as a gunner, and still yearning for that adrenaline rush. They told me about volunteering for a second tour to Iraq just to capture that same sense of validation and purpose in their life that, suddenly, only war could fulfill. Soldiers told me about struggling with their faith and feeling tortured by their conscience because they had killed an innocent Iraqi man at a checkpoint, a man they didn't know was innocent at the time. "I can't bring myself to go back to church," they sobbed.

Soldiers sat in my office crying, head in hands, clutching the disfigured dog tags of a battle buddy who was burned alive after his Humvee was hit by an IED. Soldiers told me they were beginning to think that they liked the killing. "Big," "tough," "boys" cried in my office when thinking about their unit members and how much they missed the daily camaraderie that could only be experienced in a combat zone.

This wasn't the life they had known before going to war. But it seemed to be the only life they knew now. I heard the same sentiment over and over again: "I had no idea it would be this hard when I got back." Veterans often confided that their old life seemed a distant memory to them. Though I'm not sure they could articulate it, I believe they mourned the loss of their old selves. So did their families. These soldiers were unrecognizable not only to themselves but to everyone around them.

Veterans struggled to reconcile their view of themselves and of humanity with what they had done and what had occurred around them during war. They couldn't just go to a bar and have a drink with their buddies because they didn't relate to their peers any longer. They were no longer concerned with the latest Porsche model, the pretty girl sitting across from them, or their co-worker's newborn baby. After all, some of them had missed their own children's birth while deployed. Truthfully, they could care less—not because they were or insensitive or rude . . . but because they were simply numb. They didn't have the ability to feel the way they once did. And their perspective on life had changed, without them necessarily wanting it to.

As the daily nuisances of life became an exhausting mental and emotional struggle, the soldiers began to yearn for the simplicity of the combat zone, with its regimented schedule, established chain-of-command, automatic bonds among a band of brothers (and sisters, of course) like no comparable bonds in the civilian world, pre-prepared meals (ok, maybe not those), and lack of time to process what was happening. Things happened because they had to happen, without conscious effort on the soldiers' part. Otherwise, they would not have survived.

But when soldiers come back home, they find that neither their old ways of living nor what they learned in war serve them well. In fact, wartime instincts only exacerbate their problems. Anger and rage are useful techniques in conquering your enemies, but not so popular when dealing with your family and co-workers. And being stuck between two worlds—the world you knew before the war and the world you lived in during the war—leaves you nowhere but burdened by your post-traumatic stress disorder. Or your depression. Or your alcoholism. Or your bereavement. Or your sprained vertebrae. Or your traumatic brain injury.

So when the soldiers I treated looked at me and asked, "You probably think I'm crazy for wanting to go back, don't you?" I was able to look them straight in the eye and respond, "Not at all."

I finally understood it.

15

AT HOME OUTSIDE THE WIRE
The Story of Marine Corps Corporal William Berger

"We'd divide into SWAT teams, go house by house, kick in the doors, shout . . . when you're clearing rooms, getting shot at, you're in fight or flight mode. But there's no place to run to. You don't really think about it. I'd kill some guy and then I'd rush right on through. Sometimes when I realized later what I'd done I'd throw up."

Besides securing towns and doing construction, 20-year-old Marine Corporal William Berger had other responsibilities when he was deployed with the Army's 420th Engineer Brigade in February 2004. "We were attached to the 8th Engineer Support Battalion but then our unit got sent over to the 420th to provide security while they were building bridges outside of Balad, right in the middle of the Sunni Triangle. The convoy would go out for two or three days at a time.

"They were supposed to have gotten one of those high-tech mobile robots that neutralize IEDs, but the DoD, I don't know; they'd run out or something so we had to improvise. When someone thought they saw an IED in the road, two Marines would run up and toss a grenade on the supposed IED and then we'd just run like hell to get away." The typical charge of an IED was 16 sticks of C4, a significant blast. "You had to time it just right so that you didn't get blown up yourself," William confides. "But it was impossible to miss the shock wave."

By June the convoy faced daily blinding sandstorms amidst 150-degree heat. "It was like dry wall dust. There was no place, no crevice on your body it didn't get. We were all coughing up blackish brown mucous because of that sand." Travel became a balancing act between being comfortable and being safe. "The Army guys liked to drive with the AC on and the windows up, so that became a problem. When I'd

85

ride shotgun I'd roll the window down and the guy driving would say, roll it up. I'd say, hell no, I'm not going to be a sitting duck, so he'd get pissed, I'd get pissed, but in the end I was going to have my rifle ready to go." However, when it came time to secure a village, everyone was on the same page. "We'd divide into SWAT teams, go house by house, kick in the doors, shout . . . when you're clearing rooms, getting shot at, you're in fight or flight mode. But there's no place to run to. You don't really think about it. I'd kill some guy and then I'd rush right on through. Sometimes when I realized later what I'd done I'd throw up.

"On the base the Army and the Air Force lived in trailers but us Marines, we lived in tents. It was so damn hot in there, at night you didn't want to stay inside even when the sirens went off and the mortar rounds would start . . . even when the explosions got closer and closer. I remember one night they hit the satellite dish 20 feet from where I was sitting in line to talk on the phone."

William doesn't remember how many confirmed kills he had or people he injured but he has recurring nightmares about them which got progressively worse as time went on. "They're not normal nightmares like the boogey man is going to get you. They're big and awful. I wake up and the bed is soaked. I get up, take a shower, eat a sandwich and wait for daylight. I don't go back to sleep after one of those nightmares."

Tami Berger, William's mother, lists her son's symptoms in the matter-of-fact tone of someone who served as an Army Medic for six years and as a Registered Nurse since her time in the Army. "He has short-term memory loss. You tell him something and he'll forget it two minutes later. He's lost his sense of smell entirely. He flies off the handle occasionally for no apparent reason. And then there's the depression and the migraines. But it's his seizures that are frightening. I remember one time a year or so after he'd gotten back from Iraq, he was taking a shower while getting ready to go to the funeral of a fellow Marine. I heard a big bang. I went in and he was face down in four or five inches of water having a seizure. He could have drowned. I turned him over; he was blue in the face. I called 911. By the time the EMS got there, William was standing in the bathroom, both legs in one leg of his PJ bottoms. He didn't want to be humiliated."

The seizures began after William was apparently exposed to a nerve agent, although no one in the military will verify the incident, and William's not quite sure himself exactly what happened.

One night in late June William was with an Army convoy outside the base. He was on fire watch when insurgents attacked. He remembers heavy mortar fire and then feeling his knees give out and falling to the ground. When he came to, he had no idea he'd had his first Grand Mal seizure. For the next few days, the seizures increased in number. "I'd twitch, black out for a few seconds, and then come to and find myself on the ground. I never knew when it was going to happen. Finally I went to my Corpsman, and I said, 'You gotta get me out of here. I'm a liability.'" The next day William was Medevac'd to Landstuhl Medical Center in Germany.

But despite days of tests the doctors could find nothing physically wrong with him. "They told me the seizures must be coming from deep inside my brain and there was nothing they could do." He was sent to Camp Lejeune in North Carolina, prescribed nothing for his migraines or seizures and put to work full time as a Combat Engineer.

Two months later William had another seizure at a party and fell to the concrete floor, fracturing his skull. His best friend, a fellow Marine, stayed with him, applying CPR until the EMS came. "I would have suffocated on my own puke if he hadn't been there," William says. He was flown to a trauma center in Greenville, NC, where he spent the next two days in a coma. "When I got there, he was sitting in a chair strapped down, totally unaware of what was going on, recalls Tami, "and he was like Houdini. The nurses told me he had pulled out the tube that they'd inserted to keep him breathing and had also yanked out the catheter. They finally put restraints on him and stationed a Marine in the room to help keep him under control. The nurses were great, letting me stay. About the only thing that seemed to calm him was my standing there stroking his head."

A short while later when orders came to transfer William back to Camp Lejeune, Tami went ballistic. "I said, 'Over my dead body, you're taking my kid. There's still blood on his head; he's only been seen by an internist, not even a neurosurgeon . . . I'll get an attorney." William was allowed to stay in the hospital and then return home to his parents' house to recover. He was taken to a local neurosurgeon, neurologist and psychiatrist who all agreed to help him.

On March 1, 2007, William was honorably discharged from the Marine Corps. He was given the choice of accepting 40 percent disability due to Traumatic Brain Injury or risk the 40 percent to negotiate for more. He accepted the offer. Over a year later the regional Veterans Administration would determine he was due 90 percent disability benefits for his physical injuries, TBI and PTSD combined, a monthly income that wouldn't start for another year. For the first time since he left for the Marine Corps Recruit Depot at Parris Island at age 18, William was on his own as a civilian. He moved to Suwannee, Georgia, sharing a house with a new girlfriend, an environmental scientist he had met at a party. He got a job at the local lumberyard, bought a truck and enrolled in classes at Gainesville College. "I told myself that I could keep it together, even though I was pretty crazy at times. I thought I could outsmart my emotions."

But his short-term memory loss made it difficult to be on time at the lumberyard and follow through on tasks, and he lost the job. He started going to a VA TBI therapy group in Atlanta, but his symptoms got worse and his relationship with his girlfriend turned sour. "I was very childish and irritable. I had trouble being intimate with her; I would withdraw and she wouldn't know how to bring me out of it. Then I'd get frustrated and we'd have these fights. I wouldn't even know what they were about sometimes. I'd just fly off the handle. I'd have panic attacks. I remember we rented the Mel Gibson movie, "We Were Soldiers Once and Young," and I had to leave because of the shooting. I freaked out over loud noises and pops. I was on anti-depressants, anti-seizure drugs. She didn't know me prior. I'd get so frustrated at the doctors for giving me one drug, then another drug, then another drug. She just couldn't understand it all." Their arguing escalated when William decided he wanted a dog, and soon after that they broke up.

William rented an apartment in Oakwood, Georgia, a few miles from his parents' house, and got himself a four-month-old Austrian Shepherd who he named Raider. He was still enrolled at the University, but was having trouble with his courses because of the memory loss. "Seems like no matter how great my notes were, I'd still forget important material." When he sought help for his learning problems associated with TBI, the University turned him away. "When William was in sixth grade, he was always getting into trouble," Tami recalls, "so we had him tested at the Sylvan Learning Center, and he was reading at a college level. He was just bored. It kills me that this kid who served his country and who had to fight for everything his whole life, they wouldn't give him the tools to learn with. I was very angry that they would not accommodate him." Soon after that, William dropped out.

He continued to respond to local job listings and was puzzled when his application to be a security guard at a correctional facility fell through. "Maybe it's my health record. The thing is, no one is going to make something of my life except me. When you have something like TBI that most people don't recognize or understand, you're on your own. You got to have patience and strength. It's not physical strength I'm talking about that's going to lift you emotionally." The Armed Forces Foundation gave him career counseling and helped with rent and truck insurance.

For a long time William searched for an alternative to the Southern Baptist church he went to throughout his childhood. "I was looking for a place where you're not just scolded for what you've done all week." He finally found a small nondenominational church where he feels comfortable. "It's pretty low key. They use a version of the King James Bible that's understandable. You can wear blue jeans and a collared shirt. I like the people there."

He keeps his hair cut like it was in the Corps. "Seems like I have to dig deep to keep my sanity. If I had longer hair I'd probably pull it out." What does he miss the most from his TBI? "The smell of my mother's cooking."

William eventually got a job with T.J. Max, but like the lumberyard, it became too much for him. He moved back in with his parents in Cummings, Georgia, and enrolled in La Nier Technical School to learn how to become a welder.

On December 16, 2008 William was on his way to Camp Le Jeune to be re-evaluated for additional symptoms of TBI when his car broke down in Jacksonville, North Carolina. The repairs were expensive and would take a few days. With no money to speak of, and unwilling to impinge even more on his family, William was at a loss. He contacted

Semper Fi and received a donation, but it only covered the cost of a hotel room for a night. Knowing that the Armed Forces Foundation has a policy of only helping veterans out once, due to the numbers of people asking for help, William didn't contact them. He spent the next two nights in a House of Pancakes sitting in a booth until finally, exhausted and desperate, he called AFF, prepared to beg for a donation. The foundation immediately paid for his car repairs and a hotel for him to stay in until they were completed.

MEDALS

Combat Action Ribbon, Global War on Terrorism Expeditionary Medal, Global War on Terrorism Service Medal, 2 Letters of Appreciation, Marine Corps Good Conduct Medal, Sea Service Deployment Ribbon, National Defense Service Medal, Navy Unit Commendation.

16

WINNING HIDDEN BATTLES

Defense Centers of Excellence for
Psychological Health and Traumatic Brain Injury

By Bill Yamanaka

I have had the privilege of working in the Office of the Deputy Assistant Secretary of Defense for Force Health Protection and Readiness since June of 2006. My work focuses on information sharing, and this has given me the opportunity to contribute to an effort that collectively strives to improve conditions for our people who are sacrificing so much. A large part of my task had me supporting, in its formative months, the Defense Centers of Excellence (DCoE) for Psychological Health and Traumatic Brain Injury. A new organization, the DCoE is leading the effort to make life better for service members who may be dealing with psychological health issues such as Traumatic Brain Injury or Post-Traumatic Stress Disorder.

As a former naval officer and now an organizational communicator, what I am seeing is genuine compassion in the attitude of Department of Defense officials and military leaders. Task forces, presidential commissions and independent committees, as well as the National Defense Authorization Act of 2008, presented hundreds of recommendations to address the psychological health and TBI concerns of wounded warriors. In keeping with the intent and specific recommendations, and in charting a course for the DCoE, the emphasis for renewed efforts held steady on a continuum of care. Through the DCoE's collaboration and what they refer to as "network orchestration," the Department of Defense is effectively addressing the recommendations to improve the military health system.

It is history in the making. Prior to the DCoE becoming official, the Deputy Assistant Secretary of Defense for Force Health Protection and Readiness, Ms. Ellen Embrey, was responsible for a line of action on TBI and PTSD, reporting directly to a Senior Oversight Committee. That committee is co-chaired by the Deputy Secretary of Defense, Gordon England, and the Deputy Secretary of Veterans Affairs, Gordon Mansfield. In my eyes, it is without question that this nation's defense leadership sincerely believes psychological health is of prime importance to overall good health in America's armed forces. This is why the DCoE came into being.

The line of action was referred to as the "Red Cell," and was formed in June of 2007. One of eight lines of action to improve medical care for our troops, Red Cell worked nearly around the clock to battle an enemy that could only be seen through the effects of brain or psychological health injuries. It began with 17 representatives from the medical community of each service, and experts from the staff of Force Health Protection and Readiness. Also integral to the team effort were two officials from the Department of Veterans Affairs, as well as representation from the US Public Health Service. With a sense of urgency, they developed the plans, policies and procedures to address the needs of service members and their families affected by deployment-related brain injury and psychological health. It quickly became clear that what was needed was a national "center of centers" to identify, continue and create programs for TBI and psychological health.

Doors to the DCoE opened on Nov 30, 2008 under director Brigadier General Loree Sutton, Medical Corps, US Army, who is also the Special Assistant to the Assistant Secretary of Defense (Health Affairs) for Psychological Health and Traumatic Brain Injury. A psychiatrist herself, General Sutton has a gift for metaphor, skillfully using words to illustrate and emphasize key messages for the DCoE. Working fast, a small support staff (initially less than ten) created a center unique within the military health care system, the core of a "continuum of care," from initial accession to separation and discharge, for all its service members.

The DCoE is charged with building and orchestrating a national network of research, training and clinical expertise. To do this, they integrate organizations, defense programs and other federal and civilian entities. Since its small beginnings in November 2007 the staff has grown to more than 80, and is projected to exceed 125 by October of 2009. General Sutton's enthusiasm for service to country, and for the people who sacrifice so much in duty, has helped ensure that under her guidance the DCoE has incorporated a balanced mix of uniformed and civilian staff members, making for a diverse but talented staff.

The mission is clear: by coordinating efforts with the Department of Veterans Affairs, the US Public Health Service, and other agencies, the DCoE is increasing the number of mental health providers working with the wounded warriors and personnel returning from Operations Iraqi Freedom and Enduring Freedom. The DCoE is also improving access to psychological health care, and trains in tandem with the Department of Veterans Affairs so that the needs of service personnel and veterans with TBI and psychological health issues are best met.

So much of what is said in public circles would lead one to think TBI is usually of the severe variety; yet, the fact is that a TBI may range from "mild" (a brief change in mental status or consciousness) to "severe" (an extended period of unconsciousness or amnesia after the injury). TBI can also be "moderate," a condition between mild and severe. A TBI is caused by a blow to the head or a penetrating head injury that disrupts the normal function of the brain. Not all such blows to the head result in a TBI. Mild TBI is far more prevalent, and its causes are far more often from common circumstances than war zone incidents. Sports injuries and everyday accidents at work, school or recreation often involve mild TBI instances.

Mild TBI is also called "concussion." Yet, although mild TBI is the most common, it is also the most difficult to assess of the three TBI conditions. It needs to be emphasized that, as with civilian circumstances, mild TBI can be difficult to identify and diagnose in the combat zone. A concussion, or mild TBI, may not be readily apparent, and there may not be obvious symptoms as found with moderate to severe TBI cases. An automobile accident or football injury could produce such a brain injury, with little or no outward signs present but clinically measurable if sufficient follow-up is carried out. Among those diagnosed with mild TBI, nearly 90 percent have no lasting residual effects. They fully recover and return to normal lives.

Moderate TBI is clearly recognizable. It has a broad range of symptoms and signs. It may include casualties with no residual symptoms but with x-ray imaging evidence of injury, perhaps as a result of a blast incident. Severe TBI is obvious with a penetrating wound to the head. Service members with this type of injury are given immediate emergency surgical treatment and then ongoing treatment in the US at either a military medical center such as Walter Reed or Bethesda or one of four Department of Veterans Affairs Polytrauma Centers. For example, in the story of Army Specialist Walter Blackston, a relatively "normal" but very busy day turned into a nightmare due to a land mine. Both TBI and PTSD are often medical issues which manifest themselves after initial diagnoses. Specialist Blackston's experiences lay out a process, not uncommon, that goes from battlefield explosion to head injuries and unconsciousness, to initial care, return stateside, follow-up care, then longer term repercussions of the head injuries.

Military medicine, in collaboration with the Department of Veterans Affairs, has a strategy to improve the entire continuum of care for TBI. It involves training health providers in the latest clinical practice guidelines and giving care that is based on many proven methods. Those "evidence-based" methods of care examine clinical cases and documented treatments so that patients with TBI have the greatest chance of recovery. The shaping of that improved program is taking place today.

PTSD is an even more common occurrence than TBI. The term is increasingly viewed as a misnomer by using the word, "disorder." Traumatic stress causes reactions, and the impact of the traumatic stress or incident on an individual's mental state can vary greatly. To say every case represents a "disorder," however, can be misleading.

As time goes on we are seeing an increasing reference to "combat stress reaction" and "post-traumatic stress syndrome" when discussing behavioral health following traumatic stress. The reasoning? People may exhibit reactions that are actually reasonable to horrific situations. It really only becomes a "disorder" if left untreated.

Researchers from the Uniformed Services University of the Health Sciences are working on ways to prevent and treat increasing numbers of combat troops suffering from TBI and are improving methods of diagnosing and managing PTSD. The staff at the DCoE believes it is important to note that how we label people—what we say about a "condition" or a "disorder"—has a big impact on an individual's self-perception and their healing ability.

You can't grasp the magnitude of the military's response to TBI and PTSD unless you at least get a sense of how it's addressing these profoundly significant health issues. There are six major components making up the DCoE. To begin with there's the Defense and Veterans Brain Injury Center which, since 1992, has made significant contributions to overall knowledge of TBI. It provides core functions for the DCoE. For example, it has a participating network of military and Department of Veterans Affairs sites, and worldwide expert contacts. They create clinical practice guidelines for the management and treatment of brain-injured patients.

The DCoE also collaborates with the Center for Deployment Psychology of the Uniformed Services University of the Health Sciences. They train military and civilian mental health professionals to provide high quality deployment-related behavioral health services. Participating training sites involve Army, Navy and Air Force medical centers.

The Deployment Health Clinical Center, established in 1994, developed the Specialized Care Program for those Gulf War veterans whose health concerns and symptoms presented unclear causes, often associated with the unexplained Gulf War illnesses but increasingly related to PTSD as well. These are patients who have had other treatments for PTSD (or perhaps depression) but continue to experience symptoms that interfere with functioning. It is also for patients who have no other treatment available to them. This center's responsibilities have expanded with the wars in Iraq and Afghanistan to include clinical care for veterans of all conflicts, as well as deployment-related health research, education and training for patients and families. Here in Washington DC you'll find them working at Walter Reed Army Medical Center helping small groups of service member patients in three-week cycles every month. Earlier in this book, Richard Gutteridge told of being admitted to the Specialized Care Program in the story about coping with PTSD.

The Center for the Study of Traumatic Stress provides knowledge, leadership and applications in preparing for, responding to, and recovering from the consequences of war, operations other than war, disaster and trauma. Their scope reaches from laboratory to bedside, field and clinic, as well as in operations and public policy.

The National Intrepid Center of Excellence is designed to provide leading-edge services for advanced diagnostics, research, initial treatment planning, family education, introduction to therapeutic modalities, referral and reintegration support for warriors with PTSD, complex psychological health issues, and/or TBI. The planned 75,000-square-foot facility is being funded by the Intrepid Fallen Heroes Fund, a not-for-profit agency that raises money to support military service members and their families. It is expected to be complete in the fall of 2009 in Bethesda, Maryland, the current home of the National Naval Medical Center and future site of the new consolidated Walter Reed National Military Medical Center.

 The newest component to formally be included in the DCoE core network is the Tele-Health and Technology Directorate and Center, also known as "T2." This emerged from the need to have high-technology, advanced state-of-the-art care through innovation. This center fosters comprehensive programs that develop, standardize and deploy technologies for psychological health and TBI. It ensures psychological health and TBI providers are available to all service members and their families on a 24/7 basis, and effective access to care will be provided in underserved areas.

The conflicts in Iraq and Afghanistan have brought challenges not anticipated from past wars. Ironically, it's because of incredible advances in battlefield medicine and selfless devotion to duty that more service members are surviving battlefield injuries that would have been fatal in previous wars. The DCoE is currently moving forward with a unique momentum as the Department of Defense organization providing our service members and their families with the best possible care for psychological health and traumatic brain injury.

17

A NEVERENDING BATTLE
The Story of Army Corporal Jonnei Campaz

"Out of desperation we got together all our jewelry, more than $2,000 worth, and pawned it for $300 to pay our gas and electric bills."
But they couldn't pay their rent. Jon wrote his Congressman. "I said, 'I'm a disabled veteran and my family is going to get thrown out of our house.' They wrote back that they were not a federal agency so there was nothing they could do. No one wanted to help us."

In 1993 when Army Corporal Jonnei ("Jon") Campaz was honorably discharged after spending eighteen months at Walter Reed Medical Center recovering from injuries received during Operation Desert Storm, the subject of brain injury or Post-Traumatic Stress Syndrome never came up. "No one sat me down and talked to me about mental conditions. They classified me as 20 percent disabled due to my injuries, but I was walking again. I was outta there."

Figuring his migraines, nightmares, flashbacks, irritability and jumpiness were "just part of what happened when you were in combat," Jon assumed that he had no choice but to tough it out. He'd joined the Army right out of high school. Now, three years later, he was 21 and on his own.

He married a soldier whom he had met at Walter Reed when they were both patients. They moved back to Merchantville, New Jersey and tried to make a life for themselves. They had a little boy, Korey, but Jon's mental state started to impact their life together almost from the beginning. "I didn't adjust well to civilian life and I took it out on everyone around me. I'd left the Army so bitter. I was angry at everything. I couldn't concentrate. My wife and I fought all the time. Maybe I was bipolar, I don't know. There were a lot of highs and then low lows. I had migraines, like some sort of chronic hangover headache, almost every day." Jon and his first wife divorced. Afterward Jon, who had custody of his son, started dating Dee, an English woman and single parent of Donoven, four years younger than Korey. Everyone got along so well that it soon became obvious theirs was a family in the making. They got married in 2001 and rented a townhouse in Lumberton, New Jersey, with an option to buy. Jonnei started making good money in the mortgage industry and Dee got a job as a file clerk.

Ever since he'd returned from combat Jon had had recurring nightmares and flashbacks to the evening of February 16, 1991, the last time he can recall being in the Gulf. "We were driving along about 22 miles outside of Kuwait, and everyone was relaxed, just joking around. Suddenly the Bradley in front of us exploded. Boom. It was on fire; people were screaming. We jumped out of our Humvees and took positions. Then another Bradley was hit. Boom. We started running toward the vehicles.

"It was complete chaos, dark. It was crazy. We were taking fire and shooting back. You could see gun flashes. I remember trying to pull a guy out of one of the Bradleys. He was on fire and I could smell his flesh burning. Then I heard another explosion and I felt something hit me and that's the last thing I remember." Jon was later told that a canister on one of the damaged Bradleys had exploded and hit him on the head and neck. He also suffered a gunshot wound in the back. A day later he was Medevac'd out of Kuwait to Walter Reed Medical Center. "My right arm was paralyzed. I couldn't walk. It took a long time for everything to come back, but it did. It was the mental stuff that they couldn't fix."

Eight years later, happily married to Dee, Jon was still often irritable and jumpy around loud noises. He had trouble remembering things. In crowds he was guarded and anxious. "I couldn't stand the smell of barbeque. Still can't. It reminded me of burning flesh. It's a sweet smell. You could smell a burning body a mile away." "I tried to sympathize with his mental problems," Dee says. "We didn't know he had PTSD so it never occurred to us that he could get benefits from the Veterans Administration."

Then in the spring of 2004 Jon's health started to deteriorate. He was diagnosed with diabetes in March, the same month their daughter, Veronique, was born. Dee quit her job. "I was making $9.50 an hour and it just didn't make sense to keep on working with a new baby." Jon continued to work but in August he had a stroke. "My health just went south. For a while we survived on savings, but the money ran out real fast. We kept getting farther and farther behind." His recovery in the hospital was complicated by Gastroparesis, a diabetic condition that affects the nerve endings in the stomach. "I couldn't hold anything down. You gotta eat extremely small meals and liquids. The conditions worked against each other. I needed to get strong and do physical therapy, but at the same time I was getting weaker and losing weight from the stomach allergy."

When Jon finally left the hospital, his health was still in jeopardy but his mental state was worse. He tried to cope with an increase in nightmares and the worst migraines he'd ever experienced. Unable to work or take care of the children, he stayed at home, depressed and angry. "No one understood what I was going through. When I'd try to explain, they treated me like crap. They'd say, 'Go out and get a job and support your family.' The family was living on $1,300 a month from state unemployment and $220 a month from the VA.

An old customer urged him to apply for an increase in benefits from the VA, and in 2005 he finally did. "It must have taken ten trips to the Veterans' Center in Philadelphia and Newark to get them to even consider me," Jon recalls. "At first they said, my deployment was so long ago, it would take some time to get all the documents and a long time to process, and there were no guaranteees." Once he was screened and retested Jon was classified 60 percent disabled with severe PTSD. But by then the two wars in Afghanistan and Iraq had created a two-year processing logjam before applicants began to receive benefits. It would be April 2007 before the Campaz family would see a dime. Meanwhile Jon was diagnosed with bowel cancer.

"I think it was during Jon's chemotherapy at the end of 2005 that we were at our lowest point, Dee says. "We almost separated. We had so little money that we sent Korey back to live with his mom. Both younger children missed their brother terribly. I just kept thinking, 'We got to find our way through this. There's got to be a way.'" They applied for food stamps. "We went into the office," Jon recalls, "and the woman looked out the window and saw my 1997 Ford Explorer and said, 'If you own that car, you make too much money for food stamps. Sell it and come back.' She was rushing us out of the office. I was humiliated."

Jon went to a local charity center to see if he could qualify for any amount of money to tide them over, but when a representative from the center made a home visit and saw a two-year-old wide screen television and an "X" box Jon had purchased for his children during better times, she denied his request. "No one would believe that we couldn't pay our bills. Out of desperation we got together all our jewelry, more than $2,000 worth and pawned it for $300 to pay our gas and electric bills."

Jon wrote his Congressman. "I said 'I'm a disabled veteran and my family is going to get thrown out of our house.' They wrote back that they were not a federal agency so there was nothing they could do. No one wanted to help us." What the Congressional office did do, however, was recommend that Jon seek an independent human services agency. "Through a Google search I found the Armed Forces Foundation. One phone call later, the rent was paid. They also provided the name of other agencies such as USA Cares, which enabled us to get some of the past due bills paid to get back on track." In early 2006 Dee got a job as a floor manager at Linens and Things, and the Campaz family received additional help from the American Legion. Somehow the family, including Korey, who had returned from his mother's, hung on until Jon's benefits kicked in.

Today Jon and Dee are both going to school, Jon to get his degree in social work, and Dee to become a certified medical assistant. After a lengthy to-and-fro with the VA, Jon was finally screened for TBI and has now been certified 100 percent disabled, but that will never stop him from going after a career. "I've been working since I was sixteen, and I want to provide for my family. I think I'll make a good social worker because I've been there. I know what it's like to have problems no one will recognize. I know what it's like to be on the verge of being homeless."

Life is still a battle. Jon takes 20 pills a day, not counting two types of insulin. He must use a sleep apnea machine, and the doctors at the VA have yet to find a remedy for his migraines. And the Campaz marriage has its ups and downs. "We've learned how to be more patient with each other, more supportive. The kids get us going sometimes but they're good kids. I love my kids. We still argue but we won't ever give up. I believe in my family. Family is everything."

Jon continues: "I do not blame any one for what happened to me; I chose to be a soldier and I am proud to have given it my all. As a soldier I chose to put myself in harm's way. As J.D. Sallinger wrote in *Catcher in the Rye*, 'The mark of the immature man is that he wants to die nobly for a cause, while the mark of the mature man is that he wants to live humbly for one.' I choose to live humbly for one. My family knows that without the darkness we cannot appreciate the light."

MEDALS

(Among others) Bronze Star with "V" attachment, Purple Heart.

"In many cases these caregivers have had to sell the family home, quit their jobs, and move their families to be closer to hospitals. The result is that taking care of their disabled loved one becomes their full time occupation. They end up putting on hold their careers and lives and in some cases they are dealing with a person that does not resemble the love one before the injury. Gaining access to the limited benefits is time consuming and not at all easy."

—"The Challenges of the Caretakers of Disabled Veterans," Ginny Estupinian, April 30, 2008, VeteransTransitionweblog

18

THE REAL STORY BEHIND YOUR STORY

By Dr. Rick Levy

Bill Moeller, a 58-year-old veteran of the Vietnam War, called my office for an appointment, saying I was his last hope after he had seen a TV news feature on my work. Bill had served in the First Cavalry Division, one of the most decorated units of the war. He was a hero by anyone's standard, awarded the Bronze Star, the Vietnam Service Medal with Bronze Star, the Vietnam Campaign Medal, and the National Defense Service Medal, though he is quick to deny he did anything exceptional during the conflict.

After Vietnam, life was torture. For 35 years he was sleepless every night, consumed by rage and a visceral fear that haunted him; he couldn't walk down the street of his hometown without feeling like he was under attack. He suffered from flashbacks in which he relived the worst moments of his military career, like the day one of his friends was blown up beside him. And he endured chronic guilt because he couldn't save his friend or the other members of his troop. Bill succumbed to alcoholism, a battle he waged and won. But his erratic behavior was harmful to the people he loved. His marriage and his relationship with his only child became further casualties of the Vietnam War.

Bill succeeded in business in the years that followed. But finally, the stress of corporate America combined with the strain of undiagnosed Post-Traumatic Stress Disorder began to take a life-threatening toll. He had a pulmonary embolism, followed by a massive heart

103

attack. He was unable to work, and would struggle just to walk, which left him winded and suffering from angina. But Bill had the heart of a lion. Armed with state-of-the-art methods from the field of mind-body medicine, we used the power of his mind to free him from the psychological and physical wounds of war, lead him to health, and help him to create the life he most wanted to live.

Bill's physical health problems were caused by his PTSD, but the cause of his PTSD was secreted away in his mind; therefore, one of our primary clinical goals was to find it and dismantle it, which we did.

"Every disease begins with dis-ease"—this is an essential tenet of mind-body medicine. When reality clashes with our needs and expectations, as it had repeatedly for Bill during his time in Vietnam, dis-ease arises in the mind in the form of grief, anger, terror and distorted thinking. Sometimes we can resolve our dis-ease while it's happening, but for the soldier that isn't possible. A soldier must devote all of his or her energy to survival—there is simply no time to process and deal with the constant trauma and anguish that arises 24/7.

If we can't resolve our dis-ease while it's happening, we can sometimes resolve it later using psychological methods. In Bill's case, he had never been afforded this opportunity. (The clinical methods I use in my practice today weren't available in the late '70s, or even the '80s.) If we can't find a way to resolve our dis-ease, and it persists, the subconscious mind will place it symbolically in the body in the form of illness. The subconscious mind does this not to hurt us but to communicate that there is something wrong that needs our attention.

The bottom line from a clinical perspective is that every illness (mental or physical) has a related root in the mind: find that root and pluck it out and recovery time is reduced or eliminated. Some people find this hard to believe because they don't realize how much of their "thinking" is going on at an unconscious level. Most of us rely only on our conscious minds (everyday thoughts and feelings) for self-insight, but the conscious mind is the smallest part of the mind. The subconscious mind—a storehouse of memory, feeling and deep self-knowledge—is almost three times the size and power of the conscious mind. Among other things, the subconscious contains a record of the experiences, feelings and thoughts of a lifetime, reaching as far back as infancy. You probably can't remember what you were doing on

New Year's Eve when you were three, but the subconscious mind has it all tucked away in high definition with surround sound.

For the veteran with PTSD, repeated exposure to life-threatening trauma saturates the subconscious mind with the experience of terror and helplessness to such a degree that it chronically invades the conscious mind—it creates the conscious expectation that ordinary, everyday events will be life threatening and heartbreaking, and that 'there isn't anything I can do about it.'

It is easy to see how Bill's experience in Vietnam led first to PTSD and then to heart disease. His subconscious mind was densely populated with the continual experience of tragic death, unresolved grief, guilt and helplessness. Consciously, Bill was home, living a seemingly safe existence. But subconsciously, his life was a "heart-rending" battle. In my clinical opinion, any one of the traumatic experiences he endured in Viet Nam would cause psychological instability and physical illness in the average person. This is Bill's story, as told in his own words . . .

In April of 1970, I arrived in the Republic of South Vietnam. It was about 3:30 am when the Captain of the chartered Boeing 707 announced we would be landing soon. I looked out the window, and for as far as I could see there were fires everywhere. At first I thought they might be campfires that were keeping our troops warm, but as we got closer, I could see they were buildings and huts that were ablaze. The pilot came back on the intercom and announced he was going to circle around the airbase and land to the west using no landing lights, no cabin lights and a very steep approach—something he had to do because the airbase at Bien Hoa was under attack.

When the door of the aircraft opened, the most acrid odor I have ever smelled assailed me. It was cordite—jet fuel used to burn human feces, backed by the smell of burning buildings and jungle rot. The sound of artillery shells exploding and the roar of fighter aircraft was deafening. We were met by an Air Force enlisted man who told us to hurry into the terminal and huddle close to the walls because the perimeter of the building was surrounded by sandbags. The humidity was so bad that by the time we got in the terminal our clothing was sticking to our bodies and the sweat was pouring off us. We were told not to worry, we would get used to it. I got used to the sweat, but I never got used to the smell or the explosions. After my return from Nam and for three decades to follow, bad smells and loud abrupt sounds would trigger uncontrollable fear and flashbacks in me.

I was trained in Avionics at Fort Gordon Georgia for eight months before arriving in Vietnam, so I was sent to the Avionics hooch at the Cav Rear. Our shop and hooch were just behind the main hanger, and I was often on the flight line. Soon after my arrival, I was on the line taking the radios out of a Loach helicopter. Another Loach came in for a landing. The pilot taxied the bird to his respective spot, put the engine on idle, and the Crew Chief got off the aircraft to load something on board. As I was watching, I observed the Crew Chief getting too close to the tail rotor blade. I started to scream at the top of my lungs to warn him, but the noise of the engine and his flight helmet prevented him from hearing. All of a sudden he walked backwards into the tail rotor, which split his head and helmet into a million pieces. I rushed to help him, along with many others. After he was medevac'd out I returned to the safety of my hooch and cried for hours. For the first time in my life I saw someone die, needlessly.

In May of 1970 we were sent into Cambodia to seek and destroy the enemy that was using Cambodia as a warehouse for arms and safe refuge. We quickly set up operations in Tay Ninh, a Vietnamese town on the Cambodian border. I was sent to set up a makeshift Avionics shop and to do whatever was needed. Pilots and crews were flying around the clock. The medical people were grounding pilots and crews for spending too much time in the air, and we were losing huge numbers of men and aircraft to heavy ground fire. There came a day when the CO asked for volunteers from the maintenance group to fly as door gunners. The only requirement was you needed to know how to handle an M-60 machine gun. I decided to volunteer, as long as I could keep my day job (I didn't want a MOS change). I received one day of pilot training from a guy named Larry. Other procedural things, like hanging from a MacGuire Rig, were learned quickly, and before I knew it I was helping to insert and extract personnel from the jungles of Cambodia as a Huey machine gunner.

I don't know how many helicopter missions I flew during my tour, or how many firefights I was in on the ground. They all seemed to take on a sameness after a while: get shot at, shoot back, kill the enemy, watch your buddies get shot-up, watch them die a gruesome death, sometimes hold them in your arms while the life ebbed out of them, knowing there was nothing you could do about it. One day one of my buddies was shot to pieces while he was standing right beside me. The agony that followed while I helplessly watched him die, and the guilt I felt at not being able to save him, have dogged me to this day. Of the many flashbacks I endured over the years that followed Vietnam, this one haunted me the most.

We lived with the constant fear of incoming rockets or mortars. It was something you had no influence over. You couldn't control when, where or what they would hit, and you couldn't control whether you'd be anywhere near a bunker when the firing started. There was simply nothing you could do to protect yourself from "incoming." The fear was so intense it was often paralyzing. Often there was no bunker in site when the shelling began, and all you could do was hit the ground and pray "this one" doesn't have your name on it.

After I came home I had a feeling down deep inside that something was very wrong with me. I couldn't explain it to anyone or even to myself. I would see a car accident and start to cry uncontrollably. A friend or relative would die and I would be out of sorts for months on end, as if I never learned how to mourn. I seemed to be hyper-sensitive, yet I was always looking for a fight. It didn't matter with whom, or how big the other guy was. My drinking became excessive. I couldn't sleep for more than an hour a night without getting tanked. Because of it, I lost my wife. She left me and took our daughter with her. At first I thought, "How could she leave me after all we've been through?" But today, I see just how smart she was and just how screwed up I had become. God Bless You, Georgia.

As the years went on, I was able to lock-in a good career in sales and sales management with different Fortune 500 companies. The last of these assignments was with a large telecom company where I was the Director of Sales for the Mid-Atlantic Region. Because of my work habits, I spent less and less time with family and friends. Over the years there have been very few people who ever got close to me. I could never trust anybody enough.

I still couldn't sleep. I always felt detached and estranged around other people and preferred to be alone. I even lived in a basement apartment for thirteen years, because it was underground and it had the feeling of safety like the bunker near my hooch in Nam. These feelings and symptoms became severe enough, and lasted long enough, to significantly impair my daily life. Depression, substance abuse and problems with memory and cognition became the norm. After a while, I had no ability to function in social or family life, and occupational instability set in.

I got clean and sober and quit smoking by sheer willpower, but my mental health remained lousy, and eventually my physical health failed. In November of 2003 I was admitted to the hospital with a pulmonary embolism, and then just six months later I had a major heart attack. I was completely disabled and couldn't work. I was a wreck.

At the Veterans Hospital I found some help, but more important I found a whole hospital full of guys just like me. We were all diagnosed with Post-Traumatic Stress Disorder, or PTSD. I asked the doctors, "How do we treat this thing? How does one live with it? What do we do?" Basically, I was told they were going to try several different types of medication that might help until they found one that would work for me. In addition, I was assigned to a group for therapy.

At the height of my treatment at the VA hospital I was taking upwards of 40 pills per day. I was taking pills to get up in the morning. Then by afternoon if I felt I wasn't functioning I could take pills to pep up even further. But of course, by nightfall I had to take pills in order to come back down. Then if I couldn't sleep, I had pills for that. Too many pills during the day made my stomach upset, so I had pills to solve that. I had pills for heart, blood pressure, cholesterol, blood thinning, anxiety, pain and water retention. I had more pills than the average size pharmacy in a small third world country. And I had a small cadre of medical experts at the VA willing to give me even more.

Despite "better living through modern chemistry," my PTSD symptoms didn't abate; I was extremely depressed, physically ill and still disabled. I couldn't work. At about that time, I was watching TV one night and saw a Fox5 News feature on the work of Dr. Rick Levy, a clinical psychologist who specializes in mind-body medicine. His patients were getting better from heart disease, cancer, stroke, diabetes and other problems that conventional medicine has few solutions for. The idea that you can use the power of your own mind to heal yourself made sense to me. I called his office the next day to set up an appointment.

When Bill arrived in my office, I assured him that mind-body medicine would help him. For any illness, up to 40 percent of your solution can come from conventional means like surgery, pharmaceuticals or physical therapy, but up to 60 percent of your solution can come from your mind. Bill had received a great deal of conventional health care, and good conventional care is absolutely critical—but if you use mind-body medicine in addition, you can enjoy a 150 percent increase in healing effect. Good mind-body methods don't just make you feel better, they change your biochemistry, eliminate the effects of negative environmental influences, shift unhealthy behavior, and can even counter a hereditary predisposition to illness. They make the crucial difference between life and death, a full or partial recovery, joy and despair.

Using psychotherapy and clinical hypnosis, I helped Bill dismantle the chronic stress-response syndrome that had been fueling his emotional and physical ill health. He began to sleep at night, felt happier, substantially reduced his reliance on medication, and made huge gains in strength and stamina.

The rest of our work involved helping Bill to discover the Story Behind the Story. Everyone is living out a unique, epic journey in self-discovery—The Story Behind The Story. To heal yourself, you have to discern what your life has been trying to teach you, discover your native talents and your most noble aspirations, and live them out, free of pain or confusion from the past. That is the purpose of life itself. Living outside your story, by repressing your experience or misunderstanding it, or failing to pursue your highest dreams, is the root cause of suffering. For Bill's entire adult life he'd been fighting the war in Vietnam. He was never able to discover who he really was, fully explore his innate gifts and talents, or develop a vision for how he wanted to live his life.

We used clinically guided meditation to help Bill attain deep levels of self-awareness, where he found the peace and joy that had so long eluded him. He began to meditate regularly, pursued the relationship with God that he'd aspired to, and found a religious community where he belonged. He found his story behind the story and began to live it out authentically—his personal quest was to move away from being a warrior into being a deeply spiritual man. With progress on this part of his journey, Bill's heart and lungs improved to the point where he was asymptomatic of pulmonary problems or heart disease. He conquered what remained of his depression and anxiety, and came into joy. He realized that he had the power to map out his future and make it happen.

Now 60, Bill is down to just three pills a day and is free of the symptoms of PTSD, heart disease and pulmonary problems. He sleeps through the night, has regained his stamina, is pain free, has a vibrant social life and has re-united with his daughter and grandchildren. He is still a hero, but these days he campaigns for justice armed only with compassion, as an advocate for veterans and their families.

19

AGAINST ALL ODDS
The Story of Marine Corps Corporal Joshua Hoffman

"He kept asking, 'What happened to me?' and no one wanted to tell him, so finally I said, 'Right now you're paralyzed. It sucks, but you're home and you're alive.' I tried to lighten it up a little. I said, 'Josh, I realize you really wanted to come home, but did you seriously have to take it this far? Don't you think this was a little extreme?' Josh laughed."

Joshua Hoffman figured joining the Marines would be a good way to get the money to eventually go to aviation school. At the time he was attending Western Michigan University, but he dropped out to enlist. He had a couple of exotic assignments: Djibouti on the horn of Africa, and South America, and then came back home to Kentwood, Michigan and joined the reserves as part of the Grand Rapids-based Alpha Company, 1st Battalion, 24th Marine Regiment. His father, Jim, a career Army NCO who had just returned from a deployment in Iraq at the start of Operation Iraqi Freedom, was living in Texas with his stepmother. But his mother, Hazel, lived near Kentwood with her son, Michael, and so did Josh's younger brother, Jacob.

Even though it had been years since he'd lived in Michgan, Josh wasn't worried about making friends. He'd had to start from scratch in Juneau, Alaska and then Newport News, Virginia after he started living with his father when he was twelve. Moreover he'd met Heather in that fall of 2004 and she was the strongest argument of all that he'd made the right decision to settle down in Kentwood. As far as being called up, which was something his dad worried about all the time, he was in the reserves for chrissakes. But it turned out his dad's apprehensions were correct.

By October 2006 he was in Iraq's Anbar province attached to the battalion's Weapons Company in Fallujah. On January 6, his patrol of the city's narrow alleyways was going as usual when a man carrying a rocket propelled grenade appeared out of nowhere and then ran off. SOP required that Josh and his teammates chase him down. Josh was point man for the group, an assignment he carried out on a regular basis. No one saw the sniper. When the shot rang out the men took cover and then, a few seconds later, checked to see if everyone was okay. They saw Josh lying face down in the dirt. A Corpsman, disobeying orders to wait for smoke to camouflage his movements, rushed out into the street, knelt down and turned his buddy over. Josh was able to open his eyes and speak but he couldn't squeeze the Corpsman's hand. The bullet had entered the front left side of his neck and exited out his right shoulder, severing his spinal cord. The Corpsman kept his finger in the bullet hole to stop the bleeding until the medics came. The Corpsman would later tell Heather it was the longest ten minutes of his life.

Heather:

"When I first met Josh he was twenty-two and I was seventeen and I just knew he was the one. For me it really was love at first sight. I wasn't going to be eighteen for five more days, and I was afraid he would consider me too young for him. It took a couple weeks after my birthday for me to really win him over." But it quickly became apparent that they shared the same sense of humor and keen appreciation of small town life in western Michigan. She had short brown hair, a beautiful smile and infinite "can do" enthusiasm. "They called him 'The Ox' at the landscaping company where he worked. He was like a human forklift. One time he pulled up a ten-foot-tall tree weighing 300 pounds and planted it exactly where his boss wanted it in a client's yard. He didn't even break a sweat." Heather and Josh hit it off. They dated for a few months and then moved in together in an apartment complex in Kentwood, and for the next two years life was sweet. "He used to take me out three times a week on 'dates' even though we were living together."

Jim:

"From the time Joshua was three until he was twelve, I didn't exist for him. He thought I was dead. But he got my social security number from his mother, and he found me. Once I got custody of my boys they lived with me pretty much full time. I remember our first Christmas together I was stationed in Alaska, and I must have bought $15,000 worth of toys for them to make up for all those Christmases we'd lost. We had a big long living room and it was a third filled up with presents. It took us three hours to open them all. At the end there were three boxes left: one for Josh, one for Jacob and one for me. So we all opened them together and there was a helmet in each one. Josh was groaning, 'Ah Dad, does that mean we have to go skiing?' because he didn't like learning how to ski, and I said, 'No, these go with something out in the garage.' So I took them out to the garage and there were three four-wheelers, one for each of us. You should have seen the look on their faces." While Jim was stationed in Newport News, Josh developed into an all star high school wrestler. "I went to all his wrestling meets. He made it to the high school state championship; I took him camping and hiking on the weekends. We were so close. We were making plans to go to Disney World after he got back from Iraq, but you know everything went out the window."

Josh:

Josh was flown to Balad for three days of emergency care, then Germany's Landstuhl Medical Center for a week to stabilize, and then finally to Bethesda Navy Medical Center. When surgeons operated they discovered that the few membranes connecting the two sections of spinal cord were not enough to regenerate, so they cut them. Josh was paralyzed from the chest down. Permanently.

Heather:

"I was driving home from work when I got a call on my cell phone from Josh's sister-in-law. She said, 'Call me when you get home.' And I said, 'What's going on?' 'I can't tell you.' 'I'm pulling over. Okay, what's going on?' 'Josh was shot in the neck and he's in critical condition.' I was so confused. I called my parents, and they already knew. Everyone knew but me. No one wanted to tell me." Heather and her father flew up to Washington, DC so she could be at Bethesda Navy Medical before Josh arrived. When she got there she came up against hospital protocol. "I could hardly wait to see him. I was terrified, excited and exhausted beyond belief. Josh was there but the hospital staff wouldn't let me see him because I wasn't a member of the family. I tried to explain but they said absolutely not. I was beside myself." Once Hazel and Jacob arrived at the hospital Hazel told the staff that Heather should be allowed in Josh's room.

At first Josh seemed paralyzed, but shortly thereafter a doctor asked if he could move, and he grabbed Hazel's hand and squeezed it with his thumb and first finger. "He said 'Whoa' and I nearly passed out when the doctor asked him to squeeze again and he did. He could raise and flex his right arm, and even curl his toes. He kept asking, 'What happened to me?' and no one wanted to tell him, so finally I said, 'Right now you're paralyzed. It sucks, but you're home and you're alive.' I tried to lighten it up a little. I said 'Josh, I realize you really wanted to come home, but did you seriously have to take it this far? Don't you think this was a little extreme?' Josh laughed."

Jim:

"It was terrible when I got the call. It was around 2 p.m. on the 6th. I was shopping with the wife in the PX when my cell phone rang. Josh had put me down as his point of contact. At first I couldn't catch my breath. I had to get both of us out of the store before I could tell my wife Carmen, because I knew she'd become hysterical." An ice storm in Texas would delay Jim's plane to Washington for a day and a half after the rest of the family had arrived. Jim had met Heather before on a six-day trip his son and Heather had made to San Antonio, and he had spoken to her on the phone a couple of times, but when they met at the hospital Jim drew a blank. "To be perfectly honest, I didn't remember who she was. We knew Josh was living with a girl, but he had so many girlfriends. I like Heather, but as time went on during those first few weeks and months there was a lot of friction between us." There was also a lot of confusion as the prognosis for Josh worsened by the hour. Surgery was postponed because Josh "coded" when he was positioned on his stomach. There was a serious possibility of meningitis.

Josh:

Five days later, after surgeons were finally able to operate on his injury, Josh developed an infection and a fever. The fever went from 102 to 105, then during the night spiked to 108.8. First ice packs were placed around his body, and then he was wrapped from head to toe in an ice blanket, but by the time the fever broke it was too late. The high temperature had literally cooked his brain, giving him severe Traumatic Brain Injury. He went into renal failure and was put onto life support. His body ballooned to three times its normal size. His eyes were swollen shut, and his lower lip was so big that it touched his nose. His body was covered in blisters from the fever. Jim, Hazel, Jacob, Carmen and Heather assembled in a waiting room and listened as doctors told them Josh had 24 hours to live.

Jim:

"It was the biggest mess. No one had power of attorney or the authority to make medical decisions. Hazel and I were coming from different perspectives, and Heather had her own opinions. If there was a message I would give families of deploying troops it is: get your legal house in order before your soldiers or Marines go. We've had so much heartache because during that time we had differences about what to do." Jim felt strongly that Josh would not have wanted to be resuscitated. "Before Joshua left for war he said, 'Dad, if I have to come back missing my legs, I don't want to come back.' The doctors said it was possible that he could spend the rest of his life tube-fed, on a catheter while his brain atrophied. What kind of quality of life is that?" But Heather and Hazel felt differently.

Heather:

"Once they finally put the ice blanket on him and got his temperature down below 100, I prayed he'd be like he was before, but he was so sedated he looked right through us." Heather prided herself on her strong faith, and when the family was called together to say their goodbyes, she refused to give up hope. "It felt wrong. I just knew he wasn't supposed to die. He had a life to live. We had a life to live together. I can't explain knowing this except that it was God's way of telling me not to worry. He mouthed to his mom in the very beginning, 'Mom, I want to live.'" She would spend the next few months fighting to show he was mentally competent. "After that day I promised him that I would never leave his side. Even though he couldn't talk, he kept mouthing to me when nobody else would listen, saying that he wanted to live."

Josh:

Josh was moved to the Veteran's Administration's Maguire Hospital in Richmond, Virginia, where he would remain for 14 months of rehabilitation, six months longer than the average stay. For every step forward there were five steps back. He was continually in and out of the ICU with pneumonia (five times), urinary tract infections (ten times), and problems with his feeding tube. Every day was a struggle.

Jim:

"I was traveling back and forth from San Antonio to Richmond, and every time I got to the hospital and saw Josh I would get depressed. He was suffering so much, and I couldn't do a thing. The doctors were saying that even if he made progress, he was going to plateau at some point and that would be that."

Heather:

"I told people there was no way I'd go home. I'd rather sleep in my car and eat moss. Maguire didn't have a Navy Lodge so they put me and Josh's mom up in a hotel. The Red Cross paid for my first two weeks at $55 a day, but then after that I used my savings. So Hazel said, 'Well I get $93 a day from the military because I'm his mom, so move in with me.'" The two women rented an efficiency suite at a nearby Marriott for $91 a day. Eventually the Wounded Marine Semper Fi Fund found out about Heather's dilemma and started sending her money. "I felt lower than scum taking money from that fund, but I wasn't going to leave Josh's side, and no one would grant me family privileges." The staff wouldn't let her stay the night and were inflexible on visiting hours. "It was a constant struggle because Josh never wanted me to leave, so I would be there as much as I was allowed, but even that upset Josh. He would always say that it wasn't long enough. He would beg me to stay."

During this time Josh almost died when he choked on a mucous plug that got stuck in his throat during the removal of his tracheoto-my tube. "When they pulled his trach, the oxygen to his blood start-ed going down from 97 to 89 percent . . . I ran out into the corridor and yelled, 'We need someone, now!' By the time people started work-ing on him, it was 57 percent. The doctor looked me straight in the face and said, 'You saved his life.'"

Dealing with Josh's PTSD proved to be almost as big a challenge as any of his physical injuries. He started having such extreme night-mares that he was given medication so he wouldn't remember them. Then he started hallucinating when he was awake. "He would stare up at the ceiling and see things floating around in the air. He thought he was captured in Iraq. He would start crying and freaking out. It was horrible. We didn't know what to do." Ironically, it was Josh's PTSD symptoms that Heather used to argue to psychologists that his brain was healing itself. "The psychologists said, 'It's TBI. He doesn't understand.' The psychiatrists said, 'It's PTSD, not TBI.' I kept saying to all of them, 'He hates white coats. When I'm in the room alone with him, he's Josh, but when you come in he shuts down.'"

Josh:

In September 2007 Josh received a medical discharge from the Marines. He was still getting food from a feeding tube, but he was communicating to Heather and Hazel with blinks of his eyes for "yes," "no" and to spell out words or names. He was given 100 per-cent disability and, after a struggle, 24-hour nursing care from the Veteran's Administration. Jim was given legal guardianship for Josh and control of his pension.

Jim:

"I wanted to take him back to a veteran's hospital near me in San Antonio, but Heather was determined to take care of him herself in west Michigan. I couldn't imagine it." Heather made a strong case. She came to the final meeting with Jim and Josh's medical team armed with a three-ring binder with comprehensive research covering every possible facility, service and emergency support in Kentwood. Jim opened the binder, glanced at the index page, and gave in. "I realized if I brought him to Texas, Heather wouldn't come down there. I thought, 'She makes him happy so let him have whatever happiness he can get. I got to let him live his own life.'"

Josh:

On March 25, 2008, Josh and Heather returned home. In the homecoming ceremony in a hangar at Gerald R. Ford International Airport, Josh was welcomed by hundreds of supports. Dozens of Marines in dress uniforms from his old unit were also there to cheer as he was wheeled on an American flag–covered gurney to the ambulance.

Heather:

"I told them that if they'd just let me take care of him we would be fine. It's about love, not money. I hate it when people say, 'She's in it for the money.' We're in love. Josh can talk now, not all the time but enough, and he mouths words and spells out whatever we can't understand." He knows I love shoes so he keeps saying 'I want to buy you shoes,' and I say 'I don't need shoes.'"

Josh:

The organization Homes for Our Troops is building a wheelchair accessible four-bedroom home for Josh and Heather in Middleville, Michigan, about twenty minutes away from where they live now. The ground breaking was August 18, 2008. Josh proposed to Heather on her birthday, and gave her a diamond ring. They will be married next year after moving into their new home before Christmas.

MEDALS

Joint Service Achievement Medal, Navy Presidential Unit Citation, Marine Corps Good Conduct Medal, Armed Forces Expeditionary Medal, Purple Heart, Combat Action Ribbon, Joint Meritorious Unit Award, Navy Unit Commendation, Marine Corps Expeditionary Medal (with gold star), National Defense Service Medal, Iraq Campaign Medal (with gold star), Global War on Terrorism (Expeditionary), Global War on Terrorism (Service), Navy Sea Service Deployment Ribbon (with gold star), Armed Forces Reserve Medal, Navy, and Marine Overseas Service Ribbon.

20

A VETERANS' GUIDE TO MENTAL HEALTH SERVICES IN THE VA

By Ira R. Katz, MD, PhD, and Bradley Karlin, PhD

The Veterans Health Administration (VHA) is one of the three major components of the Department of Veterans Affairs (VA) that, together with the Veterans Benefits Administration and the National Cemetery Administration, serves the needs of America's 23,800,000 veterans. VHA provides health care in 153 VA medical centers and 737 community-based outpatient clinics located throughout the country. In addition to health care, VHA provides readjustment counseling services to combat veterans in 225 Vet Centers.

VA medical centers and clinics serve the 7.8 million veterans who are enrolled in VHA. Last year, they treated approximately 5.5 million veterans. Soldiers who are returning from service in Iraq or Afghanistan are eligible for preferential enrollment during the first five years after returning from deployment. As of the end of 2007, 837,458 service men and women had returned from Iraq and Afghanistan. Fifty percent were former active duty troops, and 50 percent were National Guard and Reserve members. Of these, 324,846, or 39 percent, had come to VA medical facilities for care. Although there is a major focus on services to returning veterans, VA serves veterans of all eras. In fact, about 40 percent were over age 65.

VA is the largest and most organized health care system in America. It has been recognized throughout the country and the world for its commitment to providing quality care. To ensure that every patient has a provider that can get to know them, as well as their

119

health problems, VA emphasizes the importance of primary medical care. However, the health care system includes an extensive array of specialists focusing on essentially every area in medicine.

About 30 percent of all the veterans who were seen last year expressed a concern about a mental health issue. This number reflects VA's commitment to providing ready access to high quality mental health services, and to do so in a manner that minimizes embarrassment or stigma about mental health issues.

Of the veterans from Iraq and Afghanistan who were seen at VA medical centers and clinics, mental health conditions were the second most commonly diagnosed problems (after musculoskeletal conditions), and were present in about 40 percent of patients. Of these, one specific condition, Post-Traumatic Stress Disorder (PTSD), represents about half.

PTSD is more common among veterans than other Americans, and VA has pioneered its recognition, diagnosis and treatment. However, PTSD doesn't represent the whole story about mental health for either veterans returning from Iraq and Afghanistan or those who served in prior eras. Conditions like depression, other anxiety disorders, and problem drinking that are common in other Americans are also common in veterans.

In addition to mental health conditions, there are a range of lifestyle or behavioral issues that are often very amenable to psychological treatment, including chronic pain, sleep disturbance, weight management, and coping with health conditions or disability.

Care for all of the mental health and behavioral conditions that affect veterans is available in VA's specialty mental health or behavioral health services. Access to these services can be either through referral from a primary care provider or through direct requests from patients. In addition, most VA medical centers have programs for integrating mental health with primary care, to support treatment of common conditions like depression and problem drinking within primary care clinics.

Vet Centers provide a different type of care. They focus on counseling for problems in readjustment rather than on treatment of specific conditions. They use a wide variety of individual and group counseling methods, including relatively informal drop-in strategies.

However, they can also provide specific types of evidence-based psychotherapy for PTSD and related conditions.

Only combat veterans are eligible to receive services in Vet Centers, but the centers are able to provide care without requiring formal enrollment in the VA system. When individuals need care that is not available in Vet Centers, when there are symptoms that do not respond to care, or when there are diagnosable conditions that are beyond the scope of what they can provide, Vet Centers refer individuals to medical centers or clinics for further evaluation and treatment as needed. In turn, medical centers may also refer veterans to Vet Centers.

The diagnosis of PTSD and other mental health conditions requires a clinical evaluation with a trained provider, usually a mental health professional such as a psychiatrist, psychologist, social worker or a nurse with advanced practice training. In many cases, the evaluation and diagnosis can be done by a primary care provider.

Clinical evaluations can be triggered by a request from a patient, or by a screening examination. For example, VA screens patients to identify those likely to have PTSD by asking specific questions when patients are seen, at least once a year for the first five years after people come to VA, and at least once every five years after that.

The screening procedure begins with a stem question about whether the veteran has experienced traumatic events and, if so, it follows up to ask about their impact: "In your life, have you ever had any experience that was so frightening, horrible, or upsetting that, in the past month, you:

1. Have had nightmares about it or thought about it when you did not want to?

2. Tried hard not to think about it or went out of your way to avoid situations that reminded you of it?

3. Were constantly on guard, watchful, or easily startled?

4. Felt numb or detached from others, activities, or your surroundings?"

If the patient indicates that he or she has had a trauma and answers "yes" to at least three of the follow-up questions, the screening examination is considered positive. A positive screening evaluation does not mean that a patient has PTSD, or that he or she requires treatment; however, it raises concerns that he or she may have the condition, and it points to the need for a clinical evaluation.

Many veterans who experience distress related to a stressful or traumatic experience may have what is referred to as an "adjustment reaction." This is an extreme reaction to a stressful life event that causes significant distress. An adjustment reaction does not involve the full range of symptoms or duration of PTSD, but it can cause significant life disruption. Like PTSD, it is very treatable.

A counselor or mental health professional at a Vet Center or medical center can identify whether the symptoms a veteran is experiencing is related to PTSD, an adjustment reaction, or possibly another anxiety or depressive disorder, which can share similar features. There are screening evaluations, comparable to the screening evaluation discussed above for PTSD, to help detect depression. Again, positive screening evaluations do not make a diagnosis, but they do point to the need for further evaluations.

Several types of effective treatment are available for most mental health conditions. For PTSD, for example, both certain medications and specific kinds of psychotherapy have been shown to be effective. This does not mean that the treatment alleviates symptoms completely in all patients. In fact, it can frequently require first one treatment, and then another, and maybe even another before patients are doing as well as they can.

The medications that have been shown to work for PTSD include certain antidepressant medications. Both sertraline (Zoloft) and paroxetine (Paxil) have been approved by the US Food and Drug Administration as being safe and effective for the treatment of PTSD. When medications work, they usually lead to a substantial decrease in symptoms within three of four months. Psychotherapy can also be effective, and the evidence for the effectiveness of psychotherapy is strongest for two specific treatments: Prolonged Exposure Therapy and Cognitive Processing Therapy.

With the availability of several types of effective treatments, the initial step is usually the formulation of a treatment plan. In developing these, patients and providers meet, often with the patient's family when that is his or her choice, to discuss the range of effective treatments that are available, and to prioritize which should be done first and which should be done later, as needed. They should also plan how they would monitor the outcomes of treatment, and both how and when they would decide if it is working or not. Moreover, they should begin thinking about how they would modify care if significant symptoms remain after they have given the treatment enough time to work.

Each of the common mental health conditions can be recurrent conditions. For example, people who have recovered from one episode of PTSD are likely to experience repeated episodes, especially if they underwent repeated traumatization from highly stressful events. Treatment planning should go beyond considering what can be done to help patients get well to also considering what should be done to help them stay well.

Veterans, in general, live within communities that include their families and friends. And it is they who may first become aware that returning veterans may be suffering from a mental health condition. Talking about concerns can be helpful, and it can be useful to suggest that veterans try out services in a Vet Center, or a VA medical center or clinic. If the veteran is reluctant to go for an evaluation, it may be useful to negotiate a time frame, as discussed above. Other alternatives include finding out more about the VA resources for the mental health conditions that are common after employment to be able to provide more detailed guidance, or seeking professional help, for example, from a Vet Center, from a community-based provider, or others.

There are often questions about the extent to which VA can treat veterans' families. The mission of the VHA is to provide care for the veteran; however, families can be included in treatment when the veteran requests it or agrees to it, as long as the treatment is provided to benefit the veteran. Within this context, VA can include families in a range of mental health services, including consultation, counseling (including marriage and family counseling) and training, as needed for the effective treatment and rehabilitation of the veteran.

Veterans returning from Iraq and Afghanistan should recognize that it is important for them to enroll for care in the VA during their five-year period of preferential eligibility. Enrollment makes the entire VA health and mental health care system available during the five-year period with no co-payment requirements for conditions that could be related to deployment. Moreover, enrollment during the five-year period establishes the veterans' access to VA care throughout their lifetimes.

Often it can be clear to veterans or family members whether they are doing well after deployment, or if there are obvious signs of PTSD or another mental health condition. However, there are many veterans for whom it is less clear, and for whom it can be difficult to tell the difference between a normal period of readjustment and the beginning of a condition that may need treatment.

The scientific evidence indicates that the earlier treatment is provided, the more effective it can be in alleviating symptoms and, even, in preventing the development of full-blown illnesses. Therefore, most experts recommend that patients should go for evaluations whenever there are concerns about possible diagnoses, and that treatment should be initiated sooner rather than later, for mild-to-moderate as well as more severe conditions. However, it is important to recognize that there are, at times, differences between the experts' opinions and the veterans' own preferences.

One way to deal with uncertainty about whether or not an individual veteran has a mental health condition that requires treatment would be to bypass the question. Veterans could go to Vet Centers, and get counseling for issues related to readjustment. Another would be to go to a VA medical center or clinic and ask for an evaluation. Admittedly, however, some veterans prefer to wait it out to see if they bounce back on their own, and to seek help only if it is clear that they need it. For these people, it is important to recognize that getting an evaluation is only one step in a process.

Even if a provider makes a recommendation for treatment, it is still the veteran's choice about whether to begin immediately or to continue to wait and see. Moreover, when patients and providers agree that it is time to start treatment, treatment planning provides many opportunities for veterans to provide input by indicating their preferences about different strategies.

But what happens if mild symptoms persist? Time may go on, the veteran may not bounce back, but, in spite of symptoms, suffering and impairments, there may never be a time when the veteran feels that it is right to go for an evaluation or to seek treatment. The answer may be for veterans, maybe together with family or friends, to set up a time frame when they first notice symptoms. Maybe they should decide that it would be time for an evaluation if the symptoms are still there in two months. Maybe it should be three months, or four. Regardless, it is important to pick a time and stick to it.

Some basic principles are well established. For PTSD and other mental health conditions, treatment works, and it is readily available within VA. When mental health symptoms lead to significant suffering or impairment, they should be treated. When they lead to danger to patients or others, they must be treated. Beyond these principles, decision-making is more complex, and it is VA's role to be a resource for veterans, helping them make informed decisions that will enhance their lives.

Veterans need to recognize that VA health care is an important resource available to them, and should take advantage of it—first, by talking about a problem or concern with a provider with whom the veteran feels most comfortable. This may be a primary care provider, a Vet Center counselor, or even the veteran's eye doctor. The door is open, now more so than ever before.

VA facilities have extended hours on evenings and/or weekends at its mental health clinics. In addition, VA has greatly enhanced its mental health care system over the last three years. As part of this effort, over 4,000 new mental health workers have been added, and services have been expanded to promote recovery-oriented, evidence-based and innovative practices.

VA is committed to providing the best mental health care to veterans, both to honor our nation's heroes and enable them to live the most meaningful and productive lives possible.

"More than 80 percent of a sample of Air Force women deployed in Iraq and other areas around the world report suffering from persistent fatigue, fever, hair loss and difficulty concentrating, according to a University of Michigan study. . . . In general, Pierce and Lewandowski found that those women in the Reserve and Guard reported more symptoms than active duty personnel. Enlisted women reported more health problems than officers did."

—"Women and War: The Toll of Deployment on Physical Health," *Science Daily*, August 15, 2008

21

WHEN MOMMY COMES HOME
The Story of Army Sergeant Devore Barlowe

"They had us set up our computers in a bombed-out concrete building, and we were just settling in when they bombed the mess tent. It was awful. But then I saw a lot of things that were awful . . . an Iraqi soldier with one side of his body gone, wounded and dead soldiers."

Devore Barlowe is only 38, but she walks with a cane at the pace of a woman forty years her senior. Her year long tour of duty in Iraq left her with bronchial asthma, chronic neck and back pain from slipped disks and bone chips, hearing loss in her left ear, carpel tunnel syndrome, arthritis, mild TBI and a severe case of PTSD. She is so on edge that her two young sons are reluctant to hug her without asking first if it's okay for them to approach. From the time she enlisted in the Army in 1993 to when she was an E5 logistical supply sergeant in Mosul in 2004, up to her current status as a "drilling reservist" with 30 percent disability from the VA, she has served her country proudly and well.

Devore's deployment to Iraq started in 2003 when she rushed out to meet the UPS deliveryman who she thought was bringing a box of books she needed to complete her semester's courses in criminal justice through the University of Phoenix. Instead he handed her a manila envelope stating that, as a reservist, her contract with the Army had been extended and she was to report to Pennsylvania for "SRP" (Standard Readiness Program) immediately. Mother of two little boys, Devorian, age 4, and Dakie, almost 2, Devore was living in Killeen, Texas working at a correctional facility. "I was at my ten-year mark and counting down. I was going for my degree and a career. I had it all planned out. Was I stupid or what?"

Six months later she'd moved her family to Pennsylvania, put her boys in military day-care and started learning electronic purchasing at the local Wal Mart Distribution Center as part of Army Unit 318, Logistics and Communications. "They made me an E5 and gave me four MOS's combined into one: logistics supply. After a year I asked if I could leave and they said, 'No, Devore. We need you. Your contract has been extended through 2005. You've been involuntarily attached to the 818th Maintenance Company. You're deploying to Iraq.' I remember the next day I was having a birthday party for Dakie who was turning three on August 29th. Through the entire party I kept wondering, 'Will I ever see my boys again?'" Two weeks later her sister Monica came and took Devorian and Dakie back home to Wilmington, Delaware, while Devore left for Washington, DC and then to Fort Bragg, North Carolina.

On December 15th the 818th flew from Fort Bragg to Iraq, via Kuwait. "It didn't sink in until they locked us down in a bunker in preparation for boarding the plane. That was when I thought, 'Holy s***; this is happening to me.' When we landed in Kuwait they put us on a bus to Camp Victory, one of the US staging areas. The bus had curtains over its windows, which were kept drawn 'for our safety.' It was 120 degrees outside." Even with Hardees, Baskin Robbins, Pizza Inn, and "beach" volleyball games, amenities courtesy of the American military while settling in for the long haul, Camp Victory was still a grim, hot, sandy tent-city in the desert.

"No one had prepped us for Kuwait. No one had said, 'Don't go into the bathrooms or showers unless you post someone at the door because women have been assaulted.' No one told us about the heat, the sand. A Special Ops guy came over to me when we were packing up for Iraq and said, 'What size equipment you got on, soldier? That's falling right off you.' I'm five feet and I was issued a Kevlar vest two sizes too big for me." The 350 soldiers of the 818th were broken down into units and sent throughout Iraq. Devore was one of seven soldiers, four women and three men, tasked out to handle automated supply and warehousing for all of Iraq at Forward Operating Base Endurance, home of the 1st Brigade, 25th Infantry Division (Stryker Brigade Combat Team) just south of the city center of Mosul in northern Iraq. There was no way for her to "prep" for what would happen as she arrived.

The *New York Times* reported it this way on December 22, 2006:

"A powerful explosion killed 22 people, including 18 Americans, when it ripped through the mess tent of a large American military base in Mosul during lunchtime on Tuesday, in one of the deadliest attacks on American forces in Iraq. The noontime blast, which also wounded 72, sprayed shrapnel into a line where American soldiers, civilian contractors and Iraqi troops were waiting to be served lunch. Pools of blood streamed out from the tent as soldiers rushed to evacuate wounded."

Devore's "secured base" had been the target of a major battle (for Mosul) in early November when hundreds of insurgents along with foreign fighters coming in from Syria attempted to take over the city. The fierce fighting lasted a week with hundreds killed, including four US soldiers, before the insurgents retreated to the western part of the city from where they would continue to conduct hit and run attacks for the next year. The mess tent explosion was the work of a suicide bomber. "They had us set up our computers in a bombed-out concrete building, and we were just settling in when they bombed the mess tent. It was awful. But then I saw a lot of things that were awful . . . an Iraqi soldier with one side of his body gone, wounded and dead soldiers."

Devore's unit barracked and worked out of the same blown-out building. "The Army had contracted repairs of the building to local Iraqis. They were painting and plastering. There were even detainees working construction. At first there was no water because everywhere they dug they'd hit oil instead. We had no choice but to set up our computers and start ordering supplies. Those were 18-hour days. On Christmas Eve I don't think we even noticed when someone dropped off a little Christmas tree. No one expected much in the way of morale boosting." Telephone calls home to her boys were few and frustrating. Her youngest son was so angry at her for leaving that he refused to talk to her at all.

Mosul was "destabilized," as the military put it, during Devore's entire tour of duty. "We got used to the sound of helicopters coming and going and the bombs . . . that heavy 'boom!' sound. In fact, if we didn't hear bombs, we panicked because one time, after a period of no bombs, a mortar hit the room next to the sleeping area. It shook the building so hard that we were thrown out of our beds. It took the breath right out of me. My ears were ringing. There were times when they'd say to us, 'We're going black.' That meant 'cut off all communications. One of our soldiers has died, and we're going in to the area to get him back.'"

After the first few months, Devore started feeling the stress. "I was anxious all the time, lashing out at people, not sleeping. I remembered what my mother told me when I joined the Army in 1994. 'It's not going in to the Army that you need to worry about. It's coming out. Don't lose yourself either place.' My uncles had fought in Vietnam, and when they came back they had a lot of issues with drugs and alcohol. My mother was afraid the same thing would happen to me."

Devore's mother was killed in a car accident during her daughter's Advanced Individual Training at Fort Hood with the 1st Cavalry. Instead of telling her himself, which was his responsibility, her squad leader left her a message taped to her door to go see the Battalion Commander who assumed she already knew about the tragedy and butchered the news. Ten years later, in Mosul, she experienced mindlessness on a greater scale when she and other black female soldiers reported countless incidents of sexual harassment and racism, to deaf ears. "If you didn't sleep with them, they said you were gay." But there was a war going on, and harassment was not high on the list of issues to attend to.

"We were constantly hit upon, but when we'd say something to our superiors we were told, 'They don't mean any harm.'" Showering was a nightmare. "Once when I was showering, two soldiers pulled down the curtain and just stood there. I was petrified but I stared them down. I still get panicky every time I take a shower." Her anxiety was compounded by breathing and back problems. When she wasn't at her computer ordering supplies, she was outside loading and unloading heavy cartons, carrying them from trucks to the warehouse. She injured her neck and back from jumping on and off the trucks, but worse than her slipped disks was the gradual onset of bronchial asthma. The sandstorms didn't help. "The air was always dirty. After a sandstorm you knew you had been breathing in sand because the inside of your nose was filthy." By the summer of 2005 Devore was having serious breathing problems. When she eventually passed out one night in late July, the Army decided to medevac her home.

Devore spent the next year at Walter Reed Medical Center being treated for her spine injury, asthma and PTSD. She lived at the Malone House, on-base quarters for wounded soldiers and their families, with her sons, and then "on the economy" in an apartment in Silver Spring, Maryland. "But they didn't increase my housing allowance so I couldn't pay the rent."

Her sons went back to her sister Monica in Wilmington while she continued her treatment for PTSD and began the fight for benefits. The VA was offering her disability benefits for her physical injuries but nothing for her PTSD, although her symptoms—depression, irritability, sleeplessness, hallucinations, nightmares and withdrawal—were well documented. "If I didn't have to fight as hard as I did, my PTSD wouldn't be as high as it is. I know the military says to suck it up and drive on, but they can't give me my lungs back again or make me whole mentally."

At home in Delaware, Devore works to overcome her distrust of the world around her. "I used to drive down the middle of the street, I was so anxious. No one can come up behind me without me getting jumpy. I lock all the doors. When I walk down the street, I'm analyzing every little thing. I have trouble connecting with my kids." She cites her faith as the reason she's managed to keep going. "That summer in Mosul I was targeted as a trouble maker. I remember that one night I was drinking heavily. I was so depressed. I was suicidal. And I prayed to God, 'I'm putting myself in your hands to take me home.' Three weeks later I was on American soil."

Devore is taking vocational education classes and attends group therapy for her PTSD at the Wilmington Veterans Center. Finances continued to be an ongoing problem. The Armed Forces Foundation gave Devore some money for clothes so she could attend college. "When I got back to the civilized world from war, I didn't know how to get back into a regular routine. I was so hyped up on adrenaline. I don't think I'll ever really blend back in. When I put on my military uniform for drill I feel such anxiety; no, worse, I can barely get myself to put it on. They call that a 'trigger' and I have a lot of them. As I said to my social worker, 'I can't do the things Devore used to do. I'm not the person Devore used to be. I'm making up a new person. I just hope that person is up to the task of being a mother and having a life." Devore has become a spokesperson for the Veterans Administration, giving advice to wounded warriors like herself on how to cope with their PTSD.

MEDALS

2 National Defense Medals, Global War on Terrorism Service Medal, Iraq Campaign Medal, Army Service Ribbon, Overseas Service Ribbon, Armed Forces Reserve Medal (with "m" device), Good Conduct Medal, Army Achievement Medal.

Above:
Army Chief Warrant Officer Richard Gutteridge at his combat outpost, outside the city of Hit, Al Anbar Province, Iraq.

Right:
Michael, Suki, Aaron and Kenzie Mills.

Below:
Army National Guard Sergeant Michael Mills before his "Alive Day," June 14, 2005, outside of Tikrit, Iraq.

Above left:
Army Sergeant Brent Bretz serving in Mosul, Iraq, 2004.

Above:
Brent Bretz at his mother, Kathy Pearce's, home in Mesa, Arizona with his niece.

Left center:
Brent Bretz surrounded by children in Iraq.

Bottom left:
Brent Bretz meeting with his family at the airport.

Right:
Brent Bretz with General Peter Schoomaker, Chief of Staff of the Army, receiving his Purple Heart.

Above right and far right:
Brent Bretz at Walter Reed Medical Center.

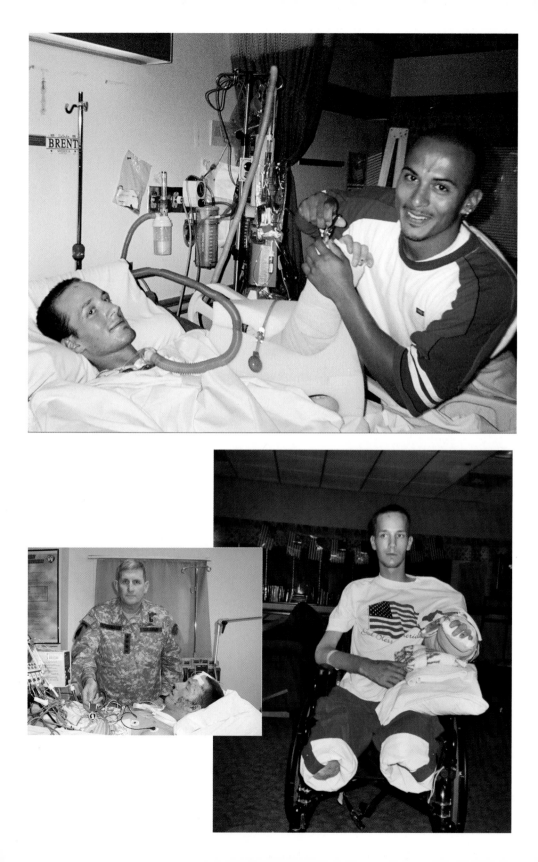

Above and right:
Army Sergeant Nathan Toews outside of Kabul,
Afghanistan before his "Alive Day," June 13, 2006.

The Campaz family at Disneyland—Donovan, Korey and Dee holding Veronique.

Army Corporal Jonnei Campaz,
Gulf War veteran.

USMC Corporal Joshua Hoffman and his fiancée, Heather Lovell.

Right and center:
Army Sergeant Devore
Barlowe in Mosul, Iraq,
2005.

Bottom:
Devore and her son,
Devorian.

Above left: The Armed Forces Foundation has been recognized on many occasions by the White House, Department of Defense and the Department of Veteran's Affairs. AFF President and Executive Director Patricia Driscoll is seen here with President Bush and his wife Laura Bush.

Above: Jose Pequeno, Nellie and Elizabeth Bagley, Patricia Driscoll, and Governor Deval Patrick of Massachussetts.

Left: The Armed Forces Foundation does much to aid wounded service members suffering from TBI and PTSD and it also provides comfort and care to the families of those troops.

Below: Former Congressman Jim Saxton (NJ) with a wounded Marine at the monthly AFF hospital dinner at Bethesda National Naval Medical Center where most of our wounded service members are treated for TBI and PTSD.

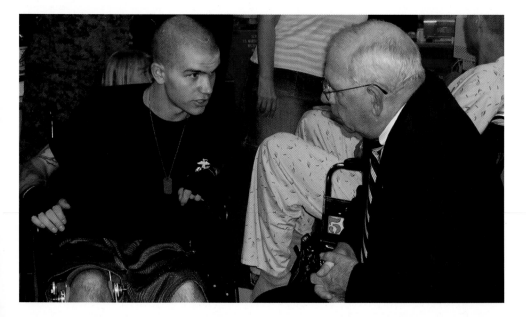

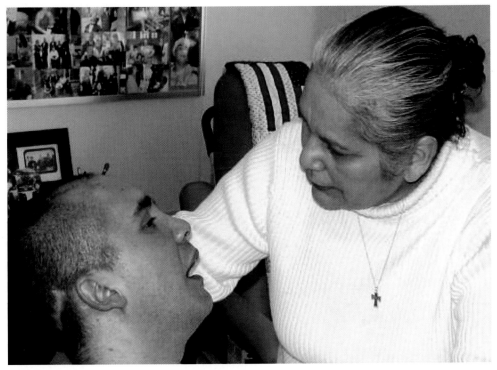

Jose Pequeno and his mother, Nellie Bagley, at the VA's Polytrauma Rehab Center, Haley Hospital, Tampa, Florida.

Hilary Duff appears with a wounded service member at the Bethesda National Naval Medical Center while partnering with the Armed Forces Foundation.

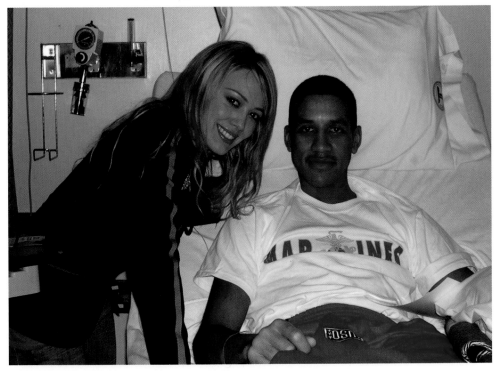

Left:
Army PFC Rob Kislow while deployed to the border between Afghanistan and Pakistan, north of Khost, before his "Alive Day," June 10, 2005.

Above:
Rob receiving a Purple Heart for his head and arm wounds at Walter Reed Medical Center.

Right center:
Rob on his motorcycle in Pennsylvania, after leaving Walter Reed.

Right bottom:
Rob showing his catch on an AFF-sponsored fishing tournament.

USMC Sergeant Chris Harmon and his wife, Kathy.

Judge Julie Mogenis (far left) heads the Armed Forces Foundation's Outdoor Sports Program, which serves as a unique form of therapy for many service members suffering from TBI/PTSD.

Above:
John with his wife Lindsey and children Ashley, Mary Sue and James (on lap.)

Right:
USMC Sergeant Cody Sepulvia with her dog, Durango Kid, and at home, in her truck.

Below:
USMC Sergeant Kelly Meister.

This page and opposite: Army Specialist Walter Blackston in Kabul, Afghanistan, with friends and in his quarters before his "Alive Day," May 24, 2003.

Above:
Sylvia Blackwood-
Boutelle and her son
Holden at home in
California between multi-
ple deployments to Iraq.

Right:
Beverly Young, the wife
of Congressman C.W.
Bill Young salutes our
troops at an AFF event
in Washington, DC.

22

WHY ARE YOU SO ANGRY, MOMMY?

Children in Wartime—How to Know When Help Is Needed

By Michael Genhart

In their incredibly honest accounts of when a mother leaves for war, US Sergeant Devore Barlowe and Second Lieutenant Blackwood-Boutelle both document in these pages how destabilizing it is for an entire family when the primary caretaking parent is deployed. These stories of PTSD, characterized by symptoms ranging from panic attacks and paranoia to suicidal ideation, are extremely compelling as well as unnerving. They illustrate how no one in a family is left untouched by war—including the children.

Although the impact of wartime on military families has been well studied, it is not uncommon to overlook the stress experienced by children in these families. Because all members of a family—the soldier, the spouse and the children—will have psychological and emotional reactions to wartime situations, it is important to know how to "see" that a child is in trouble and in need of help.

From a child's point of view, war means that there will be a separation from the parent leaving to go into service. The period of separation can extend a long time, and in many cases indefinitely. Often there are multiple separations, as the parent leaves, returns home, and then leaves again. A child also sees that the parent left behind at home can be stressed and sometimes overwhelmed and depressed. Children worry about the parent who is away dying during the separation, as well as whether the caretaking parent will be able to run the household and take care of him or herself and the family. There are also adjustments and transitions, not only when a parent leaves for war, but also when that parent returns home and the routine must change again. The strain of war sometimes leads to marital stress and divorce. The child can also be witness to a returning parent whose behavior is unusual or uncharacteristic, and even odd at times.

Both mothers in these cases report relatively abrupt departures from their families and children. They describe feeling unprepared for what they eventually experienced in wartime. Their stories poignantly express how the entire family experiences a shock to the "system" and how everyone goes through a powerful adjustment when a parent leaves for war. Indeed, casualty treatment for when a soldier/parent comes home with PTSD is the necessity to learn "how to be" a parent again when their inner foundation has been cracked.

Re-entry into the family was particularly painful for both Sgt. Barlowe and 2nd Lieutenant Blackwood-Boutelle. They experienced a loss to their identity as "mother" and feelings of dissociation and depersonalization which dramatically affected relating to their children. Painfully, their children saw their mothers as quite different, fragile and rather alien. The children protected themselves by keeping an emotional distance from their mothers once they returned home. In the case of multiple comings and goings of a parent, children may defend against the emotional toll this takes by withdrawing and retreating from the relationship.

So how does a parent know if their child is feeling what might be considered "normal" reactions to the stress associated with a parent being away during wartime? What are the symptoms of depression or anxiety? And how resilient are kids anyway, no matter what they have experienced?

Let's start with the last question: resiliency in children. According to popular belief, children who have experienced stress in their environment (such as their parents' separation and divorce) are affected, but then "get over it." We sometimes take refuge in this understanding and fail to look more carefully at our children and the ways they react internally and externally to the events in their lives. So while many children, like adults, have strengths and ways of coping with life's stressors, they are not totally immune to stressful events. Children are touched by the drama around them.

To assess the level of psychological or emotional distress a child is experiencing, parents should ask themselves the following questions: (1) "Is my child's behavior and mood unusual for my child?" That is, use what you know about your child as a kind of yardstick to determine if he or she is acting in uncharacteristic ways; (2) "Is my child's behavior unusual for a child or teen of this age?" That is, reflect on what is normal behavior from a child of a certain age and whether your child is acting within the range of behavior that is expected from this age group; and (3) "What are my child's teachers, coaches, siblings and so on, saying about my child during this time period?"

Children range in their ability to communicate in words if they are troubled by something. Many children who are less verbal will resort to action as a means of expressing their internal distress. Some will express their feelings in a piece of writing (such as a poem or class essay), while others will create a drawing. Some children who are more inclined to be obedient, quiet, "good" kids become even more compliant because they do not want to cause the adults around them any further upset; these children are easily overlooked. It is also important to consider gender differences in how a certain boy or girl expresses emotional upset. Many times what is shown on the outside is not what a child is necessarily feeling on the inside—an angry child can be masking his or her worries and sadness through overt aggressive actions.

What would a parent look for to determine if their child is experiencing depression or anxiety? Regressive behavior is a hallmark indicator that something may be nervously stirring in a child. For example, a child free of nighttime accidents may begin a period of wetting the bed. Children sometimes report psychological stress in terms of how they feel physically. That is, a child may complain of tummy aches, headaches, body soreness, or fatigue. Changes in sleep patterns and appetite can also signify a problem, such as when a child reports insomnia, nightmares, oversleeping, lack of appetite, overeating, or eating for "comfort." Also, there might be a general lack of interest in things that were once fun—like sports, dance and music. School grades that slip more than expected may be a reflection of a child's shutting down. Social withdrawal and retreating; angry outbursts and fighting with siblings, peers, or adults; attention-seeking behavior;

clinginess and fears of separation; possible drug use; and sexual exper-
imentation or inappropriateness are all signs that a child or teen needs
to be looked at more carefully.

Most of all, children want to feel protected, safe and understood
by the adults around them. They also want to feel that their well-being
and whereabouts are being tracked and considered at all times. It is
important that returning parents talk to children or teens and let them
know that they are available to them. But assessing their internal state
is not necessarily an easy task, and parents should not be afraid to ask
for help. Consulting with other adults in their child's life (other
observers like teachers, coaches, and parents of friends) as well as professionals such as behavioral pediatricians, mental health workers and
school personnel, is a good way to gain better understanding if a child
needs additional psychological help at this time.

Tragically, Sgt. Barlowe and 2nd Lt. Blackwood-Boutelle experienced tremendous stress not only in battle but also once they returned
home. The "battles" at home consisted of dealing with the causes and
symptoms of their PTSD as well as having to fight for the support they
needed to deal with their trauma and pain. Enormous efforts are
required to help heal and repair the emotional, psychological, physical, social and familial wounds that soldiers suffer. This, of course,
extends to the families these soldiers return to. The children just want
their "mom" back, and in these cases, the person who returns from
battle can be (from a child's perspective) a scary, unstable and sometimes unrecognizable version of the person who originally left for war.

Now that both Sgt. Barlowe and 2nd Lt. Blackwood-Boutelle have
completed their deployments overseas, they have taken the first important steps toward re-engaging with their children. They understand the
value of taking care of not only themselves but the families to which
they have returned. Furthermore, they appreciate how important it is
to reflect on how every soldier may have brought a significant piece of
the war home.

23

A GOOD WACKING

The Story of US Army Sergeant David Emme

"When we got to Talafar, I noticed that there were no children out and about, only teenage boys. I saw several of them give us the 'cut your throat' sign. At the time I thought they were doing this because they wanted to see harm come to us. But after thinking about it, I wonder if they knew something was planned and were trying to stop our convoy or warn us. The thing is, if they had tried we probably would have ran them over or even shot them."

Dave Emme joined the Army in May 2001. "I was a retread. On June 14, 1990 I was standing on the yellow footprints of Parris Island, South Carolina at the tender age of 17. I spent five years in the Marine Corps, three of them in Okinawa. I kept extending because of the great church there, Maranatha Baptist Church. I found that I liked reading and studying the Bible as well as discussing and teaching it. For those reasons I thought it was only natural to go into a full-time ministry as a preacher."

After getting out of the Marine Corps, Dave enrolled at Pacific Coast Baptist Bible College in San Dimas, California, but the college was going through a period of transition. There were large debts to be paid off, the curriculum was disorganized and the faculty at odds with one another. After a couple of years, Dave became disillusioned and dropped out.

Over the next few years he drifted through a series of low paying jobs. "I was lost. In the end I went back to what was familiar. I grew up watching war movies, reading books on war, playing war as a kid. Plus I'd already served five years in the Marine Corps. I figured going back into the military was a no brainer. I figured I could do 15–25 years serving my country while getting a degree or two from Liberty

University—say a double Bachelor's in Business Management and Religion. That way I would have my bases covered. I would end up with a ministry in a small church that would not be able to pay my salary. I would be a blessing to a church without wondering where my next paycheck would come from."

Dave joined the Army. He was assigned to Supply and Logistics and stationed in Ft. Lewis, Washington with a unit that was transitioning from a heavy combat brigade to a sleeker, lighter Stryker Brigade (1st Brigade, 25th Infantry Division). He had previously been in a tank unit (1/33 Armor Battalion). "I left Joint Readiness Training Center in Fort Polk, Louisiana for Fort Lewis. We turned in the tanks and transitioned to a RSTA (Reconnaissance Surveillance Target Acquisition) Cavalry unit, known as 2/14th Cavalry."

He became a supply sergeant for six months and then went to the arms room as the unit armorer along with conducting supply operations. "I picked up rank quickly because of my experiences as a Marine NCO, and in December 2003 I was promoted to sergeant. I was given the supply room of Charger Troop. In the nine months before deployment, I trained up with the 'trigger pullers' while working full time as a supply sergeant."

On September 30, 2004 Dave deployed to Mosul, Iraq as part of an advance party to set up the billets and equipment for his troop. On October 19th, while preparing his unit for a move to Talafar, he was wounded in a mortar attack. "I heard the first mortar drop about 25 meters from my position. Being mortared twice a day, we got used to hearing mortars coming in. This one was different, very close. I jumped into a mortar shelter with about 15–20 infantry dudes piling in behind me. I was the most protected but I got wounded the worst."

A mortar hit one of the trailers where the soldiers lived, and shrapnel came into the entrance at an angle, bounced off the cement wall and missed every soldier except Dave and one other. "I ended up with shrapnel in my arm, hand and leg. My platoon sergeant, SSG Jason Forgey ran out and opened the door to the CP and shouted to the XO to give him a medical bag, yelling out that 'Emmis' (my nickname) was hit." Another mortar hit at a tree nearby and wounded SSG Forgey in the back of the head. "We all survived and returned to duty the next day. We were the first soldiers wounded from our troop."

The unit (2/14 CAV) went to Talafar. After four weeks Dave was put on a mission to truck Iraqis the US had recruited for the national police force to Mosul for training. Without enough personnel and equipment, so far they had not been able to train them.

"We loaded them up on FMTVs, big square supply trucks. Since I was the supply sergeant and commander for the supply vehicle, I was gunning on a .50 cal. When we got to Talafar, I noticed that there were no children out and about, only teenage boys. I saw several of them give us the 'cut your throat' sign. At the time, I thought they were doing this because they wanted to see harm come to us. But after thinking about it, I wonder if they knew something was planned and were trying to stop our convoy or warn us. The thing is, if they had tried we probably would have ran them over or even shot them since almost anyone who tries to stop a convoy in Iraq intends harm.

"I got on the radio and told people what I had seen and warned them to keep an eye open because I felt that something would happen to our convoy. We entered an Iraqi traffic circle. My vehicle had crept up on another FMTV. I told my driver to slow a little when going around the circle to keep our distance. That is the last thing I remember. An IED exploded on the left side of our truck. I happened to be scanning on my weapon system to the right and was totally exposed to the blast."

When Dave regained consciousness, he was still in the vehicle. Shards of metal pierced his left eye and his left ear drum was blown out when shrapnel from the blast penetrated his head. He had no sense of where he was or what had happened. "My driver started yelling at me to get out of the vehicle. I cried, 'No my head hurts too much!' He dragged me down and I fell about six feet. I was wondering why in the h-e-double hockey sticks did this guy cause me to fall six feet. He picked me up by my equipment and put my hand on his shoulder and told me to run with him. Then I heard my .50 cal go off and that was that."

Months later Dave's battle buddies told him what had transpired. "When the IED blew, several things happened. First, there were about 25 insurgents trying to shoot up my vehicle. I was the most severely wounded; no one else got shot. With bullets snapping at our feet I got out of the vehicle. SFC Podplesky got on my .50 cal and started blasting everything—cars, people, buildings. There were insurgents shooting from the ground floors, windows and from on top of buildings. Several insurgents started rushing the vehicle, and some NCOs on the ground shot them at point blank range. There were at least four insurgents shooting RPGs at us, two shooters in front of us and two to the left. A car bomb sped toward our convoy.

SFC Podplesky and two or three others with .50 cals and small arms fire took the suicide vehicle out before it could do any damage. When we got word back to the base what was going on, reinforcements headed out immediately. When they did, insurgents started clogging the road with traffic to stop them. Our guys began smashing vehicles off the road and causing cars and trucks to crash and flip. Quite a few insurgents in those vehicles were killed. Apparently the plan had been to destroy the whole convoy. Needless to say they did not succeed."

Meanwhile, Dave and his driver reached the safety of a Stryker vehicle and took off. "While we were in the Stryker I got some of my vision back in my right eye. It had taken us about forty minutes to get to the spot where we were attacked, and about ten minutes to get back to the Forward Operating Base. The only thing I could think of was, 'This will get me some time off work.'" Once Dave got safely back to his FOB he tried to walk down the ramp of the Stryker. "I thought I had passed out again after walking down that ramp, but apparently I was still awake and kept on asking the medics if I was okay."

When the medics started ripping off his equipment to check for wounds, Dave "coded." His heart stopped and his breathing ceased. "I didn't see a white light nor remember floating over my body, probably because I was immediately given CPR by the medics." He "coded" a second time on a medevac chopper. "I remember waking up and thinking, "Never rode in a chopper, want to see what it is like—cool!" I tried raising my body and head and was unable to. So I started tracking the blades against the mountains we were weaving in and out of. I got dizzy and passed out again, and that's probably the second time I died."

Dave awoke ten days later from an induced coma at Walter Reed Medical Center. He had been medevac'd to Mosul, loaded on a C-150 and flown to Baghdad where he was operated on, then flown to

Landstuhl Medical Center in Germany, and finally Walter Reed. "I didn't know where I was when I woke up. Doctors told me that they had taken a good-sized hunk of skull off on the left side because my brain had swelled up twice the size of a normal brain."

Dave had shrapnel in his brain and over 50 percent loss of hearing. To replace the part of his skull—a bit bigger than the size of a hand—he was given a prosthetic skull in the procedure called a cranioplasty. "They told me I had serious Traumatic Brain Injury. Although I got most of my mental faculties back, I still have word aphasia, which means you can't remember what things are called. Sometimes I get lost in conversations for no apparent reason. People tell me jokingly that losing their train of thought happens to them all the time. I know they are just trying to comfort me—but it doesn't help."

The cartilage in his neck was also ruptured. While it has healed, Dave still has some slippage of neck bones which at any time could guillotine his spinal chord and perhaps cause paralysis. Contact sports like touch football became a fond memory. "I have a major loss of hearing in my left ear and some loss in my right ear. My vision is now different in both eyes. Consequently, sometimes when reading something on paper or the computer I occasionally miss what is written. The hole in my leg has healed. I have some cool scars on my face. Chicks dig scars; you can tell any story you want of how they got there."

Dave left Bethesda to recover at Walter Reed Medical Center for the next two years. He could barely talk and went through months of intense speech therapy to learn how to recognize and remember words. Like Rob Kislow, who tested out different types of prostheses, he was asked to participate in clinical trials having to do with TBI. "I was asked if I would go through an experiment with a drug called X to see if it would help in my recovery. I had no idea if I had the drug or something else but I said yes. In the clinical trial, I had to go see some nurses to do weekly and monthly testing, and I was constantly taking different kinds of mental exams which forced me to think. That was a good thing. "

"In the meantime I tried reading, doing logic puzzles and playing Mahjong on a PDA. My best friend, Steve Smith, called me every day and we talked from one to three hours a day for eighteen months.

Talking with Steve did a lot to get my mind working. Without him, I don't think I would have recovered as much as I have."

After getting his prosthetic skull he got a job at Walter Reed. "I started working with Mr. Kitt in the baggage room. Storing baggage was one of my responsibilities as a supply sergeant. This was a minor task in the Cavalry, but a major one at WRAMC with so many soldiers filtering in and out of the hospital." After he worked there for about four months the job started becoming easy and he knew he was ready for the next step.

"I took over the supply room for the Medhold Company. They had no equipment accountability or ordering system, so I started building the systems to reclaim accountability of equipment and start the flow of office supplies. Before I got there you were lucky to get a pen, a notebook or printing paper. For example, we were supposed to get a new uniform issue once in Medhold Company, but when you were coming from the battlefield you got nothing like that. It took me over a year to get a new issue. That was because once in the supply system, the Brigade S-4 just kept things bottled up there in the bureaucracy. I convinced the S-4 officer to put this process in my hands, which he did. After I took over it wasn't long before a soldier could put in for a new uniform and literally have the paperwork to go to the PX to get it the same day."

A few months later, Dave worked with the Wounded Warrior program to return to the civilian workplace. His first job was as an unpaid intern at the Federal Highway Administration in Washington, DC. His hope was that an internship might turn into a full-time job.

"The first interview I went to was with Paula Ewen of the Federal Highway Administration. I told her that I did not see myself holding a stop and go sign on the side of the road, that I wanted to work for a logistic branch of the government. She not only offered me a position but grabbed hold of my arm as I left and told me she would not let go 'til I said yes. I believed her and relented and it was one of the best decisions I made. I became a sort of personal assistant to her. If I can ever work again, she is the type of boss I want." By far the biggest challenge Dave faced during this time were his headaches, constant migraines that kept him home for days at a time. "Once, I felt so guilty not going to work that I did not go back for six weeks. Paula called me at home and told me she understood that I was going through some bad times and to come back any time I was ready. I was not to feel any guilt about the time missed. She and the agency were there for me, not me there for them. The next day, I reported back to work."

Dave retired from the Army in September 2006 with 30 percent benefits. He was approved for Social Security disability and received 200 percent from the VA.

Today he is attending Muhlenberg College. "Heather Bernard of the American Council of Education told me about Muhlenberg and helped me get into the school. My goal is to overcome some of my TBI issues so I can successfully re-enter the work force." His first year was a resounding success. "I always thought that people would follow me to class protesting the war, or penalize me for having a conservative viewpoint. This is not the case at Muhlenberg. Professors and students want to hear your stories and show their appreciation and support regardless of politics. Because of the support of many professors I've succeeded in my classes, with only one B, the rest A or A- and a 3.82 GPA. I feel it's important to tell people my GPA and the courses I'm taking, not because I want to boast, but to clear up the fact that though some of us veterans were affected by TBI, we can still accomplish great things."

Dave is optimistic about his future. "It would be easy to say, 'I have done enough in thirty-five years to take it easy; certainly, I have earned this.' But God has a purpose for me, to be a blessing to someone, and that takes work. Through all my experiences since I've been injured I have found it pays to be proactive and to push to rehabilitate myself. If nothing else I will have gained the satisfaction that I know I have lived a good life and framed my living to be a pleasure to my Lord and a blessing to others."

MEDALS

Army: 2 Purple Hearts, Army Commendation Medal, 2 Army Achievement Awards, 3 Army Good Conduct Medals, 2 National Defense service Medals, Global War on Terrorism Service Medal, Non Commissioned Officer Professional Developement Ribbon, Combat Action Badge.

Marine Corps: Meritorious Unit Commendation, Good Conduct Medal, Sea Service Deployment Ribbon with one star.

"Little is known about the epidemiology of mild traumatic brain injury during deployment and its association with adverse health outcomes after deployment. Many troops reportedly have persistent post concussive symptoms such as irritability, memory problems, headache, and difficulty concentrating."

—"Mild Traumatic Brain Injury in US Soldiers Returning from Iraq," *The New England Journal of Medicine,* January 31, 2008

24

THE MENTAL TRANSCEIVER

By Norman McCormack

Like other communications systems, our brains receive and transmit messages. As is the case with any transceiver, the human brain contains many electrical circuits—each devoted to a particular task or set of tasks. How clearly messages are received and sent out depends on how well our brain circuitry works. Disruptions (e.g. open circuits, short circuits, power fluctuations) interfere with both reception and transmission—in other words messages get garbled.

Unlike man-made transceivers, our brain circuitry does not rely on transformers, diodes, resistors and the like. The flow of electricity is modulated by chemicals called neurotransmitters. If the actions of these chemicals are disturbed, the electrical signal—the message—is interrupted.

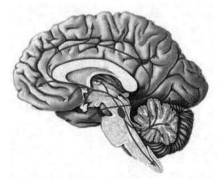

The Norepinephrine Circuit

This drawing is of one of many neurotransmitter circuits in the brain. If this circuit malfunctions, electrical signals that rely on it are disrupted.

Disturbances in neurotransmitter circuits can result from physical injury, illness, drug abuse, or psychological trauma. For example, it is well established that the circuit connecting the thalamus (information clearinghouse), the amygdala (emotional memory, survival response) and the pre-frontal cortex (seat of reason) often malfunctions in those who have been exposed to severe trauma (such as military combat). This malfunction is in the nature of a short circuit. Instead of proceeding from the thalamus to the pre-frontal cortex and then to the amygdala, the signal is shunted directly from the thalamus to the amygdala, where the message is interpreted solely by emotion. This process—called emotional hijacking—frequently leads to inappropriate responses to the original signal.

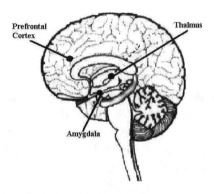

Brain structures involved in emotional hijacking

Stimuli from the environment are interpreted by "unresolved" emotions stored in the amygdala. The prefrontal cortex is "locked out" of the loop. As Jonnei Compaz's story demonstrates, a stimulus, the "smell of barbecue," is "mis"-interpreted as the smell of "burning flesh." This "mis"-interpretation resulted in behaviors necessary to survive combat, but not appropriate to his hometown.

Troubleshooting brain circuitry is not as straightforward as it is with man-made devices; oscilloscopes and digital VOMs are of no use to us. The "diagnostic tool" we use is behavior. If a person has trouble controlling anger, or avoids involvement in previously enjoyed activity, we can use these as crude measures of disrupted circuitry.

By exploring with someone how he or she interprets and responds to messages from the environment, we can "drill down" and focus on specific circuits. Once identified, we are then able to help people repair and re-energize disrupted circuits.

Sometimes it is necessary to use medication to help repair mental circuitry. Just as we may use a jumper wire to temporarily bypass a short in a man-made transceiver, medications help by giving us time to re-energize a neurotransmitter circuit that has been disrupted by trauma.

25

I'LL NEVER LEAVE YOU

The Story of National Guard Sergeant
Jose Pequeno and His Mother, Nelida Bagley

*"After Jose got injured I had to fight for a way to be close to my
son. There were nights when I really did believe they were going to
throw me out and then I would sleep in the waiting room.
I had to prove myself."*

There is a lioness living in Jose Pequeno's hospital room at the James
A. Haley Veterans Hospital. Nellie Bagley is protecting her cub after
he was returned to her from Iraq with a portion of his brain blown
away, his left arm shattered and two shrapnel holes in his back. Since
March 3, 2006 when she "got the call," her fierce, almost unfath-
omably single-minded love for her son has been the driving force that
keeps him alive.

"Back then I worked nights. I got home at 7 am but I couldn't
sleep that day. Around 1 p.m. there was a phone call. 'We need to noti-
fy you that your son had an accident and is in surgery.'" But they
couldn't tell her any details so she hung up, called her daughter and
Jose's dad, and then kept calling Casualty Affairs every fifteen minutes. "They kept telling me that when they knew something I'd know
it. It seemed like hours before they said, 'They're flying him into
Germany.' When he got to Germany, they told me there was a severe
injury to his head. I kept asking them, 'How bad is it?' They kept saying, 'Until he's getting cleaned up we won't know the extent of the
injury.' I finally got to a nurse and begged her to tell me what was
going on. 'I'll have a neurosurgeon call you' she said."

At two o'clock in the morning, Nellie received a call from the neurosurgeon. "'I'm still evaluating your son. I'll call you when I'm done.

I asked, 'How long are you going to be?' 'I've got twenty minutes to go,' he said, and I said, 'You've got twenty-two minutes. I'm his mom, for God's sake.'"

Twenty-five minutes later Nellie got a call. "The same male voice said, 'Is Jose Pegueno your son?' I said, 'Yes.' 'Such a beautiful son,' he said. 'What a terrible waste, a young man with such a life ahead of him, and he's going to die.' Right there, a piece of me just left. 'You're such a liar!' I yelled. 'Of course my son is going to make it.' After that, I asked, 'Are you finished with your evaluation? Tell me exactly what's wrong with my son. Please.' And the surgeon said, 'He has a severe brain injury, severe bleeding; he's lost the bottom two lobes of his brain.' I started throwing things. My next-door neighbor came running, and I sat down and cried and said, 'I can't do this.'" But she could.

In 2001 former Marine José Pequeno was the youngest police chief in the state of New Hampshire and the sole officer of Sugar Hill, population 600. He supported a wife and two school-age children as well as a preteen daughter from a former relationship. He ran five miles a day, hunted, fished and loved motorcycles and snowmobiles. The New Hampshire "north country" townspeople gave him a surprise going away party at the local meeting house when his National Guard military police unit deployed to Iraq in the spring of 2005. He'd be back in a year.

Almost exactly one year later, on March 1, 2006, just a week after his 32nd birthday, Jose was manning an Iraqi checkpoint. "Insurgents had blown up an Iraqi police station in Ramadi with a car bomb and Jose was there calling it in to the base," Nellie explains. "They threw a grenade through the open part of his Humvee and it exploded directly behind him." The blast blew Jose out the door. His driver was killed instantly, the gunner was shot, and Jose ended up half out of the truck so that the lower part of his body was still inside the Humvee but his head and parts of his brain were on the sand. The explosion had gone under his helmet. When medics arrived less than two minutes later they assumed Jose was dead and went to help the gunner. But they heard the gurgling sound of the "dead" soldier choking on his own blood. They cleared his airways and yelled "Sergeant P!" and Jose opened his eyes.

The first surgery was in Balad. The next few were at the Landstuhl Medical Center in Germany where Nellie would be told, for the first of six times in twenty-nine months, that Jose would die. The following day Nellie was flown to Bethesda Navy Medical Center along with Jose's wife Kelley and his sister Elizabeth to meet her son. "There were so many tubes, wires and halos, I could hardly find a place to touch him, but I did and his body was warm. 'You're going to make it,' I said. 'I love you.' At 3 a.m. Kelley had returned to Fisher House, the hotel where families of patients are housed, when a doctor came into the ICU room and asked to speak to family members. Nellie and Elizabeth were the only ones present at the time.

He took them into a conference room nicknamed the "Nutty Room" by families because it was where doctors told them the bad news. "There's no way he'll make it," the doctor said, "and if he lives, the only thing he'll be able to do is open and close his eyes. He'll be a vegetable. I don't give him two days, so be realistic and accept it." Nellie was furious. "You've no right or power to make that call," she shouted. "Go back and do your job." Months later the doctor would tell Nellie that his encounter with her "Changed the way I dealt with families from that point on."

Two weeks later Jose opened his eyes. One week later his breathing equipment was disconnected. He was transferred to Walter Reed Medical Center where he would stay for the next five months. It wasn't long before Nellie gave up her job in North Woodstock, New Hampshire to be with her son twenty-four hours a day. There were questions about her presence at Walter Reed around the clock while Jose's wife was living at the Malone House for patients' families. "Walter Reed was the worst period of my life after Jose got injured. I had to fight for a way to be close to my son. There were nights when I really did believe they were going to throw me out and then I would sleep in the waiting room. I had to prove myself." Meanwhile her son's weight dropped from 205 to 126 pounds.

She quickly depleted her savings. She chose to exchange living in the home she was renting in New Hampshire for the temporary living quarters provided by the Army next to Walter Reed. "The first eight months I received $59 per day for expenses. I ate very little and used the money to pay my bills. I tried to keep up the rent on the house, but

I got behind." Elizabeth, 21 when her brother was injured, dropped out of college to help her mother care for him. "He is my brother, my father figure, my protector, He took care of me my whole life. How can I not take care of him now?"

After he transferred to Haley Hospital, part of the VA Polytrauma Rehabilitation Center in Tampa, Florida in August of 2006, Jose was retired from the military, and the $59 per diem stopped. For the next eighteen months, Nellie slept on a recliner at his side, showered and dressed in his bathroom and bought the skimpiest of meals at the hospital cafeteria. Whatever money she had came from veterans aid groups. But she was thankful because at Haley Jose had access to as many as twelve specialists in medicine and pain management, and ten people specializing in occupational, physical, vocational and speech therapy. Staffers convinced her to become a volunteer, and to write a newsletter for families like hers. Haley officials gave Elizabeth a paying job as an assistant in the nursing recruitment office. The hospital became their entire world.

On July 22, 2007 Jose was back at Bethesda Navy Medical Center for his first cranioplasty, but the procedure would fail when infection set in and his body rejected the plate. A second cranioplasty in April of 2008 would fail for the same reason. "It was one step forward and two steps back because everything had to come out, and each time we were at square one," Nellie recalls. The surgeons at both Bethesda Navy Medical Center and Haley Hospital in Tampa, where Jose and Nellie returned to at the end of May, agree that a third attempt can come only after Jose has spent a full year infection-free, an almost impossible goal in the infectious environment of a hospital.

Yet Jose's responses give her hope. His eyes move when he hears a familiar voice, made louder and clearer after he was prescribed a hearing aid for his left ear. He utters sounds that convey frustration, anger or love in answer to questions and conversation from his mother, his sister and particularly his 13-year-old daughter, Mercedes. "Mercedes spent a lot of time with him, and she would scold him, 'You need to hurry up and talk. You're supposed to be my parent.' You should have seen the look on Jose's face. He positively beamed."

Seventeen operations and two and a half years later, Jose was allowed to go home on weekends in a wheelchair to Elizabeth's rented apartment in Tampa, ten minutes from the hospital. One evening in July 2008 he was lying on the bed watching television. "He was doing fine so I left for five minutes and then went back to check on him and there was blood everywhere. He'd pulled his feeding tube out. I can't imagine how painful that must have been to do." Nellie and Elizabeth called an ambulance and he was rushed back to the hospital. "I believe he was just frustrated and fed up with life," Nellie says. "And I don't blame him. He hadn't had the luxury of dealing with the emotional part of himself."

Two weeks later, on July 28th, another crisis occurred when Jose developed an infection around the shunt in the back of his head. Doctors removed the shunt and put in an outside drain, twice. In the process, an intravenous line became infected, and that infection spread throughout his body. Nellie found herself back in the ICU with her son on three antibiotics tending to his 102-degree temperature and praying. "During that time Jose was fighting harder to stay alive in the ICU than he ever did in Iraq," she remembers. On August 12, 2008, Jose was operated on again to remove a newly discovered piece of shrapnel from his brain, possibly the reason his body rejected the first two cranioplasties.

Nellie admits that as a caregiver, she too probably suffers from a secondary form of PTSD. "The big things I can handle great. It's the little things that hit me. I don't have the patience to deal with the details. I get frustrated by all the paperwork, and how nobody will give me a direct answer about my son." In Nellie's opinion, Jose's doctors are vague about how much more he will improve once his skull is rebuilt, assuming a third cranioplasty takes place and isn't rejected. However, Jose's doctors may be clearer than she is willing to admit that his quality of life will never be anything near what he experienced before he was injured. Yet Nellie is determined that her son will eventually leave the hospital for good.

"No matter what the doctors say, I know he knows what is going on," Nellie says. "He and I will get through this together, no matter how long it takes." Elizabeth and Nellie are looking for a house in Tampa near the hospital where they can live with Jose and care for him. In the past two years the Armed Forces Foundation has given several thousand dollars to support Nellie's housing needs, as well as several hundred dollars to Jose's wife Kelly. Jose and Nellie were also honored at the Armed Forces Foundation's 2008 Gala.

MEDALS

Army Service Ribbon, 2 Purple Hearts, 3 National Defense Service Medals, Army Achievement Medal, Army Commendation Medal, Army Good Conduct Medal, Army reserve Component Achievement Medal, Global War on Terrorism Service Medal, Armed Force Reserve Medal with M Device, Non Commissioned Officer Professional Development Ribbon, 3 New Hampshire National Guard Service Bars, Iraqi Campaign Medal, Combat Action Badge.

26

THE FACES BEHIND THE FILES
VA's Polytrauma System of Care

By Barbara Sigford, MD, PhD

Glen Vanitallie's life hung in the balance after an improvised explosive device (IED) struck his Humvee in Baghdad. Now, five years after his injuries, he is back in his community, going to school, studying photography and snowboarding.

Caroline Carter, a single mother, saw the Army as an opportunity, a fresh start. However, her future changed when she was exposed to multiple IEDs in Iraq. Now, she suffers from a severe Traumatic Brain Injury (TBI) and has lost sight in one eye. She is working hard to rehabilitate her body and mind and to reconnect with her son.

Sean Bianca turned 19 years old in basic training, 20 in Iraq, and 21 at the Minneapolis Veterans Affairs (VA) Medical Center. He was hit by an IED. Some thought he would not live, much less be able to sit on top of a horse. Through aggressive rehabilitation, Sean is learning to do the basic tasks while living at home with his family in a handicapped accessible house.

These three are among the hundreds of veterans and members of the Armed Services faced with life-altering challenges who have received care for severe TBI or polytrauma in the Department of Veterans Affairs' Polytrauma System of Care.

Glen, Caroline and Sean are in different stages of recovery after undergoing polytrauma/TBI rehabilitation tailored to their specific goals. Their determination and desire to recover from their wounds provides inspiration to us all.

The clinicians, therapists, counselors and staff who work with these patients are committed to providing these brave and inspiring people with "the best care anywhere." At the VA, the clinicians, therapists and professional staff who work with these patients do so because "we really want to do this challenging work. It's not just a job for us. We are truly committed to helping. We want to make a difference."

Active duty service members and veterans such as Glen, Caroline and Sean may enter the Polytrauma System of Care at any of the more than 100 polytrauma care centers, depending on the extent of their injuries and the treatment and care that is needed. Those with the most severe injures will be referred from a Military Treatment Facility (MTF) run by the Department of Defense (DoD) to one of four VA Polytrauma Rehabilitation Centers. Those with less severe injuries may be referred from the military treatment facilities, or other DoD or community providers, and obtain care and treatment at any medical facility in VA's Polytrauma System of Care.

VA's Polytrauma System of Care is a tiered system comprised of four components: Polytrauma Rehabilitation Centers (PRCs); Polytrauama Network Sites (PNS); Polytrauma Suppport Clinic Teams (PSCT); and Polytrauma Points of Contact (PPOC). This system balances access and expertise.

Four regional rehabilitation centers (PRCs), provide care for those with the most intense needs and severe injuries. The 21 network sites provide care for individuals who are medically stable but still require the support of a full rehabilitation team of services at a complex medical center.

The support clinic teams are typically at smaller VA facilities. Each has a full dedicated rehabilitation team, but may not have all medical and surgical support services. The points of contact are sites with a dedicated care manager who is able to connect the veteran with the required level of care.

To support rehabilitation efforts across the entire system, VA developed the Polytrauma Telehealth Network, which allows remote clinical and educational activities by way of state-of-the-art multipoint videoconferencing. This ensures that polytrauma and TBI expertise are available throughout the system and that care is provided at a location and time that is most accessible to the patient.

Coordination of care for veterans and troops with polytrauma and TBI is ensured through a network of social work and nurse case managers. Every patient seen at one of the polytrauma programs is assigned a case manager who coordinates care, identifies resources for emerging medical, psychosocial, or rehabilitation problems, and provides psychosocial support and education.

From the experience of the Polytrauma Rehabilitation Centers, VA has learned that inpatient rehabilitation is only the beginning of a long road toward recovery for many polytrauma patients. An extensive continuum of care is vital to enabling patients to achieve the highest level of function possible.

The cornerstones of VA's Polytrauma System of Care are the interdisciplinary teams that work together in the assessment, planning and implementation of a patient's care. Each VA rehabilitation professional has specific skills and knowledge, gained through firsthand experience, education and clinical training. These professionals are licensed and certified with respect to their discipline requirements and receive additional training in specific treatment areas for TBI and polytrauma.

These areas include visual rehabilitation, cognitive rehabilitation and neurorehabilitation, as well as the latest and best in medication and equipment. New therapists receive mentoring from experienced therapists, and they attend training conferences sponsored by VA, the Department of Defense, and the private sector on state-of-the art techniques and treatments.

Members of the interdisciplinary team include, but are not limited to, a physician specializing in physical medicine and rehabilitation (physiatrist), a rehabilitation nurse, neuropsychologist, rehabilitation psychologist, physical therapist, kinesiotherapist, occupational therapist, speech language pathologist, social worker, recreational therapist and a military liaison.

The patients that we treat and care for are either veterans or service members who are still on active duty. These patients were highly trained people, in the best shape of their lives, who led very active lives before they were injured. The primary goal for rehabilitation is to return to a full, active, independent life. In addition to returning to work and school, they want to play basketball, ride bikes, go hiking, swimming and increase their endurance and build their muscles.

While they cannot do many of these activities the way they used to, rehabilitation therapy programs can provide ways for them to take part in and perform active tasks while also serving to help them regain their basic motor skills, cognitive skills and self-care skills while adjusting to their limitations. Success for individuals such as Glen, Caroline and Sean often comes literally in very small steps. Through the combined application of different therapies, however, small steps can lead to big changes.

For example, Glen Vanitallie had multiple injuries, including severe brain injury, a shattered femur and severe soft tissue damage. He went through physical therapy and learned to walk again. Occupational therapy helped him learn to manage his day. Speech therapy helped him use his mind.

Glen now leads an active life. He lives at home. He just finished his first year of college, and he has a girlfriend. He goes skiing and snowboarding and took part in the recent National Veterans Winter Sports Clinic. VA considers him a model for disabled sports.

As a result of his determination, he exceeded all expectations; however, he still faces challenges every day. Glen has memory problems and does not manage his own finances. He still receives therapy to help with interpersonal skills, such as interacting with others. Glen benefited from the interdisciplinary approach, applying a variety of TBI recovery programs, as has Caroline Carter.

After being exposed to seven IED blasts while serving in Iraq, Caroline thought she had a minor concussion. Then came severe headaches. When she arrived at the VA in Palo Alto, California, she was stumbling and falling. She could not complete a sentence. It took her as long as 20-minutes to answer a question.

Caroline Carter went to aggressive therapy five days a week. She benefited from therapies such as occupational therapy, recreational therapy, visual therapy and cognitive therapy, which range from performing simple tasks such as putting away dishes, to playing basketball to painting by numbers.

After working hard and undergoing a full course of rehabilitation, she returned home to Kentucky. She now is able to play with her child and can conduct a conversation the way she used to before being wounded. She still goes to the hospital for physical therapy. Upon seeing her with a patch over one eye, her young son wanted to know if she was a pirate. "Yeah," she said, "I am a pirate."

Sean Bianca was semi-comatose when he came to the VA for care. His face was broken. The only thing completely intact was his lower jaw. In fact, the medic on the scene where the IED had exploded did a great job of keeping Sean alive. He was sent to Bethesda Naval Medical Center. His parents and brother were told he might not survive. He had to be fed through a tube. He went into ICU. They wanted to send him to sub-acute care. Observers said his head was as big as a basketball. His parents were only able to recognize him by his freckles and by his feet.

When he arrived at the Minneapolis VA Medical Center, he was confined to bed. He received the full complement of rehabilitation therapies, and doctors noticed he had incredible resilience and a drive to succeed. Those with severe TBI often have trouble doing simple tasks such as feeding themselves. But he pushed on, and went to physical therapy. When he started he could not sit up straight in a wheelchair. Now, he is able to sit on top of a horse.

The official term for it is hippotherapy. Eleven months and 11 days after he was wounded, Sean left the VA hospital, sitting straight up in his wheelchair. He hopes to be able to walk on his own some day. He also went to speech therapy. There was not a dry eye in the hospital when he was able to repeat what the nurses taught him to say: "I love you, Mom."

Sean went home to Eau Claire, Wisconsin, where they gave him a welcome home parade. Motorcycles and convoys drove past, and people lined up along the roads. A group on the bridge held up a sign, "WELCOME HOME, THANK YOU FOR YOUR SERVICE."

The VA provides a continuum of rehabilitation services. The facilities in the Polytrauma System of Care have a shared system of managing medical information, and an integrated system of care management, including access to several Transition Patient Advocates who can travel with veterans to their points of care as needed. Extensive support to families is also available, and the environment of care is modified to meet the needs of young patients and their families. Combined with the special programs, the rehabilitation services provided are unique to the VA.

The therapies and treatments available through VA's Polytrauma System of Care reflect those services utilized by Glen Vanitallie, Caroline Carter and Sean Bianca. The three are featured in a recently released DVD produced by VA called "The Face Behind the File: The Long Road Back."

27

PORTRAIT OF RESILIENCE
The Story of Army Sergeant Brent Bretz

"The Landstuhl surgery was a low point for me because Brent had lost so much blood, and the medical staff wouldn't guarantee anything. I was afraid we would lose him."

So far, 26-year-old Brent Bretz has had sixty surgeries, more minor procedures than he can count, and several close calls with death. Yet his journey to recovery is headed in the right direction, as Kathy Pearce, his mother who has been with him every step of the way, points out again and again.

"The reason I tell and retell the story of my son is in the hopes it will help other families that are going through the same thing. To let them know it takes prayer, faith, hope and courage to get through every day. Everything we experience in life changes who we are; it is up to us to see the silver lining of each experience. The silver lining in this story is that my son is alive and he is rebuilding his life."

Brent was a sniper and team leader in a platoon attached to Charlie Company, 1st Batallion, 5th Regiment out of Fort Lewis. They deployed to Iraq in the fall of 2004. An extrovert who missed his huge Ford F-150 truck and 4-year-old daughter Celeste back home in Mesa, Arizona, Brent was popular and respected by his teammates. He was the kind of soldier who covered watch patrol shifts for his buddies and took on the tough assignments. The excitement of participating in an operation and coordinating sneak attacks on the enemy that required him to slip in, shoot, and then slip out appealed to him.

"Brent is the youngest of five children, with three older sisters and one brother, and he was the mischievous one, a handful. Although I

159

knew that Brent and his unit were doing what is right and what Americans have stood for from the beginning of this great country, it was hard to send him off to war." A devout Mormon and single mother (Kathy and Brent's father were divorced when Brent was very young) it was Kathy who he called once he was in Iraq. For the first three months that fall of 2004 she hung on each phone call, e-mail or instant message for proof that her youngest was "safe for another day."

On December 19, 2004, Brent was patrolling the desert outside of Mosul. He'd just been certified to drive a massive five-ton supply truck called an FMTD and he was behind the wheel with his platoon sergeant when the truck hit an IED. He remembers nothing about the day, the truck or the explosion. The blast severed both his legs, ruptured his spleen and broke his left elbow. He suffered severe head trauma, fractured facial bones, nerve damage and hearing loss in his left ear, second degree burns over half his body and collapsed lungs. At each of the various stops at military emergency units, along what has become a tragically familiar route to stateside medical care at Bethesda Navy Medical or Walter Reed Medical Center, the doctors did not think he would live.

"On Saturday night, Dec 18, 2004, Brent e-mailed me so I knew he was okay, but the next morning I received a phone call from the Department of Defense saying that he'd been very seriously injured." Brent was taken to the makeshift hospital in Mosul where the first surgeries took place to stabilize him. "With every phone call and each passing day the only good news was that he was still alive. I wanted nothing more than to be with my son and touch him and let him know that I was there and loved him and would stay by his side, but it wasn't possible."

While in Balad, Iraq, Brent's lungs filled with fluid, his blood failed to clot and he had bleeding and swelling of the brain. It would be 48 hours before he could be put on a flight to Landstuhl Medical Center. "I received a phone call saying we had been cleared to go to Germany and be with Brent. I left Arizona with his brother and two sisters, and my other daughter left from Utah and we met up in DC so the kids could get their passports. I was beside myself and it truly was only my faith that kept us going. The whole family was determined to be strong for Brent. "

They arrived in Germany on Dec 23rd, but by the time they arrived Brent had been taken to Koblenz two hours away. When they finally got to see him the next day he appeared to be in a coma. "We entered the room two at a time, and I know he heard our voices. His sister Shilo was in the room with me, and the doctors were concerned he might not keep his left arm, so Shilo was massaging his hand and forearm to help with the circulation. Shilo asked Brent if he could squeeze her hand and he did, but to make sure it was not just reflexes she asked him again and he responded again." Progress.

"We spent the next three days traveling to Koblenz to be with Brent before he was transported back to Landstuhl. They had tried the day before to move him back to Landstuhl, but bad weather made it impossible. On the day they transported Brent, we were torn as to whether to travel to Koblenz or stay at Landstuhl. The skies were gray and looked like snow. If this happened he would not be transported, but if we drove to Koblenz we might miss him. After many prayers, the skies open up and it was a sunny day with blue skies. Soon after the helicopter landed at Landstuhl the skies turned gray again and it snowed the rest of the day."

During his first evening at the Landstuhl ICU, Brent started running a fever. "His eyes and skin were starting to look rather yellow. Within thirty minutes his liver started shutting down, and his fever spiked to 107. The doctors were preparing to take him into surgery later in the day, but instead operated immediately." Brent almost died. "The Landstuhl surgery was a low point for me because Brent had lost so much blood, and the medical staff wouldn't guarantee anything. I was afraid we would lose him." But after two more surgeries he was actually stable enough to be flown stateside. After the family had left the hospital and Brent was on a gurney, General Pete Schoomaker, Chief of Staff of the US Army who happened to be at Landstuhl, presented Brent with the Purple Heart.

Kathy was taken to the airbase to fly home with Brent. "The flight home was excruciating. Brent's temperature rose again and the doctors were watching his pressure, the bleeding on the brain and his fever. He would have gone to Walter Reed but every bed in the ICU was full so they took him to Bethesda." Over the previous eight weeks, 1,927 soldiers had been wounded. On January 10th doctors lifted the induced coma and Kathy could finally talk to him. Bethesda Navy Medical was followed by more weeks of procedures at Walter Reed as doctors worked to save his left arm and reconstruct his face. Six feet tall, Brent lost half his body weight. "So much of his recovery was determined by the amount of pain he was in," Kathy remembers.

Almost as lethal as the blast that destroyed his truck was the condition that now developed inside Brent's body: heterotopic ossification, or HO. Brent's body formed bone around his wounds instead of tissue. It grew in painful lumps on the ends of his legs and his injured left arm, making it impossible to use his prosthetics. Uncontainable, it pushed the plates in his elbow through the skin. Besides the heterotopic ossification, Brent had sores from his braces and infections from his skin graphs, and ringing in his damaged left ear.

Five months after he was injured, Brent and Kathy moved to Brooke Army Medical Center in San Antonio. Brent was terribly weak from lack of exercise, but he gamely began the physical therapy he was sent there to do. Yet as daunting as his physical recovery was proving to be, emotional healing proved to be equally as challenging. "As the physical parts of his body healed, then it was time for his mental healing to begin. While he was in rehab at Brooke he was diagnosed with clinical depression, not PTSD. I thought it was because of all the pain medications he'd been on. When I mentioned to his caregivers that I thought he wasn't depressed but had PTSD, they were surprised to hear that I would think that. But it was so clear. He was having sleepless nights, nightmares; there were days when he'd be in a constant state of anxiety."

By May 2005 he had become an outpatient, living with Kathy in a two-room suite at the Powless Guest House and driving an electric wheelchair, a far cry from his huge 1999 Ford F-150 truck with 13-inch lifts and tractor tires, but better than being pushed around by his mom. "I knew it was hard on him to be so dependent on me, but I also knew I was his best and very often only advocate." Brent was also struggling with memory loss and chronic headaches from his TBI. But he gradually gained his strength back so that in July he was able to move back home to Arizona.

Once home, Kathy and Brent found that living in the same house was difficult. Brent was alternately angry and depressed, often mixing his pain medications with alcohol. "It was his little girl, Celeste, that kept him going," recalls Kathy. "And his nieces and nephews. You know children are so spiritual, whether Brent had legs or not couldn't have mattered less. They'd come into the house and ask, 'Where's Uncle Brent? How's he doing?'" In September Brent moved into a ground level, two-bedroom condo in Tempe with his cousin, Jason. In the fall of 2007 the Armed Forces Foundation gave Brent $125,000 toward a down payment on his own house ten minutes away from Kathy.

Brent continued to struggle to regain his independence. "It took a while before he could travel any distance without having a panic attack. To travel by airplane was very difficult." In October 2005 the men of the 1st Battalion, 5th Regiment had a reunion to celebrate their homecoming from a year-long tour of duty in Iraq at the Greater Takoma Convention & Trade Center. Brent had been the first of the 160 in his company to be seriously injured, and he wanted to go.

"I remember it took four days before he made his flight. Between the effort it took to even get to the airport and the anxiety of dealing with checking in, dealing with his wheelchair, prosthetics, security, the actual flight and the number of people at the airport, it was all very stressful. I had to keep changing his flight. On the fourth day I finally accompanied him to the airport and helped him get checked in and waited at the gate with him to board before leaving. This was one of his first trips by himself, and it was a very important step for him to make."

Kathy became so wise and well known as Brent's mother that she was asked to work with the Military's Severely Injured Program to help other wounded soldiers and their families make the transition back into their communities. She took the job. "To witness the things these brave soldiers cope with as they recover from their wounds is beyond the imagination. To undergo surgery after surgery like Brent has is beyond my comprehension. Yet he wakes up every day with a renewed determination to move on, and I believe that ability to overcome what life has dealt him is because of his faith and belief in God, family and country. Brent was once asked by a reporter if he regretted his service and the loss of his legs. He replied, "How can I compare the loss of my legs to millions having freedom. The job is not done, and we should stay until it is." Brent continues to struggle with his PTSD, yet he says he would reenlist in a second if he could. His friends say that Brent isn't in denial about what has happened to him, he just doesn't let it define him.

MEDALS

NCO Professional Development Medal, Iraqi Campaign Medal, Operation Iraqi Freedom Medal, Global War on Terrorism Medal, Combat Service Medal, 2 Good Conduct Award, Army Achievement Medal, Army Accommodation Medal, Purple Heart, Bronze Star, Combat Infantry Badge, Expert Marksman Badge, Expert Infantry Badge.

28

FAMILIES OF HONOR

By Dr. Mary Car-Blanchard

In a split second, the lives of Marine Jose Pequeno and Army Sergeant Brent Bretz were changed forever. Few people may realize that the lives of the soon-to-be family caregivers were changed forever as well. Traumatic Brain Injury (TBI) and Post-Traumatic Stress Disorder (PTSD) have an insidious ripple effect on the entire family. With a lack of community services, it is extremely common and almost a "given" that adult patients will be returned to their spouses, parents, siblings, extended family, significant others or friends. These are regular people with regular lives that change abruptly as they become instant caregivers. As the mothers and sister in these accounts found out, their roles and lifestyles were no longer the same. Like other parent caregivers of adult children that experienced TBI, Nellie and Kathy learned that although needs and issues may differ from person to person and change over time, they do not abate.

Traumatic Brain Injury is a catastrophic event. It can happen at any time and certainly does not wait until a military member's or caregiver's life is in perfect order. Life has its ups and downs, and it seems like all we can hope for is a balance over time. TBI does not wait for an up, down or balanced period. TBI does not consider marital satisfaction, family dysfunction, caregiver coping skills, caregiver income or dependent children. It does not wait for your bank account balance, blood pressure or coping skills to be at their best. TBI can occur at any time, regardless of how prepared or unprepared a loved one is to become a family caregiver.

When a Traumatic Brain Injury occurs in the family, everyday life is in an upheaval. Who will stay with the patient, who will pick up the kids at daycare, who's making dinner? Loved ones take a crash course in Traumatic Brain Injury, hospital care and military systems, at the same time they are experiencing a wide range of deep emotions. Will he live? I shouldn't have let her enlist? What am I going to do? Is he receiving the best care? Please don't die . . .

As a person recovers from TBI, it becomes apparent that they have changed. Because TBI can change the way a person thinks, acts, moves, behaves or feels, loved ones experience a unique kind of grief, the concept of grieving a loss without death. Loved ones are challenged to grieve the "person they knew," while at the same time getting to know the new and different characteristics of the person. This is not the same man I married... Dad, it's me... He used to have such a good sense of humor... Why are you doing that? It's not appropriate to say things like that... You used to play with the kids... I used to know you cared. Why don't you act like you used to? I miss that person . . .

Depending on the severity and types of injuries, caregiving can range from direct supervision to hands-on total care. Are you prepared to change your spouses or adult child's diaper—every day? What about trach care (a breathing tube in the neck)? Can your back handle all of the lifting? Does a wheelchair fit through your doorways or do you need an accessible house? Can you get your loved one in and out of a car? Is your boss understanding? Who cares for him while you work...or need a break?

With all of the new responsibilities, it is common for caregivers to have problems adjusting to their new responsibilities, especially while still grieving. Caregivers most frequently report feeling depressed, anxious, fatigued, overwhelmed, self-doubting and physically stressed. Caregivers with lots of support, funds, respite care, and hands-on help usually report feeling better. In fact, some caregivers report adjusting to caregiving quite well. Indeed, the caregiving experience appears to depend on a multitude of factors and to be unique and complex.

Caregiving has been shown to be more stressful on spouses than it is on parents. A stay-at-home mom may suddenly find herself needing to be the primary breadwinner. Sex lives may change. Divorce is not uncommon. His childish immature behavior turns me off. This is not the same man I married. How am I going to care for him and financially support us?

It is speculated that parents return to the role of taking care of their child, but that is not to say that it is easy. As Kathy found, the love, care, concern and worry of a parent is always there, but not all adult children with TBI realize or even want to realize that their lives have changed and that they need help. She received negative responses to her concern over her son's partying and prescription medications. I don't see your name on the bottle. I'm going out partying with my friends....

Further, some family caregivers, such as Nellie, may experience secondary traumatization. They are traumatized by hearing or seeing what their loved one has gone through, and as a result feel a string of negative emotions. Face it, mothers pray that their children return safe from duty. It is any mother's worse nightmare to be told "Your son has been injured," or worse. Not only did Nellie have to process the circumstances of how her son was injured, but also how he had changed. She had the total firsthand shock of finding her son's attempted suicide. These are the things that are not supposed to happen....How much can anyone take...

The strength that caregivers need to make decisions is clearly demonstrated, in different ways, by Nellie and Kathy. Traumatic Brain Injury affects everyone differently, but changes in behavior, thinking skills and personality, such as poor impulse control, lack of insight or empathy and poor decision-making can cause the most caregiver stress. Kathy found herself being responsible for her son, who was not behaving responsibly when it came to partying. For Kathy it was too much to stand by and watch Brent's behavior and choices. She said, "I will not stand around and watch you do to yourself what the Iraqis couldn't." Caregiving circumstances are different for everyone, and it is certainly not a failure to say, "I cannot do this," and to get help from someone else.

In addition to a full spectrum of emotions, the experience of caregiving for a loved one with TBI brings about changes in roles, child rearing, family decision-making, financing and careers. It is estimated that about one half of family caregivers have to give up their jobs to care for their loved one with TBI. After a year or more, many do not have enough money to take care of the person anymore. This was the reality for Nellie, as her savings were quickly depleted and she chose to give up her house. Her daughter Elizabeth left college to help and got a job at the hospital where Jose was being treated. Like so many families, they would do anything for their loved one.

The accounts of Nellie, Elizabeth and Kathy are not isolated incidents. Does it need to be so difficult? Can more be done to help them? The reality is that there is indeed a lack of support services, community services, affordable respite care and financial support for military members or veterans with TBI and their caregivers. However, the reality also is that more and more soldiers are returning home with TBI and Post-Traumatic Stress Disorder each day. These men and women unselfishly dedicated their lives to protect the citizens of the United States and our country. In turn, are they receiving the best from their fellow-citizens and country?

29

DELTA FORCE DOWN
The Story of Special Operations Sergeant Bryan Lane

"Before I could take a breath, four of our guys were down. It was dark, chaotic and fast. Then a large explosion and the next thing I know I'm blown up into the air by the blast. I came down on my elbow. I couldn't feel my right arm; I thought it was gone."

On February 5, 2005, around 2 a.m. in a Baghdad slum, an Army SpecOps team broke through the door of "House A," surprising an extended family and other adults who were sleeping. It only took seconds, well before the Iraqi interpreter started demanding names, for the soldiers, seasoned from months of night raids like this, to recognize that the target they were looking for wasn't there. Someone called in to say they'd taken down the house and it was quiet. The unit got orders to check the place next door, "House B."

Bryan Lane was in his second tour of duty in Iraq, after he'd also served a tour in Afghanistan. "We'd deploy for four months at a time, then get sent home to decompress for six months, then deploy again. "We'd go out every night from 11 p.m. to 4 a.m., doing missions and then get out before the sun came up. We'd sleep all day, watch videos, work out and then go out again. We'd had only two nights without going on missions before the night I got injured. It was brain-busting alright."

In "House B," the insurgents waited until the Americans were halfway through the rooms before opening fire. They'd had plenty of time to arm up and position themselves for the ambush. It was close, dark and almost impossible to maneuver. "Before I could take a breath, four of our guys were down," recalls Bryan. "It was chaotic and fast. There was a large explosion and the next thing I know I'm blown up into the air by the blast. I came down on my elbow. I couldn't feel my right arm; I thought it was gone. I had other injuries—wounds to my groin area and leg—but I had no idea how bad they were. I knew my arm was bad. I got up, walked out of the house into the back courtyard and sat down against a wall, and that's where my buddies found me."

Bryan grew up in Bakersfield, California, the son of an alcoholic father. "In my family I was the peacemaker. But I was always crazy about the military. I always saw myself as a soldier." After he graduated from high school he went first to Sacramento and then to Los Angeles with big ambitions, but no money or job.

"I thought I could do anything. My plan was to be a bodyguard and hang out with celebrities, but surprisingly, no one was hiring 18-year-olds with zero experience. I ended up working for a company that sold Internet Service Providers—'ISP Investments.' It was like a scene out of the movie *Boiler Room*, a complete scam which took me months to realize, but I made a lot of money because I was great at selling." He quit two weeks before the company was raided by the FBI. After a series of short-term jobs he'd had enough, and joined the Army determined to qualify for the "RIP": Ranger Indoctrination Program. Sure enough, by 2000 he was training as a sniper, part of the Second Ranger Battalion out of Fort Lewis, Washington.

"We were the last Ranger battalion to deploy to Afghanistan. They sent us straight to Kandahar and then to an outstation right on the Pakistan border. In 2002 Afghanistan was nothing like Iraq. It was a much less complicated war and the Afghans were actually pretty good people."

There were only ten trained snipers, so Bryan bounced around from outstation to outstation as a "battalion asset." "There was generally very little to worry about on those sniper missions. We could shoot more accurately and farther than anyone, and the Taliban weren't exactly crack shots."

His first stop in Iraq was the city of Fallujah in Al Anbar province. He arrived at the end of February 2004, just weeks after insurgents had captured four Blackwater contractors, beaten them to death, lit them on fire, and then hung their burnt corpses on a bridge over the

Euphrates. "It got violent. We were supporting the First Marine Expeditionary Force under General Conway, doing some raids but mostly acting as a 'Force Multiplier'."

Against the ground commanders' better judgment, the Marines were ordered by the Joint Task Force to conduct an aggressive assault against the insurgents beginning April 3. American units, 2,000 strong, laid siege to the city with the aim of retaking it. Army SpecOps worked independently but also as part of the major campaign. They were so good at what they did that "when we took down a former General who had worked with Saddam, he complimented us on our professional behavior. In less than a minute we had him. With no noise, no lights, no shots fired, he simply woke up and there we were in his bedroom. He was shocked." Although at heart a humanist, Bryan became hardened in battle. "We were taking photographs of dead suicide bombers who we would identify later. There was one terrorist who had been shot many times but had somehow managed to drag himself from a hallway to the kitchen where I found him laying on the floor, blood all over the place, still alive. I could hear his labored breathing, and I remember thinking as I took his photo, 'I don't care about this guy. This doesn't mean a thing to me. He was a suicide bomber; I hope he stops breathing soon.'"

The firefight in "House B" in Baghdad left six Army SpecOps personnel wounded, two severely. As the Medevac helicopters were landing, Bryan's friend Scott, the medic, worked diligently on his shattered arm. "He saved it by stopping the bleeding and cleaning out all the debris." Once he was on the operating table in Baghdad, Bryan fought with the hospital staff who wanted to cut off his body armor. "When they started to cut off my vest, I screamed 'Don't touch it!' I made my vest myself, and it took me over a month to sew it up. No way were they going to chop it up."

His route to recovery went from Baghdad to the Air Force Theater Hospital (AFTH) at Balad Air Base, to Landstuhl Medical Center, Germany, where he had two more surgeries on his arm, and finally the Womack Army Medical Center at Fort Bragg. He had over a year of surgeries and intensive rehabilitation.

Bryan was at the Fort Bragg hospital all day, but lived off base in a two-man apartment. Soon after he moved in, the soldier he roomed with deployed back to Iraq. "I got very depressed—my version of PTSD. I had insomnia from all the medications. I lost my appetite. I basically withdrew from the world. Wouldn't let my parents or my girlfriend come and see me. Wouldn't get help; I felt like it was a lot easier to deal with everything by myself. At first I thought I was going back to my unit, but then I found out that wasn't going to happen because of my injuries." Even though his arm had been saved, it was a new left-handed world.

The next nine months were tough. Then he met Patricia Driscoll, president of the Armed Forces Foundation. "She was playing golf with my boss, and she asked him if he knew of any wounded soldiers who were getting out and he said, "Yeah, I know someone." We met at a Barnes and Noble in Fayetteville. She wanted me to work for AFF at Fort Bragg, but I told her nothing would keep me in North Carolina. I was getting out of there and moving to the West Coast." Two months later Patricia called him to ask if he would head up the Armed Forces Foundation Career Counseling program for wounded warriors out of Las Vegas. She'd found someone else to partner with him in Fayetteville. Bryan took the job immediately.

Today Bryan lives in Las Vegas and works full-time for the Armed Forces Foundation, managing the Career Counseling and Family Assistance programs as well as doing occasional security consulting. He is currently remodeling a house with his girlfriend, Danyel. He has also gathered together five of his friends from Army Special Operations units, wounded warriors all, to run together in the Las Vegas marathon in December 2008 to raise money for other wounded veterans. "After that we're conditioning for other marathons and triathlons, and eventually we want to climb Mount Everest," he says.

Bryan joined the Army and initially became a Ranger assigned to the 2nd Ranger Battalion in Fort Lewis WA. He was deployed to Afghanistan as a sniper, then moved to US Army Special Operations in Fort Bragg. He deployed to Iraq twice before being wounded in combat.

30

REALIZING THE PROMISE OF EVIDENCE-BASED PSYCHO-THERAPIES IN THE VHA

*By Bradley Karlin, PhD, Josef Ruzek, PhD,
and Kathleen Chard, PhD*

These are both challenging and exciting times in mental health care, particularly for veterans and active-duty personnel. Many service members when they return home face significant challenges readjusting to civilian life and reclaiming their lives of old. Even veterans who have been home for decades and have been able to "get by" can have increased difficulty coping that may suddenly appear or be worsened by changes in their lives, such as illness and loss. These difficulties, for some, may develop into full mental disorders, such as Major Depressive Disorder, a substance use disorder, Post-Traumatic Stress Disorder (PTSD), or other mental health conditions.

For years, mental health experts had limited options to treat some of the most complex mental illnesses, such as PTSD. This was the case following the Vietnam War, where despite best intentions, effective treatments were limited because the science was still in its infancy. Following the Vietnam conflict, we knew little about PTSD and its causes; in fact, we did not even have a consistent name for the condition.

The exciting news is we have come a long way in the treatment of mental illness since 1975 when the Vietnam War ended. Over the last three decades, there have been significant strides made within the scientific community to better understand mental disorders and to develop effective treatments. A variety of new medications have been devel-

oped for various mental health conditions. Several new psychotherapies, or "talk therapies," that are not as well known have been developed for specific mental health problems, and are showing great
potential.

Over the last few decades there has been increasing interest in sci-
entifically evaluating the effectiveness of psychotherapies in much the
same way we evaluate treatments for medical disorders, such as high
blood pressure or diabetes. This research has clearly shown that psychotherapy is a very effective treatment for a variety of mental disorders. This research has also shown that certain psychotherapies are
more effective than others. Psychotherapies that have consistently
been shown in controlled research to be effective for a particular condition or conditions are referred to as "evidence-based."

One condition for which research has shown evidence-based psychotherapies to be the most effective available treatment is PTSD,
according to a 2007 Institute of Medicine report. In recent years,
research has shown that two psychotherapies, known as Cognitive
Processing Therapy (CPT) and Prolonged Exposure Therapy (PE) have
been developed for PTSD and consistently shown to be very effective.
In fact, these treatments are recommended in the Department of
Veterans Affairs (VA)/Department of Defense (DoD) Clinical Practice
Guidelines for PTSD at the highest level, indicating "a strong recommendation that the intervention is always indicated and acceptable."
Both psychotherapies are fairly structured and consist of approxi-
mately twelve weekly sessions, lasting for an hour to an hour and a
half each. These psychotherapies are based on a well established evi-
dence-based set of psychotherapeutic interventions known as
Cognitive Behavioral Therapy.

Cognitive Processing Therapy, or CPT, is based on years of
research that has shown a strong connection between thoughts and
emotions. Although it is often believed that events or situations produce emotions, it is usually one's interpretation of an event or the
meaning one attributes to a situation or oneself that directly makes a
person feel the way they feel. When thoughts or interpretations of
events or oneself are not balanced or do not consider the "complete
picture," but rather overly focus on specific details at the exclusion of
others, individuals are prone to negative emotions; when this happens

repeatedly it may lead to significant psychological distress or mental illness. In PTSD, disruptive thoughts or beliefs focus around a traumatic experience and oneself as a result of the traumatic event. CPT refers to these disruptive beliefs as "stuck points," which are an important focus of the treatment.

The first stage of CPT consists of educating the patient, having them write a statement about the meaning of the trauma, and helping them begin to make the connection between thoughts and feelings. In the second stage, the patient is typically asked to write a detailed account of the trauma to access the natural emotions related to the event and to identify specific stuck points. The therapist helps the patient evaluate and challenge extreme thinking, particularly thoughts related to blame, guilt and hindsight bias, in which only part of an event is recalled, leaving out information that may be inconsistent with self-blame or guilt.

In the third part of the treatment, the therapist guides the patient in challenging their thoughts in three areas: the self, others and the world. CPT further focuses on stuck points in the areas of safety, trust, power/control, esteem and intimacy within each of the three areas. Through practice, patients learn to replace or change their extreme thoughts related to the traumatic event with more realistic beliefs.

The process of the therapy is outlined in the following case description of Mr. C, a 26-year-old Operation Iraqi Freedom veteran who was honorably discharged from the Army after five years and two tours in Iraq. He stated he was a sniper and enjoyed being in the Army and was "good" at what he did. Mr. C received 100 percent service connection for PTSD, and was referred for PTSD treatment due to symptoms related to his combat experiences, including explosions, seeing friends die, and causing the death of someone else.

He had frequent feelings of guilt, as well as thoughts about the traumatic event and about himself in relation to it. He was treated for PTSD in a seven-week residential PTSD treatment program that uses CPT in a combined group and individual format. When Mr. C was admitted to the program he obtained a Clinician Administered PTSD Scale (CAPS) score of 70 (a score of 45 on the CAPS is usually indicative of a diagnosis of PTSD). Mr. C also met criteria for Major Depressive Disorder and Alcohol Dependence in full remission.

Mr. C was very reserved during his early therapy sessions, rarely participating in group while hesitant to share information in his individual sessions. Mr. C wrote an Impact Statement about the trauma for his first session homework, and he was able to identify key stuck points, including "I am weak for having PTSD" and "I no longer fit in society." Using worksheets to connect thoughts and feelings, Mr. C began to see that his primary emotion was anger, and it was fueled by what he was thinking.

In the middle phase of treatment, Mr. C wrote about two traumatic experiences, one outlining the death of a friend and one about a mission when he killed his first enemy. He identified additional stuck points, including "I could have prevented my friend's death" and "No one respects me unless I get angry." In the third phase of treatment, Mr. C was able to challenge his disruptive thoughts, and he began to see how he was not looking at all of the details of the events when he was blaming himself. He also noted that since he returned from Iraq he was not trusting of others and did not give them a chance before he pushed them away.

Upon completion of the program, Mr. C obtained a CAPS score of 22, and he was in remission for his Major Depression. Realizing that he still wanted to pursue a military career, Mr. C petitioned for and was granted a waiver to return to the military. In addition, he asked his fiancé to attend couples counseling to discuss the impact his being in the military again would have on their family.

In Prolonged Exposure Therapy, or PE, the emphasis is on helping the patient confront feared memories and situations. The emphasis on confrontation, or exposure, is due to the fact that individuals with PTSD frequently avoid emotionally processing trauma-related memories, and also avoid situations (e.g., crowded areas, social situations) that remind them of the traumatic experience. These avoidance tendencies actually serve to maintain and even strengthen PTSD symptoms in the long run and, as noted, prevent needed emotional processing from occurring.

PE helps patients emotionally process traumatic events by providing education about PTSD, repeated and prolonged imaginary exposure to trauma-related memories, repeated real-world confrontation with feared, but safe, situations the patient is avoiding, and discussion of thoughts and feelings related to exposure exercises.

The PE treatment is typically delivered in nine to twelve 90-minute sessions administered once or twice weekly. The first session consists of an overview of the treatment, rationale for exposure, information gathering, treatment planning, and breathing relaxation techniques. In the second session, patients are asked to talk in detail about their reactions to the trauma and its effect on them. Patients also begin to engage in real-world exposure to safe situations (e.g., public places) that they have avoided.

In the third session, the first imaginary revisiting of the trauma memory takes place, followed by discussion aimed at helping to process associated thoughts and feelings. During sessions four to nine (or more, as needed), imaginary exposure, post-exposure processing of thoughts and feelings, and discussion of real-world homework assignments are continued.

The following is a course of PE treatment with Mr. B, a 32-year-old, married, African-American veteran of Iraq, employed as an office worker. He sought care after his wife pressured him to deal with his combat experiences, and, during assessment reported concerns about distressing memories, nightmares, sleep problems, hypervigilance, difficulties with concentration and sexual problems. Mr. B scored a 68 on the CAPS questionnaire and met criteria for a PTSD diagnosis. His symptoms were present for three years and caused moderate distress and severe impairment in work and social functioning. He also met criteria for Major Depressive Disorder.

Mr. B had been in treatment focused on providing education about PTSD, coping skills, and group support for several months before initiating PE. While he perceived these elements of treatment as helpful, his symptoms diminished only slightly. Initially, Mr. B was apprehensive about starting PE. He was praised for his commitment to recovery and engaged in a discussion of the rationale for PE treatment, and the therapy was acknowledged to be "difficult but not dangerous."

Mr. B considered his direct exposure to an IED blast to be most distressing among a range of stressful experiences. His leg was injured during the explosion and was bleeding badly. During the next few minutes, the situation was chaotic and Mr. B experienced great anxiety. His attention darted from his leg, to his duty to the individuals in his command, to his dizziness. He blamed himself for not protecting his men more effectively. This experience was associated with his intrusive thoughts and other PTSD symptoms.

After introductory sessions focusing on the rationale for PE, information collection, and education and discussion about reactions to trauma, Mr. B was started on real-world exposure homework assignments. He was avoiding many situations that reminded him of the attack, and reported high levels of distress in situations involving driving, crowds and loud noises. He reported performing errands during off-hour times, avoiding roads where traffic congestion might occur, and driving very fast. He developed a list, ranking these from least to most distressing, that would be used for progressive exposure tasks.

Following the first imaginary exposure during session three, Mr. B had several disturbing memories and some difficulty sleeping. He reported that he was skeptical of the treatment. His concerns were discussed and described as very common once emotional avoidance was no longer taking place, and he was encouraged to continue with the treatment. He decided to remain in treatment. Repeated exposures during sessions three through nine, coupled with in-vivo exposure homework tasks, led to diminishing levels of distress. As the exposure activities became more routine, he gained confidence in the treatment and in his ability to recover.

During the emotional processing that took place after his imaginary exposure sessions, Mr. B was able to see that he didn't abandon his duties or his men during the blast experience. When he revisited his memories of the event in detail, he realized that, despite his injury, he continued to lead his team and take appropriate defensive actions until he lost consciousness. In the ninth session, during emotional processing, he stated, "I did, in fact, do the best that I could." Through this process, his troubling feelings of guilt were resolved.

Mr. B appeared for his last session wearing his finest suit. He was proud of what he had accomplished, and showed a genuine respect for himself that had not been present at the beginning of treatment. Mr. B no longer met diagnostic criteria for PTSD or Major Depressive Disorder.

How do we "achieve the promise" by bridging the gap between research and practice? Despite the clear effectiveness of evidence-based psychotherapies and their recommendation in numerous practice guidelines and other reports, research has consistently revealed that mental health providers deliver evidence-based psychological treatments at low rates. Why are these "gold standard" treatments not frequently delivered? Primary reasons identified for this include limited systematic training and lack of administrative support.

The Department of Veterans Affairs sees a tremendous opportunity to realize the potential of evidence-based psychotherapies and bridge the gap between research and practice so that veterans have access to the most effective treatments. Accordingly, the VA is embarking on a major national effort to disseminate several evidence-based psychotherapies throughout the VA health care system, as part of the implementation of the VHA Mental Health Strategic Plan and the transformation of its mental health care delivery system.

Specifically, the VA has developed national training programs to train VA mental health providers in the delivery of CPT and PE for PTSD, CBT and Acceptance and Commitment Therapy for depression and co-occurring anxiety, and Social Skills Training for serious mental illness. In these training programs, VA mental health clinicians attend intensive clinical workshops, usually three to four days in length, followed by ongoing clinical consultation and feedback by an expert clinician and program training consultant. The VA has developed specific evidence-based psychotherapy protocols, manuals, and other materials tailored to veterans. The VA is also working closely with DoD to make these trainings and materials available to active duty military personnel. As of the end of Fiscal Year 2008, the VA has trained over 1,200 VA mental health providers and over 600 DoD mental health clinicians in the delivery of CPT or PE for PTSD.

Beyond intensive clinical training, there are numerous efforts in place at multiple levels of the VA health care system to provide administrative structures and procedures to successfully implement the delivery of evidence-based psychotherapies. This includes mechanisms for tracking the delivery of the treatments, ensuring appropriate clinical capacity, evaluating training and clinical outcomes, and providing ongoing support and education broadly in the field.

Mental health treatment has come a long way in a relatively short period of time. We now have proven treatments that work for many of the most challenging and, at one point, seemingly untreatable mental illnesses. These treatments offer great promise to individuals returning from Iraq and Afghanistan, as well as to those who have been home for 30 or more years. Moreover, they provide an opportunity to move beyond symptom reduction toward promoting true recovery in multiple aspects of life.

Science and promise, however, are not sufficient, as even the most effective treatments have no effect if they are not available in the clinic to individuals who need them. Making state-of-the-art treatments, such as evidence-based psychotherapies for PTSD, depression and serious mental illness, part of the treatment repertoire should be a national priority. The Department of Veterans Affairs is committed to leading the path in realizing the promise of evidence-based psychotherapies as part of its fundamental promise to honor and provide the best care for veterans. Truly, our nation's heroes deserve nothing less.

Editor's note: References for this chapter can be found on page 270.

31

A WOUNDED WARRIOR
The Story of Army Sergeant Nathan Toews

"I had second thoughts but I was so tired. I climbed out of the truck and slid down to a crouch, resting my back against the tire facing the inside of the perimeter we had set up. My last memory is standing back up to do something. That was when I was hit with the RPG."

The supply convoy, made up of four now-empty tractor-trailer trucks and four up-armored Humvee gun trucks, wound its way back to Kandahar from the Musa Qala district where the supplies had been offloaded for Operation Mountain Thrust. Mountain Thrust was the largest Coalition offensive since the fall of the Taliban in 2001, a US-led operation of more than 2,300 US soldiers, 2,200 Canadians and 3,300 British, along with 3,500 Afghan troops and large air support. The goal was to quell the ongoing Taliban insurgency in the south of the country. Trained as a mechanic, Army Sergeant Nathan Toews was finally on a mission that might see some action.

"I was a gunner in my Captain's Humvee. We drove for days, sleeping and eating when we could. We were targets of small arms fire now and then, but it was nothing more than a few sporadic gunshots and one incident when a car bomb was driven into one of our trucks and detonated. We didn't sustain any injuries. I loved everything about it: the adrenaline rush from the constant threat of danger, the uncertainty of how things might unfold, living rough, sleeping on trucks, all of it." After a few days they made it to their destination and dropped off supplies for the new forward operating base. Tired and hungry, they left the following morning for a multinational base set up near Kandahar.

It was mid-morning on June 13, 2006 when the convoy entered a small town in Helmand Province in southern Afghanistan, a hostile and Taliban-infested part of the country. Nathan was manning the second gun truck when a surprisingly large Taliban force sprung an ambush. Just seconds after the firefight began, one gun truck and two equipment trucks were disabled by mortar fire. Yet the team of mechanics fought back as if they were seasoned infantry. "I recall jumping up and down, screaming and cursing at my driver to get me into a better position so that I could return fire and help rescue one of our vehicles that had been cut off from us. We were engaged in combat from about ten in the morning till nightfall." About halfway through the fight air support arrived in the form of four Apache attack helicopters, and for a short time two A-10 jets strafed a nearby village where the Taliban had taken up positions. Nathan's unit formed a defensive perimeter on a nearby hilltop with what remained of the convoy. A British paratrooper unit was airlifted in to assist with holding the position until they could get the personnel who had lost their vehicles flown out.

At dusk the fighting stopped. Drained and exhausted from eight hours of combat, Nathan accepted a buddy's offer to take his spot in the gun turret. "I had second thoughts but I was so tired. I climbed out of the truck and slid down to a crouch, resting my back against the tire facing the inside of the perimeter we had set up. My last memory is standing back up to do something. That was when I was hit with the RPG."

Three years earlier, on January 20, 2003, after two years of junior college in his hometown of Kingsburg, California, Nathan had enlisted in the Army. "I joined more or less to occupy myself while I attempted to figure out what I wanted to do with my life. To my surprise I almost immediately developed a sense of pride in what I had become a part of—pride in myself as well as my country." He did his basic at Fort Knox, Kentucky, and then trained at Aberdeen Proving Grounds as a mechanic. His first posting was Fort Drum, New York with the 10th Mountain Division.

By June 2004, less than a year later, he was in Baghdad doing maintenance work on the 10th Mountains' 2nd Brigade's fleet of light wheeled combat vehicles "inside the wire." He was twenty-one and hungry for action, but other than being part of one of the last units to actually drive the two-day trip from Kuwait to Baghdad (rather than being flown in), his tour of duty was unremarkable. He returned home with a few meager war stories about incoming fire and a handful of foot patrols during particularly "hot" periods such as during Iraq's first democratic elections. "There were rough periods throughout the deployment, but I had made it home without getting injured and I was much more self-confident. I considered myself, I must admit, just about fearless. So as I neared the end of my contract I decided to re-enlist so I could deploy a second time."

He was assigned to Fort Irwin in southern California, and shortly after arriving heard about a deployment to Afghanistan. "I had not been stateside for a full year yet, so I had the right to miss the deployment, but I volunteered to go." His unit deployed at the end of February 2006 and was stationed at a large military post near Kabul. "Something I wanted to do differently for my second deployment was to be more actively involved in the combat side of the missions." He got his chance in late June.

The shrapnel from the RPG lacerated Nathan's right thigh from his hip to his knee. His right wrist was blown out of the socket. Jagged shards pierced his right eye and lodged in his brain. "I don't remember anything that happened after I was hit. Months later I was asking everyone, 'So how did I take it?' You know because everyone wants to know, 'Did I cry? Did I freak out? Did I take it like a man?'" Nathan dropped straight to the ground but then propped himself up against the tire and tried to fire back even though his weapon was disabled. "Our body armor has a handle on the back behind the collar, and I was told somebody grabbed that handle and dragged me out of the line of fire. I was yelling, 'My ears fucking hurt' and coughing up a lot of blood from the head injury."

While the rest of the convoy fought off a second attack, a British medic kept him alive until he could be evacuated. He was moved to the field hospital at Bagram, then Landstuhl Medical Center in Germany, and finally Bethesda Naval Medical Center in Maryland. His family was flown to Bethesda to meet him. His younger brother, Andrew, would remain by his side for the two and a half months he was there, through surgery after surgery.

Two weeks after arriving stateside Nathan was brought out of an induced coma. Doctors told his family to keep their expectations low. "There was no way to know what my mental condition would be. It was possible that I would wake up and have no memory of anything from my life or even be capable of speaking. While I was in my coma, I had vivid dreams, which I confused with reality. I was unaware of where I was, how I got there, or even what year it was. Most of all I was oblivious to my injuries, excluding my broken arm because I could see the splint."

After the preliminary surgeries Nathan was moved to Walter Reed Medical Center. He gradually became aware of his injuries, a process the Walter Reed hospital staff call "self-discovery." The metal fragments from the RPG blast had blinded his right eye. "But I didn't know I'd lost my eye, even though they probably told me every morning since I had been there. I was so brain injured it hadn't sunk in. So I went to an appointment with an ophthalmologist, and he said, 'I heard from your mom that you can't see out of your right eye.' And I was pissed. I said, 'What are you retarded? Of course I can see. Check it out. Check it fucking out!' So he shines a light in my left eye and I can see the light, and then he shines it in my right eye and all I could see was red satin. And that's how I found out."

Shrapnel fragments had also fractured his skull and pierced his brain. More than a third of his skull had been cut out to relieve the pressure from the swelling. "When you are missing so much of your skull, your head is misshapen and the insides actually settle differently at night when you're asleep. My head was all bandaged but finally one morning I woke up and got a chance to look in the mirror. I yelled, 'I need a doctor. There's something wrong with my head.'"

Months later he found himself undergoing physical rehabilitation at the Veterans Affairs Polytraumatic Rehabilitation Center in Palo Alto, California. There were no guarantees as to how long he would be there.

"I arrived at Palo Alto about mid-August. I still couldn't walk, was missing a large portion of my skull, and had a tube in my stomach. I asked one of the therapists how long she thought I would stay. She told me the average stay for a guy in my condition was a few years. Right then and there, I made it my mission to prove her wrong."

Within three weeks, he was running on a treadmill, eating normally and had completed all his testing which indicated that he needed no additional therapy.

"I was the first person who had previously undergone a craniotomy to leave Palo Alto without having a plate put in his head in place of the missing skull section." The next step, a cranioplasty, was a minimum of six months away, assuming Nathan had no infections. Until he had his cranioplasty Nathan wore a helmet to protect his head. "I hated that helmet but I wore it. It was custom-made for me, and it looked like an old school football helmet."

There was only one low moment during his stay in Palo Alto. "I don't think I ever gave up hope that I'd get my vision back, and when I first arrived a doctor said that because I could perceive some light, it meant the optic nerves were still working and there was a chance I'd see again. Well, I took that and ran with it. Then a week later, doctors told me, 'Forget your eye. It's gone for good.' That night was the only time so far through this entire experience that I broke down; but I'm not a believer in wallowing in self pity or 'woe is me.' Getting mad at the world or how life has been unfair is just wasted energy. The military doctors put me back together. My philosophy has always been that I made my own choices and now I have to get on with the rest of my life."

And so he did, but not without a few bumps along the way. He was permitted to go home for thirty days. He would experience daily migraines so severe he had to take anti-seizure medication in the thousands of milligrams. While he was home, he woke up one morning to find his left hand wouldn't move due to the injuries to the right side of his brain. He was flown back to the East Coast to undergo outpatient therapy and surgeries at Walter Reed and then Bethesda Naval Medical Center. "Every day for a year I attended occupational therapy to strengthen my shattered right arm and to work on getting the use of my left hand back." In February of 2007 Nathan had his cranioplasty to replace the missing section of his skull. This procedure carried a high risk and the plate would be removed if there appeared the slightest sign of infection. His "took" on the first attempt.

"A couple of weeks later my left hand started to work again. I was sitting in the old Company Area at Walter Reed, what is now the new

Warrior Transition space, and I was trying to move my hand, and suddenly my thumb moved. Then I was able to clench my fist. I think the cranioplasty had equalized the pressure in my brain. I jumped up and ran down the hallway yelling, 'I can move my hand!'"

Nathan made a miraculous recovery but will have to deal with his wounds for the rest of his life. "I am no longer permitted to serve in the military, which is something I am still struggling to accept. My plan is to get into the field of working with service members who have similar injuries. I have yet to narrow it down to a more specific field. I want to be able to help soldiers and their families, if nothing more than to just share my experiences and be an example of how well someone can recover from such severe injuries. Such jobs require a degree. So the next step in my life is to get one." Nathan enrolled at Dickinson College outside of Harrisburg, Pennsylvania as a freshman in the fall of 2008. He maintains a 3.5 GPA.

MEDALS

Bronze Star, Purple Heart, 2 Army Commendation Medals, 4 Army Achievement Medals, Army Good Conduct Medal, National Defense Service Medal, Afghanistan Campaign Medal, Global War on Terrorism Expeditionary Medal, Global War on Terrorism Service Ribbon, Army Service Ribbon, 2 Overseas Ribbons, NATO Medal, The Combat Action Badge.

32

FALLING THROUGH THE CRACKS
Why Time Is Running Out

By Lt. Colonel Cynthia Rasmussen

As I write this I am contemplating how to help the wife of a deployed service member who has been sexually assaulted. This is the second call regarding a sexual assault this week. The first woman had not told her husband that one of his good friends had assaulted her while he was away. What a welcome homecoming he will have. I find myself wondering how soon the divorce will come. (I bet those of you reading this are already saying to yourselves, "Oh she was just sleeping with him and now feels guilty so is going to accuse him of rape.") Oh ye of little faith, think again.

Looking back over the last four years that I have been mobilized as a Combat Stress Officer and Sexual Assault Response Coordinator, I realize what an amazing opportunity I've had to make a difference. I admit that carrying on the behavioral health program started by LTC Susan Whiteaker and LTC Mary Erickson shortly after 9/11 for over 26,000 service members and their families can sometimes be overwhelming mentally, spiritually, and emotionally, but it has been worth it. The problem is immense.

One of my initial cases involved a whole reserve unit that was devastated by a seriously impaired command. These were amazing young men and women brought to their knees with suicidal and homicidal thoughts on a daily basis. There was the usual alcohol and drug abuse as they self-medicated. There were divorces and break-ups of long-term relationships, financial and job issues, isolation, weapon issues

187

and homelessness, all within a single unit. I will never forget "Kevin," at the unit's family readiness picnic and stress management training, looking me in the eye and saying, " I want to go back and step on an IED and die a hero so my wife and son can get the money, because I cannot take living like this anymore. "

Then there is the service member, an NCO, who was served divorce papers while he was in Iraq. What was he to do? He was on a mission and responsible for lives and "bringing everyone home safe." And when he gets home he better handle his domestic situation without any emotion, acting out, expressing his feelings, or self-medicating, or he will be the one punished. And we mustn't forget the OIF/OEF Vets who are being discharged with diagnosed mental illnesses or who have been kicked out of the military due to inappropriate behaviors stemming from those mental conditions, and who now have little or no opportunity for good follow-up care or access to the benefits they so desperately need. They are often sent home to unsuspecting families who have no notion of how they have changed.

I cannot count how many times I have been to a unit's homecoming from Iraq and seen service members walk off the plane to find that there is no one there to greet them. Or their "significant other" greets them with the keys to their apartment and the words "Goodbye, I am leaving." For many other homecomers, their "significant other" or even their parents have spent all their money while they were deployed in theater.

One way for me to explain the state of our veterans when they come back home after deployment is by using the metaphor of a bridge. I look at the journey of a returning service member and his or her family as crossing a bridge. For many veterans the bridge is an obstacle course as dangerous—some say more so—as bridges they crossed in war zones. Instead of navigating cracks and holes created by an IED or a mortar, they must now confront new cracks and holes created by new enemies. These enemies can be fear, depression, loneliness, anxiety, anger, guilt, risky behaviors and frustration. The enemies can come in the form of "supportive US civilians," who don't really get it, employers, family and friends, and even the service members themselves. The journey is fraught with possibilities of destruction as well as opportunities for amazing growth. And yet I wonder how many veterans stand at one end of the bridge and see it going "nowhere."

If the service member and/or family member is "lucky" or meets the right people—knows the right "supply sergeant," so to speak—they may miss the more subtle holes or cracks in the bridge and make it to the other side. On the other hand, if they fail to meet the person or persons who can guide them, or lack the inner resiliency to guide themselves, they will inevitably fall through one of the cracks or holes. The cracks represent the slower, more subtle changes that occur over time after coming home, such as "I don't fit in," "I don't feel safe," or "I have difficulty communicating now." The cracks may occur because pre-deployment support systems may not be there or the veteran can no longer connect with those systems.

The cracks occur because once you don a military uniform you learn to live, function and survive using tools that are crucial to the service member/warrior, but do not work so well for the US civilian. Take anger. The physiological response to a perceived threat to self is fight or flight, responses that make sense in combat. But this isn't the best way to function when the uniform comes off.

Take trust. We teach our warriors not to trust anyone or anything except other warriors, those close to them who talk, act and dress just like they do. Yet when the veteran takes off his or her uniform to return to civilian life, an environment where "I'll watch your back and you watch mine" is considered only one of many ways to demonstrate trust, there can be relationship problems. Ultimately, for many veterans the cracks in the bridge to reentry include an inability to communicate, relate, empathize or feel. Feeling like a stranger in your own country, town and family can lead to withdrawal and isolation, self-medicating with alcohol and drugs, lashing out at others for no apparent reason, and having little or no tolerance for the mishaps of everyday life.

Holes are a metaphor for a fall through the bridge that lands a returning veteran in a more serious predicament from which recovery is difficult and sometimes impossible. Holes represent divorce, infidelity, suicidal/ homicidal thoughts and behaviors, complete isolation, prison, serious mental health issues and homelessness. "Jim," a 22-year-old veteran with mental health issues, was crossing the bridge when he got into an argument with a stranger who was harassing him. He reverted back to the protective mode of a warrior and shot off a gun. No one got hurt, but "Jim" fell into a hole called prison and now faces several years behind bars with no help for his Combat Stress, PTSD and possible TBI. His mom had to give up her job because of all her stress and is now living "hand to mouth," unable to find an advocate for her son.

So my job is to help service members/veterans and their families across the bridge, as well as try to help those who have fallen through the cracks and holes in their bridges, and it feels like time is running out. The calls we get for help, support and care are increasing. The numbers of homeless, incarcerated, suicidal (or dead) vets, and alienated families, are increasing. The desperate haunted voices are increasing. The number of "heroes" and their families on the bridges without the "supply sergeant" or the leaders they need to get across is increasing. What we must avoid is more encounters like the ones I've had with World War II veterans, with Vietnam veterans, and with Gulf War veterans who ask with tears streaming down their faces, "Where were you when I came home?"

33

COURAGE TO HEAL

The Story of Army National Guard Sergeant Michael Mills and Suki Mills

*"The therapist was the one who finally parked me in front
of that mirror, locked the brakes on my wheelchair and said,
'The sooner you deal with it, the sooner you'll accept it.' I couldn't
believe what I saw. Where was my left ear? My left eye was distorted. My mouth was wrong. How was Suki ever going to
want me looking like this?"*

When Sergeant Michael Mills volunteered to be the A driver on the convoy of HETTs on the mission in mid-June, he had no idea it was a decision that would change his life forever. The Heavy Equipment Transport Truck, one of the largest Army transportation vehicles, is built to haul 80 tons. Michael had no guarantees that the mission would be hazard-free no matter how huge the trucks were. In fact he had a clear understanding that, "The first thing you learn when you get to Iraq is that nothing is based on theory and the only one you can trust is yourself."

One job of the A driver was to look for anything the enemy could use for a distraction or hiding place for an IED or sniper. "We had twelve checkpoints to pass, each manned by either the ISP (Iraqi Security Police) or ING (Iraqi National Guard). Theoretically, we should have felt fairly confident, since both groups were trained by US Military Personnel and were placed there for our safety."

On June 14, 2005, the convoy left Forward Operating Base Spiecher outside Tikrit for FOB Warrior. The trip was uneventful. Once they got there the soldiers loaded up their HETTs with vehicles and started the trip back to FOB Spiecher. The convoy was only ten minutes away from FOB Warrior and just past the first checkpoint when Michael noticed the hole in the road filled with debris and wires. "All of the training I had gone through suddenly came flooding back as if I was on autopilot. I grabbed the radio: 'Truck #... IED my side' I heard 'Repeat.' 'Truck#... IED...'" The bomb went off before he finished the second call out. "The taste of the dirt and gunpowder are something I'll never forget. It is still unclear if I jumped from the truck or was blown from it, not that it really matters in the end." The blast had pierced the fuel tanks located under the front seats, so as he jettisoned from the truck Michael was sprayed with diesel fuel which then ignited. " I don't remember if the pain I felt was from the fire or from the impact when I landed on my left side."

The fall was so hard that Michael broke four of five bones in his left foot, tore up his left hip socket and dislocated his left shoulder. "The only thought I had was making sure my driver was OK. I got up and turned to look at the truck, and it was as if someone had placed a mirror there. I could see myself on fire. I fell back to the ground and began to rip off the body armor, which included about 500 M16 rounds. If it hadn't been for the body armor, the burns to my left side would have been much worse." When the rounds from his armor started to go off, a medic laid on top of him to protect him from the blast. "When all was secure, she began the necessary first aid to keep me alive. She saved my life." The medic had to cut off what remained of his uniform, start an IV to begin pain control and provide necessary fluids to prevent dehydration. She then covered his burn wounds with gauze and poured a saline solution over them to help retain moisture.

"The gun trucks that traveled with us formed a circle around the convoy because it was unclear yet if the rounds we heard were from my body armor or from a sniper. Once it was clear that there was no sniper or enemy to worry about, they called for medevac and were told it would be two hours out." The convoy commander turned the convoy around and raced back to FOB Warrior with the wounded soldiers.

If you had asked Michael Mills what he saw himeslf doing three years before his "Alive Day," he might have said driving trucks for the Army. "I was an Army Brat. I always knew I would end up doing something in the military. I finished high school in Mountain Home, Idaho, which is where we settled after my dad retired in 1981. I joined the Army in 1985 and spent three years in Alaska." When Mike met Suki in Alaska, she made it clear that she didn't want to raise a family if it meant uprooting them every few years to move, and so he began his National Guard career.

"I always knew my unit would be activated, even though they told us we wouldn't be because we were not at full strength. So when the stand-by call was made on Easter Sunday, April 2004, it didn't surprise me." After a training period in May, the unit reported to Fort Dix, New Jersey. Six more months of training and they deployed, arriving in Iraq on January 6, 2005. After spending ten days in Kuwait, they moved north to Iraq and settled in to what was to be their new home. "We lived at FOB Spiecher just outside of Tikirit, Iraq. I passed my 20 years of service in the military over there, and even though I was ineligible for a bonus, I re-enlisted for three more."

Back home in Alaska, Suki was one of the leaders for the unit's Family Readiness Group (FRG). She adopted a philosophy that she couldn't control what happened over in Iraq, and that worrying about what she couldn't control would only drain the strength she needed. If, and only if, something should happen, then she would deal with it. "The night I got the call we had gone to my parents so the kids could eat their "Happy Meals." I didn't recognize the number when my cell phone rang, but as an FRG Leader you answer any number because it could be a family member in need. The connection was bad at first and I still didn't know who I was speaking with. They hung up and called back. It was a Colonel from the battalion and I wasn't bothered at first because I work with his wife in the FRG. I went numb when he said they were on their way to see me, the Colonel, the Battalion CSM and the Chaplin. In training we were told that if the soldier is injured the family gets a phone call; if the soldier is killed they get a visit."

The Colonel assured her that Michael was very much alive but badly injured. Suki gave them directions to her parents and waited. "Mom and Dad had a lot of questions, but all I could tell them was that Michael was alive. Aaron and Kenzie, our children, sat so quietly, I forgot they were there. When the officers arrived they told us Michael had broken his pelvis and ankle, dislocated his shoulder, and had severe burns on the left side of his body and face. My mind went blank. My baby was burned. I wanted to throw up. I felt so helpless.

He was alone and hurt and I wasn't there to take care of him. I thought, 'Perhaps this isn't real; it's a test, yes, a test. The Army is testing my skills as an FRG Leader to see how I handle tragic news.'"

Michael was at the Langstuhl Medical Center in Germany, and at first Suki was told she had to be prepared to fly there to be with him. "I didn't have a passport, and unless they planned on putting me to sleep for the trip, I didn't think I would be able to handle a plane ride of that length, not to mention the anxiety I would endure anticipating what I was going to find when I got there. There was way too much information to think through everything. I needed to stop and take a deep breath. Plus I've been so into my own head, I haven't asked my children how they felt. They were both sitting there in shock. We tried to be as honest as we could without creating a great deal of fear, but the kids knew their daddy was badly injured."

When she got home, there was a message waiting from the Department of Defense. Now she would meet Michael at Brooke Medical Center in Texas. They had all the information she needed to contact the doctor who was with Michael. She was told how to get her orders so the Army would pay for her flight, and how to get money to live on while she was there. "It was getting late and I wanted to go to bed, but I couldn't. I had to wait for the doctor to call from Germany."

The next day was filled with phone calls, visitors and decisions. Suki and Michael's children could have been put on orders and gone with their mother, but Suki didn't think that would be a good idea. "I didn't know the set-up. They would miss school, and I needed to concentrate on Michael and not worry about them. So I needed to figure out who would take care of them and who would take care of our puppy, Rex. I needed to find someone to care for our plants and watch the house. I almost couldn't deal with all the decisions. At times I felt like I was losing it, but I needed to stay calm for the kids."

Suki's mother took charge of caring for their daughter, Kenzie, but their son, Aaron, had gone into a protective mode. "He was Michael's shadow. He wore his old uniforms including the boots, even though they were too big. His room was covered with military insignia and posters, and I remember being shocked when I went in that night because he'd taken everything down and put it into a box. I sat him down and tried to talk to him but he wouldn't respond. I didn't think he had slept at all the night before."

Eventually Suki was able to comfort both her children. Kenzie and Aaron would spend the summer with their grandparents, then stay with friends for the school year. The friends would even care for the puppy. Now all Suki had to do was get to her husband.

Michael was flown to Brooks Army Medical Center, where he would spend the next three months, the first three weeks of it in the ICU. "I don't remember most of my time in the hospital," he recalls, "and from what I am told, I guess I'm glad. I think part of the reason for not remembering is that some of what I went through was so painful both physically and emotionally, it was a way to cope. I do remember the anger I had because I was back in the States and my soldiers were still over in Iraq. I was just angry at myself for not seeing the IED sooner and getting injured. I didn't blame anyone but myself."

Although Michael doesn't remember his nightmares or panic attacks from that time, Suki does: "One night Michael was yelling at a sergeant to park the trucks in a certain area. He was trying to get out of bed and just about got over the bed rail. He wouldn't listen to me so I ran out to the desk for help." The medical staff calmed him down, but he revealed the mental stress of what he had been through again and again. "The worst episode was when Michael had wound vacs on both hands but thought he had been stabbed by a knife and wanted it out of the back of his hand. I played along and pretended like I took it out. He kept insisting it was still in there. I kept telling him I took it out. He looked at me with such blank eyes. I will never forget that look or what he said next. 'You don't fu**ing understand.' He yelled it at me. I knew he didn't mean it, but that didn't make it hurt at the moment any less. All I could do was walk out of the room."

As with many soldiers dealing with PTSD, Michael's emotions were right at the edge. He would tear up when someone sent him a get-well card, and that was hard for Suki because he seemed so vulnerable and fragile. "He was always saying he was sorry for screwing up our lives. Then there were times he wouldn't say anything at all. I know he'd been through hell, but if I didn't get him to open up, I was afraid I'd lose him."

It didn't matter what anyone said, not the nurses or doctors, not his family or even the person Michael trusted the most, Suki. "I was pretty convincing in the denial area and never really brought attention to the fact that something was bothering me, but Suki knew better."

"There was no way I was going to tolerate him feeling sorry for himself and playing the martyr. He was badly wounded but I was not going to give up until he realized it wasn't his fault." Suki talked to one of the mental health therapists and clued him in on what was happening. Once Michael started talking to the therapist and then gradually trusting him, he began to open up. "The therapist's demeanor was one of serenity and comfort, and maybe that's why I felt I could be more honest with what I was feeling. It was hard at first because of my belief that I'm a leader. I'm supposed to be strong for my soldiers and my family. I'm used to dealing with issues on my own. Yet I slowly began to realize that these issues were bigger and stronger than anything I'd dealt with before, and that opening up, talking about it and taking medication didn't mean I was weak or could no longer be a leader. I was a victim but I had a choice. I could sit back and allow the memories to destroy me and my family, or I could fight back." Michael chose not to feel powerless, and although it wasn't easy, it was worth it.

Michael hadn't yet screwed up the courage to look in the mirror. "Each day I would look away as we passed by the hallway mirror on the way back into my room. I had a physical therapist, Dawn, who knew just how far to push you and then go one more inch without you knowing it. She had a positive attitude and always seemed to find the sunshine. Suki used to call her "the other woman" because I'd brighten up when she was around. Dawn was the one who finally parked me in front of that mirror, locked the brakes on my wheelchair and said, 'The sooner you deal with it, the sooner you'll accept it.'" She walked out of the room. Eventually Michael had to look up and see his reflection. " I couldn't believe what I saw. Where was my left ear? My left eye was distorted. My mouth was wrong. How was Suki ever going to want me looking like this?" When Dawn came back in the two of them talked about the experience. "She told me how she watched Suki looking at me day after day with no hesitation. She only had the deepest love a wife could have for her husband."

Suki was always there. "The longer I was at Brooke, the more I was able to become Michael's advocate. I learned to refuse to back down if something didn't seem right." When Suki discovered an ulcer the size of a half dollar on her husband's heel, because of his cast, she stood toe to toe with a doctor when the new cast was put on and there was no area cut away to relieve the pressure where the ulcer was. "I made sure I completely understood who, what, where and why." She took on the Orthopedics Dept. at BAMC. "The burns complicated the healing of his shoulder, and it formed into one solid mass of bone. At the time we had no clear idea what was happening.

"When I would ask for an Orthopedic Doctor to come and explain it to us, no one would show up, and then the hospital staff would say they explained it to Michael at 5 a.m." Suki was not satisfied with that explanation and demanded to see someone else in charge. "I'm not sure that person was walking the same way as when he came in," Michael recalls. "Then the doctor made the mistake of talking down to her as if to convince her that he had been there at 5 a.m. That didn't go over real well."

Once Michael was discharged from the hospital, he still had months of rehabilitation ahead of him. "Michael joined me in the apartment where I was staying at the guest house near the hospital. It was scary because all the daily care the nurses had been doing, suddenly I had to do." That meant a bath, dressing change and special lotions applied to his burn injuries each day. "It was a two- to three-hour process. I remember being so worried that I would do something wrong, like not clean an area well enough and it would get infected."

"We settled into a routine that required me to go from where we were living in the guest house to have rehab at the hospital. Then my mother-in-law called one day in October to tell us she had cancer. With my rehab far from over, we knew we couldn't move back home just yet. I wasn't even sure they would let me go on convalescent leave. Suki was beside herself. She was torn between being with her mom and being with me. We both needed her."

They applied for early convalescent leave before Michael was considered medically ready to leave Brooke. That meant getting special permission from the head of Outpatient Therapy, Michael's burn doctor, the unit commander, and finding a hand therapist in their area so he could continue therapy at home. Just in time, they were allowed thirty days of leave to go home for the Thanksgiving holidays in November, and then again in December.

At the end of February, Suki was called to come home since her mother was dying. "I stayed home after my mom passed away to be with my dad. We made arrangements for Michael's sister, Brenda, to meet him down there and be his caregiver in my absence. That was so hard not to go back to Texas with him, but he was getting more independent and the wound care was a fourth of what it used to be. It was my dad now that needed me. After 50 years together with my mom he was lost. I am the only girl out of five children, and although dad never came right out and said it. We all knew I was the one he wanted to stay with him."

It would be another three months before Michael was medically discharged from the Army. "I never dreamed of retiring at my age. My goal in the Army was to retire as an E-7 just as my father did. Yet today I do not regret, nor do I blame myself for what happened to me on June 14. I have learned so much about myself, about my family and what is really important in my life. I realized that I still have so much to offer, and my passion to help my fellow brothers in arms was very strong." Michael created a web site where a veteran or family member or anyone with questions can reach out at any time of day or night and connect to someone who understands their pain. He has been asked to speak in several classrooms and at various public venues. " I try to put the focus on the struggles of life and about the challenges I have had to face and how I have faced them. Especially when I talk to children, I emphasize how important it is to ask for help and not internalize your emotions. Each time I tell my story, provide resources for someone or am able to listen to a soldier in need, I am healing."

Today, Michael and Suki do not dwell on that awful period of their lives. "We choose to remember because it taught us both so much, about each other and ourselves. We are loved, we are strong and we survived."

In January 2009 Michael was selected for Operation Mend, for a plastic surgery to his face performed by a world-renowned plastic surgeon. The project is a partnership between UCLA and Brooks Army Medical Center along with a private philanthropist.

MEDALS

Purple Heart, Combat Action Badge, 3 Army Commendation Medals, 2 Army Achievement Medals, Army Good Conduct Medal, 2 National Defense Service Medals, Iraq Campaign Medal, Global War on Terrorism Service Medal, 2 Non-Commissioned Officer Professional Development Ribbons, Army Service Ribbon, Overseas Service Ribbon, Marksmanship Badge (Sharpshooter w/Rifle), Driver and Mechanic (w/Driver-Wheeled Vehicle[s]).

"In the first of what could become many revisions in its disability ratings, the Veterans Affairs Department announced that it is changing how it evaluates traumatic brain injuires, a move that could increase disability compensation for thousands of veterans who have been injured by roadside bombs or other explosions in Iraq and Afghanistan. The new regulation describes traumatic brain injury as an injury that has immediate effects, such as loss of consciousness, amnesia, and other neurological symptoms. The problems could be temporary, but also may cause prolonged effects such as physical or mental impairment or emotional and behavior problems."

—"VA to Increase Compensation for TBI," *Navy Times*, September 23, 2008

34

TENDING, ATTENDING AND HEALING
All Together, One by One

By Dr. Joseph Bobrow

As a society, we don't take very good care of one another. Ours is a disposable culture: our children, our elders, our ill and infirm, our natural resources are often ignored, overlooked, forgotten or mistreated. But what we do not include, recognize and care for does not disappear. The impacts last for ages, and they affect everyone. The web of life is our connective tissue and what we fail to adequately care for, we do so at our own peril. Our veterans and their families, their suffering, humanity and the true costs of their service have often gone unrecognized. Since we are all of us interconnected at the core, what happens here impacts what happens there. Unattended to, the wounds of war fester and deepen, wreaking havoc on individuals, families, communities and our entire culture.

The impacts of war are legend; some are visible but many are not. Injuries that are invisible to the eye nonetheless radiate deep and wide into a person's life, health and web of relationships. TBI patients and their families have a saying, "When the hair grows over . . ." When the injuries we can see heal, the wounds to mind, heart, spirit and relationships often go ignored. I am not only referring to PTSD: thousands of veterans suffer from anguish that does not meet the specific criteria for a diagnosis of PTSD, but nonetheless is profoundly disturbing to their functioning and well-being, and their families' as well. "What's the matter, the war's over," someone once said to a veteran. "Yeah, over and over and over," the vet replied. The ever-present traumatic past crowds out the open present, collapsing hope and possibly the future.

Combat-related traumas cannot be reduced to an anxiety disorder. They impact our identity, the sense of meaning, purpose, ethics and spirituality that comprise our world view, that holds our world together. War can shatter it all. Rebuilding damaged connectivity among body, mind, heart, brain, core values, worldview; among thoughts, feelings, actions, views, relationships, speech and conduct, is critical.

It is important to learn skills to reduce symptoms of stress and anxiety and to help modulate and manage strong emotions. However it is just as important to rebuild damaged or undeveloped capacities to digest, metabolize and transform the profound impacts of trauma. And, as we rebuild internal connectivity, to rebuild connections among family members, and among family and community. This takes safety, trust, absence of judgment, and unconditional acceptance, compassion and love. How veterans are held by their community, culture and country forms a matrix that can contain and help transform trauma. What we cannot hold, we cannot process. What we cannot process, we cannot transform. What we cannot transform haunts us. It takes another mind to help us heal ours. It takes other minds and hearts to help us grow and re-grow the capacities we need to transform suffering. This is done in concert, re-weaving all together the web of connective emotional, relational and spiritual tissue that cumulative trauma tears asunder. In dialogue with other minds and hearts, with an informed, compassionate culture, it is possible, as psychoanalyst Hans Loewald wrote, to transform ghosts into ancestors.

Symptom reduction is not the only barometer of healing: ending the haunting of the present by the traumatic past, finding a container wide, deep and sturdy enough to help transform ghosts into ancestors is the X-Factor that often goes ignored. It is a factor in why some at our best treatment facilities observe, puzzled, "Vets come in once or twice, but we have trouble getting them to come back for treatment." It is not simply a matter of exploring new and alternative methodologies. There is no silver bullet. The quick fix is a by-product of narrow thinking. If war-related trauma damages human connectivity and the transformational capacities it engenders at multiple levels—individual, family, organizational and cultural—then unless we repair or grow these critical elements, our solutions will be partial, limited and transient at best. While lack of resources is certainly a concern, if the ways we think and work together are compartmentalized and limited, then our prescriptions may not work very well, even when we throw money at the problems as we construe them.

Concealed within damage often lies great strength. Resilience runs deep, but its resources need to be nurtured. It is like a seed that has been buried in a disaster; it needs tending, attending. When the great redwoods are damaged in a fire, their seedpods are not destroyed. There is clearly devastation, but often the forest can return to health with adequate protection, care and skill. The seeds of renewal and transformation are there—if we cultivate the intention to be of help, if we take the time and energy, if we realize that the responsibility for healing the impacts of war is collective. It takes a village and it begins with each of us. Each veteran, each partner, child, sibling, parent and grandparent, deserves our loving, skillful, attentive care for the visible AND invisible injuries. They don't only need a new set of techniques. They need us to harness our own humanity—head, heart, body and spirit—and our native connectivity and capacity to respond, in order to make a difference. They need us to participate in creating a culture in which the wounds of war are lovingly and skillfully enveloped as part of a welcoming community, where they can heal and be transformed. Fundamental inter-connectivity takes the form of a responsive community that holds the vets and their families in its attentive, loving embrace.

The Coming Home Project is a team of psychotherapists, veterans, family members and interfaith leaders devoted to helping restore and build connection in the individual, the family and in the wider military culture. Since 2006 we have offered a set of interconnected programs to address the mental, emotional, spiritual and relationship problems of OIF and OEF veterans and their family members. We provide pro bono, confidential psychological counseling; education, training and self-care for service providers, community forums; and innovative residential workshops that are not psychotherapy but whose effects are therapeutic. They bring together group process, stress management skills training, creative expression like writing and drawing, and outdoor recreation in beautiful places. The Coming Home Project har-

nesses the best from ancient and modern approaches and creates a culture and community of support and healing—an informed, compassionate, inclusive response. A safe place. Coming Home programs are
open to all OIF and OEF veterans and families and no particular political, ideological or religious belief or affiliation is represented or
required. Everyone is welcome as they are, and all are treated with
respect.

To give you a feel for the elusive quality of safety and welcome in community, let me close by sharing a few vignettes from our very first
workshop:

Kenny Sargent and Rory Dunn are Iraq veterans who both sustained serious TBIs. One was shot in the head, one was hit by an IED.
Both also suffer from PTSD. They meet outside the workshop and
seem like long-lost brothers. Neither sees well, a result of their
injuries, and they come up real close to one another. They began to run
their hands over one another's face and neck, touching each other's
wounds, comparing scars and experiences, forging a deep connection.
The emotions are palpable.

Stephanie Pelkey, former Army Captain, who feels isolated in
Houston where she lives with the legacy of her husband's suicide, is
taken in like family within minutes of meeting the other vets' families.

The first words of our first workshop are spoken during the opening moments of silence, as we are remembering those unable to be
with us. Ben, Stefanie's 2-1/2-year-old son, is playing with another
young child around the edges of our circle. Amidst the reverent quiet,
all 40 of us hear Ben say to his playmate, "My daddy died in Iraq."
Although Stefanie's husband Michael actually killed himself back
home, out of the mouth of babes, in the embrace of the beloved community, comes another truth: something in Ben's dad did indeed die in
Iraq.

As we're all saying our goodbyes, Rory comes my way and we
hug. I notice near his seat a scrap of paper crumpled up and thrown
on the floor. I pick it up, unravel it and ask if it's his. "Yeah, it's nothing," he says. I see three family trees. I ask him about it: "It's all the
people blown away by my buddies' ... dying." I look closer: a girlfriend, baby, church members, mother, father, sister and so on, three

little stories, three little family trees. Rory has a serious TBI and PTSD. But as his drawing attests, he can think, feel and communicate. Being able to represent his experience—and reclaim it—in a safe, and unconditionally accepting setting, is part and parcel of a transformation which continues to this day. It helps Rory—despite his many recurrent symptoms—find renewed meaning, purpose, aliveness and yes, even some joy, in living. And it allows him enough freedom to begin to help others.

"This war has imposed an enormous strain on our armed forces. These men and women are serving in harsh, nerve-wracking conditions, in a war where there are no clear front lines. Thanks to advances in battlefield medicine we are saving many more of the injured than in previous wars. There are 7.5 wounded for every fatality, compared with a ratio of under 3 in Vietnam and Korea. Many of these are grievous injuries that include TBI, amputations, burns, blindness, spinal injuries and polytrauma—which is a combination of such things. If you include all those who are wounded in combat, or injured in a vehicle accident or contract a disease, there are 14 casualties for every death."

—Hearing on the Economic Costs of the Iraq War, Testimony before US House of Representatives Committee on the Budget, October 24, 2007, by Linda Bilmes, Lecturer in Public Policy, John F. Kennedy School of Government, Harvard University

35

SLEEPLESS IN SILVER SPRING
The Story of National Guard Specialist 1st Class Duval Diaz

"Then there is our culture's whole machismo thing. Our men will never admit anything is wrong. In our culture men don't cry, so when I'd ask Duval how he was, he'd always say 'everything is fine,' but I knew it wasn't. I knew he was lost. I knew he felt alone. I think re-enlisting was a good thing for my brother. It made him feel needed, until he got hurt."

In Kandahar in mid-June 2003, a landmine blew up directly in front of the open jeep where 43-year-old Duval Diaz was riding shotgun. The driver spooked, swerved hard to the right, and Duval fell into the road, landing on his back. Since he was able to get right back up again, he didn't pay much attention to the incident. As a cook, driver and security guard with a 104th Aviation company for the past six months, his attempts to travel anywhere, countryside or city, by vehicle or foot were all exercises in the probability of being blown up by a landmine. One more explosion wasn't going to make that much of a difference. "It was business as usual, flat-out 18 hours a day until September when I hopped on a cargo plane to get some R&R in Qatar. When we landed seven hours later I couldn't move."

The injury to his spine three months earlier had been aggravated by the flight. He was sent back to Afghanistan where doctors did an MRI, gave him a prescription for Diludan and even offered an epidural directly into his spine. "When I saw the size of the needle I said, no thanks, but the next morning I was on my knees to them. 'Sure anything. Stop the pain.'" Duval was flown from Kandahar to Landstuhl Medical Center in Germany to Fort Dix, New Jersey where two months of physical therapy only made the pain worse. After a second

MRI, Duval was transferred to Walter Reed Medical Center where he would spend over two years recovering from his spinal surgery, enduring operations for a chronic sinus condition, being diagnosed, operated on and recovering from prostate cancer and coping with severe PTSD.

"That wasn't how it was supposed to turn out. I should have joined the Air Force, not the Army," he jokes. "I should have moved over to the Blue." Duval joined the Army National Guard in 1978 when he was eighteen. He worked as a cook for five years before getting out. Over the next seventeen years he worked as a security guard for liquor stores, a professional bodyguard, a cook, and a chauffeur. The morning of September 11, 2001 he had just come on shift as a security guard at Los Angeles Airport at 5:30 a.m. when he heard the television news from New York City. He reenlisted in the National Guard the next day. It wasn't just the attack on the World Trade Towers. Duval needed to find a new purpose in life. He was still reeling from the death of his father from Alzheimer's, and seven months later the death of his 10-year-old son.

He joined up with the 104th Aviation, ultimately deploying to Kuwait for staging, then to Qatar for a month, and finally to Afghanistan where the 104th's Chanute helicopters supported a handful of units in and around Kandahar. It was nerve-wracking. "When I was working in the mess hall I couldn't tell the difference between a missile attack and a landmine. But at night the landmines were so close that when they exploded our whole tent shook." He quickly learned to trust no one. "I'd be driving and another car would pass by and shoot at us. I saw a lot of bad stuff. " But the demands of the job took his mind off himself. "I was responsible for all the meals for four crews, pilots, co-pilots and gunners. I enjoyed working in the mess." He had dreams of becoming a gunner. "I was a helluva shooter."

Duvalia, his half-sister who works helping Hispanics better understand their Social Security and Medicare benefits, recalls his emails to her during this time as positive. "Duval has had a hard life. Our father left him and his mother when he was two, and their family never had much money. He was so very angry with our father. He would come over and scream at him, 'You deserted me!' but then by the time he was ready to reconcile, my father couldn't remember who he was. The same thing happened with his son. He and his wife split up and he didn't see his own son for eight years. Then right after seeing him for the first time, his son died. Then there is our culture's whole machismo thing. Our men will never admit anything is wrong. In our culture men don't cry, so when I'd ask Duval how he was, he'd always say 'everything is fine,' but I knew it wasn't. I knew he was lost. I knew he felt alone. I think reenlisting was a good thing for my brother. It made him feel needed, until he got hurt that is."

Maybe it was the stress of being diagnosed with cancer while still recovering from his spinal surgery, or maybe it was that he repressed what he had seen in Afghanistan and now it was catching up with him, but once he was at Walter Reed, Duval's struggles with nightmares increased. Night after night he'd wake up trembling, soaked with sweat. "I was on the front line and I was in charge. My job was to get my soldiers across safely but I never could do it. There were blasts and people being killed."

He also had occasional flashbacks. "I kept seeing how this one certain street looked after an explosion. There was blood and body parts everywhere." He started losing his concentration and forgetting things. He became jumpy. "I still cannot tolerate anyone walking behind me." He found himself becoming irritable over the slightest upset or postponement, whether it was a doctor's appointment or a tardy phone call from Duvalia. When he did talk to her, her advice was always the same: See one of the military psychiatrists for his mental problems while he was still at the hospital.

"I couldn't come down to DC to visit him because of my work and the new baby, but I must have spent a thousand hours talking to him on the phone. I had to make him see that all his denial was just hurting him. He had to get over the macho thing, this badge of honor not to admit weakness. He was so depressed, and I'd tell him, 'Go talk to someone. No one is going to think badly of you if you admit you're depressed. Getting help doesn't mean you're a pansy'."

"I don't think I was in as bad shape as she says I was," Duval says, "But she was a good listener, and I guess I needed to talk to someone more than I thought I did. I was very lonely." The one time she came to see me I took her to the Kennedy Center to see Aretha Franklin and Robert Goulet. I was so happy to be able to do that for her." He also reached out to other soldiers on the wards of Walter Reed. "A lot of them never left their rooms. They were on medication and drinking at the same time. There was a young kid, a Mexican-American from Texas who talked to no one and no one paid any attention to him. Finally I went into his room and said, 'You gotta come out, man. I know where you are. You're living in your head.' After a while he trusted me. We became friends. It helped us both."

It also helped to have Mercedes to talk to. Duval and Mercedes, a family practice lawyer living in Peru, had been communicating by email and phone since 2003 when a mutual friend convinced both of them that they had a lot in common. By April 2005, when Duval was recovering from his spinal surgery, they were talking daily. In July, at the first opportunity to get leave, Duval flew to Peru. Two weeks later, on July 16th, they were married at the US Embassy in Lima. When Duval was discharged from Walter Reed in February 2006, Mercedes was there to take him to their first home together, an apartment in Silver Spring, Maryland. But his living arrangements had not always been so pleasant.

At the end of 2005 a doctor presented him with a letter assigning him to Building 18, a dormitory for long-term patients. Everyone knew its reputation. "There was mold and cockroaches. Rats. The paint was peeling off the walls. It was like public housing. We all understood the area was dangerous. About the time they wanted me to move over there a chaplain had just been mugged on his way out the door. One soldier was beaten up with his own leg. There were two suicides. But what choice did I have? I went over and tried it, but my mattress was a half an inch thick, so I went back to the doctor and said, 'I can't live there. I have a back problem.' And the doctor said, 'But I've already written the letter and you have to sign it.' And I said, 'I'm not going.'" Ultimately Duval prevailed and was assigned to Building 11, which had previously housed medical students. "It was luxurious compared to 18, but that's not saying so much, you know?"

Duval was discharged with 80 percent disability from the Veterans Administration because of his spinal injury and sinus condition. He was refused disability for his PTSD and TBI, although he'd been seeing a psychiatrist at Walter Reed for both for over a year. He left the hospital armed with medications for depression and sleeplessness. "He is not the man I used to talk on the phone to before going to combat," Mercedes says. "It's not easy living with him. He doesn't sleep so I don't sleep. It's hard to be close to each other physically or mentally because he is so messed up." "Sometimes she wakes me up because I'm hitting her," Duval says, "I'm having a nightmare and I think she's the enemy." Mercedes says, "I've learned to be patient and not take it personally when he broods and won't talk to me. It's like having a child again who demands all my attention and all my love but has trouble giving it back to me."

Duval admits he's not easy. "I can hear myself acting like a kid. I have trouble making decisions. I'll change my mind ten times about something stupid like what shirt to put on or whether or not to go to a movie." The word, "leave" has become a loaded weapon. "When we argue, I'll say 'I've got to leave this house.' What I mean is I just need a break." But Mercedes interprets the word differently. "When he says 'leave' I'm afraid he's going to walk away and never come back. Alarm bells go off for me." But she remains committed to their marriage. "All I can hope is that he'll change with time; that we will be affectionate with each other again. I love him, I just don't understand him."

Duval doesn't see himself as that much changed. "I am the same Duval I always was, but what I personally, went through has made me more jumpy and irritable, I know that. It has also made me more human. I love Mercedes. I love my sister and I love Yestania, my daughter. She just graduated from college. I will get through this. It's going to be okay."

Duval has enrolled in French 101 and 102 at Montgomery Junior College in Rockville, Maryland. "I've always liked languages. Ideally I'd like to study Arabic, but I've heard it's very hard to learn, so I'm starting out with something easier. Once we save a little money, I'd like to send Mercedes to MJC full time." The Armed Forces Foundation assisted Duval and Mercedes with a number of unpaid bills.

MEDALS

Army Achievement Medal, National Defense Services Medal, Global War on Terrorist Service Medal, Afghanistan Medal Army Service Ribbon, Armed Force Reserve Medal, Unit Citation.

"Being resilient does not mean that a person doesn't experience difficulty or distress. Emotional pain and sadness are common in people who have suffered major adversity or trauma in their lives. In fact, the road to resilience is likely to involve considerable emotional distress."

—*American Psychological Association*, "The Road To Resilience— What is Resilience?"

36

THE BATTLE FOR LOVE

By Mitchell S. Tepper, PhD, MPH

US Marine Corps Corporal William Berger talks about how his TBI soured the relationship with his girlfriend. He describes how he was childish, irritable, withdrawn and unable to be intimate. His mood swings and reactions to medications became so extreme that she finally called it quits.

Chief Warrant Officer Richard Gutteridge describes how, during his struggle with severe PTSD after two deployments to Iraq, he became withdrawn from his wife and two sons. His dependence on alcohol, combined with depression and insomnia, drive him to the brink of suicide. His wife appears with his packed suitcase when he leaves the Army base to check himself in to the psychiatric ward at Landstuhl Medical Center in Germany.

After recovering from his spinal injury, Army Specialist 1st Class Duval Diaz left Walter Reed Medical Center armed with medications for depression and sleeplessness. He'd been seeing a psychiatrist at Walter Reed for PTSD and TBI for over a year. His wife, Mercedes, describes him as not the man she knew before going into combat. She finds him withdrawn and extremely childish and demanding. His nightmares are so severe that he sometimes hits and kicks her in his sleep. She says she loves him but just doesn't understand.

The trauma of war often results in wounded bodies and wounded psyches—both of which can dramatically impair a person's capacity for intimacy. For some, returning from combat and transitioning back into an intimate relationship is not a big problem. Reuniting after a long separation in combination with an overwhelming feeling of gratefulness may even fuel desire and strengthen bonds. However, for Corporal William Berger, for Chief Warrant Officer Richard Gutteridge, for Army Specialist 1st Class Duval Diaz and his wife, and for many of the tens of thousands of those who are experiencing symptoms related to deployment and combat related stress, PTSD, Traumatic Brain Injury and major depression, being emotionally and physically intimate can present a real challenge.

The RAND report Families Under Stress: An Assessment of Data, Theory and Research on Marriage and Divorce in the Military (2007) suggests that people who return from deployment with a serious physical or mental injury bear a disproportionate burden of marital stress and divorce than their non-disabled counterparts. In addition to divorce and strain on relationships, the RAND report Invisible Wounds of War: Psychological and Cognitive Injuries, Their Consequences, and Services to Assist Recovery (2008) found that failed intimate relationships contribute significantly to suicide, intimate partner violence, child abuse, reduced quality of life, homelessness and substance abuse.

The relationship between combat related trauma, risk and resilience factors, including guilt, shame and anger and the resultant impact on the capacity for intimacy is poorly understood. However, in light of just the few excerpts of stories repeated here, it is not difficult to picture how a mental trauma like PTSD and depression, or a physical wound like TBI can create significant barriers to establishing and/or maintaining intimate relationships.

The symptoms of deployment and combat related stress, PTSD, depression and TBI can erode the foundation of intimate relationships. Intimate relationships are founded on things such as communication, trust, a sense of safety, the ability to accurately perceive and tend to another's emotional needs, impulse control, vulnerability and love. The constellation of problems distilled from the collection of stories in these pages including nightmares, night sweats, sleeplessness, loss of concentration, irritability, anger dyscontrol, hypervigilance, forgetfulness, short-term memory loss, depression, denial, migraines, seizures, emotional numbing, avoidance of sex, social withdrawal and loneliness plague both the person wounded and their intimate partners.

Overwhelmingly, the partners of these returning veterans were unprepared for what they faced. It was difficult for them to understand their loved ones' radical changes in mood, behavior and reactions. Many a partner has experienced what Mercedes expressed so candidly: "It's like having a child again who demands all my attention and all my love but has trouble giving it back to me." The combination of not understanding, the feeling of being in a relationship with a child, and the experience of being the target of anger, frustration and blame makes maintaining emotional and sexual intimacy difficult.

Sexual intimacy at its core requires vulnerability on the part of both partners, and vulnerability is inconsistent with survival on the battlefield. In the vernacular, to be caught "with your pants down" means to be caught unprepared, thus vulnerable to a negative outcome; so too in sexual intimacy. To bare oneself literally, as in to get naked in front of a new lover, or figuratively, as in to share a personal fear or insecurity, leaves one vulnerable. Hence, intimate sexual relationships, like emotionally intimate relationships, require a sense of security and trust, commodities that are often hard to come by on the battlefield.

Some partners like Mercedes stick around and hope their partner will change with time and that they will be affectionate with each other again, while others who cannot or do not want to cope with the changes leave. Partners who stick around may experience a heavy caregiver burden that can result in cumulative physical and emotional stress over time, or even a phenomenon called secondary traumatization. This is a situation in which the intimate partners of trauma survivors themselves begin to experience symptoms of trauma, a major factor contributing to the breakup of William Berger and his fiancé. While patience and hope are two important factors that can contribute to resilience, these too can be elusive and are not sufficient on their own to alleviate suffering.

The battle for love does not take place within a vacuum. Research shows that people with pre-existing vulnerabilities—like less education, less supportive extended families, lower socioeconomic status, or a history of adjustment problems—may experience worse family outcomes than individuals without these vulnerabilities. Also, in the case of marriage, the quality of a marriage before the trauma is predictive of the resilience or adjustment afterward.

Our service members get some of our nation's best medical care and physical rehabilitation services, but access to mental health services is both limited and often ineffectual, as it is in the civilian healthcare arena. We need to work more aggressively to identify and get into treatment those struggling with depression, combat related stress, PTSD, mild brain injury, and spiritual issues. And we have to do more to educate and support their partners emotionally, and to lessen the burden of caregiving on them by providing adequate personal care or support services for the wounded partner.

The stories in this anthology talk of relationships that have either ended or been damaged by the veteran's wartime experiences. Overall the picture painted for intimate relationships is not a rosy one. At the moment we need to look beyond the stories of OEF/OIF veterans in this anthology and outside of the limited research literature on intimate relationship adjustment after combat, and then conduct research and develop evidence-based interventions.

We can start with the first-person story of a mental health care volunteer for Give An Hour, the non-profit organization that connects veterans with conditions such as PTSD with professional mental health care providers, 55-year-old George Alexander, the civilian son of a Marine Corps sniper during World War II. George tells this story as part of his counseling to veterans coping with PTSD. George's father "came home from the war a damaged man and turned to drinking to relieve the demons that haunted him." George describes a pattern of abuse he experienced when his father would get drunk and take out his anger on him, and the secondary traumatization he developed by age six, complete with nightmares of combat, insomnia and other symptoms indicative of PTSD. George's parents divorced when he was ten.

George's early life experiences translated into a series of fights, substance abuse, risky sex, dropping out of school and violence. By the age of 19—having already been married and divorced once—he took on a new identity and life under the witness protection program. George's new life, however, was haunted by his past traumatic experiences. After 35 years of failed relationships (including three divorces and two broken engagements) and a painful medical condition that led him to the brink of suicide, he checked himself into a psychiatric ward. There he was diagnosed with Complex PTSD and received treatment. George is now in a stable marriage, works as a veterans' advocate in honor of his father, and volunteers providing counseling to veterans.

George often shares some of his insights after reflecting on his intimate life and relationships. "I had built a wall around me to protect myself, which ultimately wound up preventing anyone from getting close enough to love me." He describes himself as withdrawn, emotionally numb, unable to trust anyone and always afraid of being rejected if a woman were to find out who he really was inside. He says he's reminded of the famous line from *Cool Hand Luke* where Strother Martin says to Paul Newman, "What we have here is a failure to communicate," since communication was a main problem. In his own words he describes "being unable to let my shield down long enough to connect, to open up to another human being for the love I so desperately wanted." He says that as a child he was never taught the skills necessary to have a successful relationship or to manage conflict, so as an adult he would just recoil and withdraw like an 8-year-old.

George thought he was doomed to spend the rest of his life alone and unloved. He says, "I was depressed most of the time and frequently turned to substance abuse to get me through the lonely nights spent trying to figure out why I couldn't maintain a loving, committed relationship with someone, which is what I wanted more than anything in the world. Then, totally by accident, I would meet the woman who would teach me what to be in a loving, committed and enduring relationship really meant, and we have now been together for the last 10 years. She also taught me the difference between love, sex and intimacy. I learned that intimacy meant sharing our feelings, our values, our thoughts and most importantly, our love. It was the love for this woman, who is his fourth wife, and their child that gave him the will to live and get help when he was in his deepest moments of physical and emotional pain."

I know of other anecdotes of individuals who have ended up in happy marriages after several tries and much heartache, and even couples who have weathered the storm together. However when we see case after case of relationships disintegrating between returning veterans and their partners, we cannot stand by and just let things happen "totally by accident." Formal research needs to be done to understand what factors contributed to successful relationships and what type of therapeutic interventions can foster success in intimate relationships before, during and after going to war.

In addition to access to Chaplain counseling, anger management, stress management and substance abuse treatments offered through the Department of Veteran's Affairs' system, we need to add classes on topics such as communication skills; conflict management; sexual enrichment strategies; adapting to changed bodies, changed minds and changed relationships; adapting to changed roles within relationships (e.g., partner as caregiver, patient instead of provider); effects of disability and chronic conditions on sexual response and expression; and access to couples counseling. Ideally, the DoVA will develop retreats for veterans battling for love just as the Department of Defense does for active duty personnel via the Army Strong Bonds program.

We can also help people explore and understand the nature of love in their relationships, specifically who does it serve and what needs does it meet. Sometimes, as in the case of Duval and Mercedes, and George and his new wife, love is the critical glue that holds relationships together. Other times, feelings of isolation and withdrawal can lead to suicidal thoughts as experienced by Richard. It is said that unselfish or compassionate love lasts forever. Compassionate love serves the other and meets the needs of the other; archetypal examples are the love of God toward man, the love of a mother toward her new baby, and the love that Jonathan and David shared in the Bible. Conversely, self-centered love is seen as conditional. If the condition is met, I feel love; when that condition is no longer present, the feeling of love is lost.

The battle for love on the home front requires a new type of bravery, a new type of hero. If we accept the notion that a hero acts in the face of fears, then we can say a hero rises above his or her nature. It is human nature to focus on what you had and what you lost, and to want to hide in shame when you are feeling vulnerable. It takes a small act of heroism to move forward into the unknown, armed only with what you have at the moment. Now our heroes—both those who were deployed and put themselves in harms way to protect the greater good and those who stayed at home and held down the ship—are fighting for their lovers and their families. This virtuous fight requires the ability to see the good, to not let evil prevail, and to not let the spirit be broken.

While we cannot expect every relationship to survive, we owe it to our wounded troops and partners to give them the support they need to have a fighting chance to avoid unnecessary dissolution of marriages and committed relationships. A lack of healthy intimacy can significantly impair recovery and contribute to ongoing mental health problems. Healthy intimate relationships add meaning to life in the face of substantial loss, and can contribute to a person's recovery from physical and mental trauma. Those who have sacrificed for our country deserve our full support in their battle for love.

"*Men and women are returning from Iraq and Afghanistan, in many instances emotionally scarred or horribly disfigured, only to find a veterans' system that is stressed to the max. Sophocles was Mr. Doerries's way to underline the issue, which obviously affects all Americans, civilians and military alike. 'A modern play about Vietnam,' he said, 'wouldn't have the effect of an ancient narrative that draws attention to the fact that PTSD, even if it wasn't called that, was very much a problem that plagued humanity from way back.'*"

—"Like War Itself, Effects of War are Hell, Ask the Greeks," Clyde Haberman, *The New York Times*, September 18, 2008

37

ONE FOOT IS BETTER THAN TWO
The Story of Army Corporal Nicholas Firth
and His Mother, Faye Firth

*"I've announced to the world that I have this mental condition
and it's not the end of the world. I know a lot of soldiers who are
receiving mental health care, but I also know a lot who are
reluctant to admit that they need it. That does them
no good in my opinion."*

Twenty-five-year-old Nicholas Firth had only one request for the doctors at Walter Reed Medical Center: Amputate his foot. "I was getting really tired of limping around with a cane. I was on so many pain meds I felt like I was in a mental fog. He was getting married to Krystil in two months in his hometown of Charlotte, and he wanted to stand at the altar on a prosthesis instead of what currently passed for his right foot and ankle—a tangled mass of titanium plates and damaged nerves that kept him in constant agony. He'd witnessed the remarkable improvements medical science has made in prosthesis for just about any part of the body except the trunk and neck for the past eight months.

"I couldn't understand what they were waiting for," he recalls. The doctors kept telling him to put off an amputation for as long as four or five years to see if the pain diminished. "They said I might regret my decision when I got older, but they underestimated me. I was ready to get on with my life." The one other person who understood exactly what Nick was demanding and advocated every day on his behalf was his mother.

Nick's "Alive Day" was June 8th, 2006. Eighty miles north of Baghdad, the vehicle he was riding in as a gunner was hit with an IED. The blast occurred directly beneath his feet. His scalp was torn off and both of his ankles were broken; the right one severely crushed. "I felt like my head split apart and then I lost consciousness." Florita (Faye) Firth got the call early the next morning from a captain at Landstuhl Medical Center telling her that her son was alive but badly injured. She rushed up from North Carolina in time for Nick's arrival from Germany to Walter Reed Medical Center. What the captain hadn't mentioned were the 47 staples on Nick's scalp. When Faye saw Nick his head was so swollen she could barely recognize him. "But I never let on that I was shocked, or fearful, or angry or depressed," Faye says, "Because I knew he was watching me. He was measuring his condition by the look in my eyes. I had to stay positive for Nick."

"I knew what had happened to me, even though I wasn't lucid," he recalls. "I was determined not to die."

"The first thing I did after giving him a hug was to remove his shoes (his feet were in casts) and clean each toe. 'You're going to heal with dignity,' I told him." Except for three quick trips home, Faye never left her son's side. She lived in family housing the military provides for relatives of injured soldiers. Week after week, month after month, she would appear, carefully dressed and made up, ready to help Nick cope with his injuries. "He wouldn't tell me that he was watching me, but months later I overheard him say to another soldier, 'I'm doing so well because of my mom...because of her strength.'" The orthopedic ward was understaffed so Faye gave Nick sponge baths and brushed his teeth. She bought him special foods, one day more than $20 worth of fried rice, because it was what he wanted to eat. When his headaches started, she brought them to the attention of the medical staff.

She managed to hold back the tears except for one brutally hot day in August when she was pushing Nick in his wheelchair across the Walter Reed campus. "It must have been way over 100 degrees and a double amputee was wheeling himself toward us. He was so young and all alone. And I started to cry because where was his family? Where was his mother?"

Besides her son's recovery, Faye's biggest problem was money. She was in the process of a divorce and living off her dwindling savings. She'd been too proud to go to Family Services, but in November when the $2,000 property tax bill on her home came due she had no choice.

It was the Armed Forces Foundation that paid $1,200 of the tax bill, and helped her negotiate payment of the rest, the reprieve Faye needed until she could find a job. By the end of the year she was working at a computer firm in Falls Church, Virginia, close enough that she could commute from Walter Reed. When Nick got a $25,000 insurance payment and offered to share it with her, she turned him down. "You keep it," she said. "As long as I can make my own payments, one car payment, one month's house payment, and pay one electrical and water bill, I'm fine."

And she keeps remembering Psalm 91. Faye's former husband was deployed with the Air Force during Operation Desert Storm. Faye and her two children, Nicholas, and Rena, then ages 10 and 7, would watch television images of Scud missiles raining down and pray. "I've never allowed myself or my children to live in fear," Faye says. "Not then and not now."

Five months after being admitted, Nick was diagnosed with mild Traumatic Brain Injury and PTSD, conditions he still struggles with two years later. He suffers from both short and long term memory loss. "I don't remember most of my childhood in the Philippines or when I was a teenager back in the states. My past is just gone. But also sometimes I can't remember what I'm supposed to be doing right now or why I've walked into a room or who I'm supposed to meet." He has acute anxiety, nightmares and flashbacks, all symptoms of PTSD that he discusses with his therapist at Walter Reed, and, at times, his wife. "She was my best friend for six years before we decided to get married. She probably has PTSD herself. I've put her through hell!"

Nick would be married on February 5, 2007 and become a father for the second time before his leg was amputated eight inches below his knee on January 7th, 2008 at Walter Reed Medical Center. "It's all about my leg now," he says from his apartment in Silver Spring. "In having to wait to get it amputated I appreciate it more. At least now I know I'm the best I'm going to be." He will spend the remainder of the year at WRMC receiving daily physical therapy for his leg and mental health care for his PTSD. "I have an amazing therapist. She's helped me and I've become a sort of spokesperson for soldiers like myself who have PTSD. I've been on CNN. I've announced to the American public that I have this mental condition and it's not the end of the world. I know a lot of soldiers who are receiving mental health care, but I also know a lot who are reluctant to admit that they need it. That does them no good in my opinion."

He is philosophical about his TBI. "The only real cure for that is time. I just have to roll with it." On May 28, 2008 he "rolled" by running a quarter mile on his new prosthesis. Nick has plans: "I have two kids, Cameron, 18 months, and Kylie, 6 months, and I need to get on with my life." Nick still has hopes of returning to duty as an infantryman, although he's fairly sure that's impossible. "I love this country, and I serve at the pleasure of the President. If someone like me can come here and become a citizen, then anything is possible in America." His alternative to the Army is to open an auto customization business with his best friend and take up his position in the heavy metal band "For Hope and Revenge," along with his buddies from high school. "I remember talking to the doctors about my foot and I said, 'Look, let's get this done so I can start my life again. There're forty operations I could have or there's just this one. Let's do it."

PSALM 91

1   *You who live in the shelter of the Most High,*
    who abide in the shadow of the Almighty, *
2   *will say to the LORD, 'My refuge and my fortress;*
    my God, in whom I trust.'

3   *For he will deliver you from the snare of the fowler*
    and from the deadly pestilence;
4   *he will cover you with his pinions,*
    and under his wings you will find refuge;
    his faithfulness is a shield and buckler.
5   *You will not fear the terror of the night,*
    or the arrow that flies by day,
6   *or the pestilence that stalks in darkness,*
    or the destruction that wastes at noonday.

7   *A thousand may fall at your side,*
    ten thousand at your right hand,
    but it will not come near you.

8   *You will only look with your eyes*
    and see the punishment of the wicked.

9   *Because you have made the LORD your refuge,* *
    the Most High your dwelling-place,
10 *no evil shall befall you,*
    no scourge come near your tent.
11 *For he will command his angels concerning you*
    to guard you in all your ways.
12 *On their hands they will bear you up,*
    so that you will not dash your foot against a stone.
13 *You will tread on the lion and the adder,*
    the young lion and the serpent you will trample under foot.

14 *Those who love me, I will deliver;*
    I will protect those who know my name.
15 *When they call to me, I will answer them;*
    I will be with them in trouble,
    I will rescue them and honour them.
16 *With long life I will satisfy them,*
    and show them my salvation.

MEDALS
Combat Infantry Badge, Army Commendation Medal, Purple Heart.

"We found the most powerful postwar predictor of resilience to PTSD symptoms was an element of social support that we called Interpersonal Connection. When men felt they could talk to someone—and more important that they were listened to and that people believed them—they tended to do better than men who felt they could not."

—"When Close Feels Far Away—Helping A Family Member Come Home," Dr. Thomas N. Dikel, giveanhour.org

38

FACING OUR FEARS

By Barbara V. Romberg, PhD

Fear affects those who experience the invisible wounds of war, their loved ones, the mental health professionals who offer assistance and our country itself as we watch the broken return home.

Anxiety is a common emotion we all experience, most of us in mild forms. Who hasn't felt an uneasiness of mind caused by the anticipation, whether rational or not, of some misfortune. By contrast, fear is defined as a distressing emotion aroused by impending danger, evil or pain. Even small amounts of fear can cause significant disturbance and can lead to a number of negative consequences.

Specifically, fear immobilizes our decision making and leads us to avoid situations that elicit that feeling in our bodies and minds. When we're afraid, we are reluctant to accept help from others since accepting assistance requires that we trust, which is difficult to do when we are afraid. Fear keeps us locked in old habits. Afraid to change, we hold on to maladaptive and destructive patterns of behavior. And fear stifles motivation and initiative—it prevents us from believing in our capacity to become fully functioning and healthy. When we're afraid of the pain of disappointment, we refuse to reach for what might have been and settle for the dissatisfaction of what is.

"Our doubts are traitors, and make us lose the good we oft might win, by fearing to attempt."—William Shakespeare

Much has been written about the struggles of the Vietnam veterans who came home from the war. Dr Jonathan Shay worked with veterans who suffered from complex Post-Traumatic Stress Disorder as a result of their combat experience. He observed that fear had a tremendous impact on the interactions these men had with the mental health professionals who attempted to help them. As a result of their fear, Dr. Shay explains, these veterans constantly tested, pushed and challenged those around them—looking for confirmation of the betrayal they suspected. The cumulative effect of years of repeated disappointment and mistreatment resulted in the destruction of their basic capacity to trust.

Vietnam veterans feared unleashing emotions that were too painful or difficult to feel, let alone express. Afraid they might experience overwhelming shame, or guilt or pain, these soldiers tried to protect themselves by avoiding all triggers and all associations. Unfortunately, as they numbed themselves to avoid the pain they feared, they severely limited their capacity to feel the love, the caring, the safety that others offered.

They also feared being deceived or used and even harmed by the incompetence of others.

Those coming home from today's war—some who suffer from complex PTSD, others who suffer less severe but still profoundly disabling consequences—also experience fear. They are afraid to appear weak to themselves or others. They are afraid of feeling weak. They are afraid to ask for help because they might be labeled "crazy." In many cases they don't understand what is happening to them and so they fear that they actually are "crazy."

The list of possible fears is long. Many returning warriors report that they are afraid of the stigma attached to seeking mental health care. Associated with this fear is humiliation for not being strong enough or tough enough to "gut it out." As depression sinks in, these returning warriors fear being overwhelmed by darkness and despair. Fearing a life filled with hopelessness, yet unable to connect with others, many withdraw from friends, family and their community. Eventually some turn to suicide to end the pain.

In addition, the men and women who serve fear for those they love. They are afraid that they cannot live up to the needs or expectations of those waiting at home. They fear intimacy—closeness makes them feel vulnerable and exposed. With so much chatter in their heads, they fear sex. One young marine told me that he had trouble holding his girlfriend's hand and couldn't imagine being intimate with her. He was terrified that he would lose her but had no idea how to talk with her about his fear. Those who return with physical disabilities have the added struggle of learning how to engage in intimate relationships with missing limbs or scarred flesh.

Some who return are afraid of harming those who welcome them home. They fear that they will be angry, aggressive, depressed, impulsive or disengaged. They also fear the numbness that sometimes replaces feeling. Being unable to feel is a blessing for some—but relationships rarely withstand the emotional detachment necessary to maintain this level of numbness. Parents of returning warriors have written asking for help in reaching their son or daughter. They report that their child returned physically intact but emotionally and spiritually vacant.

At a conference on combat stress I spoke with an Iraq veteran who had lost his leg in the war. He was unassuming, polite, articulate and very concerned about the men and women returning home from the current conflicts. I had just completed a presentation on fear. He was very interested in the topic and asked if I might consider adding another type of fear to my list. He wanted me to add the fear of dishonor. He explained how a soldier's fear of dishonoring his unit, his service and his family often keeps him silent about his nightmares, flashbacks, anxiety and depression. He expressed the hope that we would be able to help those returning from combat—some with invisible wounds such as post-traumatic stress and traumatic brain injury—find honor in seeking and receiving the help they need and deserve.

"Courage is resistance to fear, mastery of fear—not absence of fear."
—Mark Twain

Family members have fears when loved ones return from combat. I have spoken with many adults whose fathers served and fought in World War II. They tell a similar tale. Their fathers were good men who believed in service to others, honor and integrity. Many of these good men were clearly affected by the war. They rarely if ever spoke about their experience, and their children never asked. Their children were afraid to raise the issue. They were afraid to bring up potentially painful memories and afraid to unleash the rage that sometimes seemed to hover ever so near the surface.

Some family members of those returning home today report that they too "walk on eggshells." Some have become receptacles for their loved ones pain. They are distressed and burdened but they don't know how to stop the pattern. As we now know, secondary trauma is a very real phenomenon that often affects family members of those who suffer from Post-Traumatic Stress.

Family members are often afraid to speak about the changes they observe in their loved ones. Understandably, they continue to hope that their husband, wife, son or daughter will "come back" eventually. But by not acknowledging the changes, however, the warrior and the family member remain disconnected from each other. Their relationship is unable to evolve or heal. Indeed, sometimes relationships are not able to withstand the changes or the pain that accompanies the warrior home, and dissolve.

"You gain strength, courage and confidence by every experience in which you really stop to look fear in the face."—Eleanor Roosevelt

One fear often expressed by our military leaders is associated with the need to recruit and retain new warriors. If we expose the horrors of war by discussing the psychological consequences of combat, won't we risk decreasing the number of men and women willing to join an all-volunteer force? Many of us in the mental health field will argue that as long as the need for war exists, we will be better served by working to educate the men, women and families in the military community—to prepare them for the psychological realities of war. They will be better prepared for war and better able to return from it if they know the possible consequences.

"Taking a new step, uttering a new word, is what people fear most."
—Dostoevski

I am frequently asked questions that reveal the fear that Americans feel about this war. They are afraid of not knowing what to say or do when they encounter a veteran. Similarly, they are afraid of saying or doing the wrong thing. They fear getting too close to something so terrifying and overwhelming—better to keep a distance and remain safe from the pain and loss. We put magnets on our cars and hope that someone is supporting our troops.

By educating the public about the consequences of combat stress and trauma, we can help to create a culture of acceptance and understanding—so important for these men, women and families coping with the consequences of war. By creating this culture of acceptance and respect, we can normalize the veteran's experience and send the message that—unlike the reaction following the Vietnam War—our country stands ready to assist them upon their return.

"We must constantly build dykes of courage to hold back the flood of fear."—Martin Luther King Jr.

For those of us interested in helping the men, women and families to heal from the psychological and spiritual injuries of war, we too must face our fears, of which there are many. We must face our fear of failure. We might not be up to the task of healing those who have experienced such trauma. Even if we are up to the task, we may not be able to save a veteran from his or her pain. We have limitations. For those of us in the civilian community, we must face the fear that we will not be able to understand the military culture—a culture that seems at times so impenetrable. For a mental health professional, this is the ultimate failure: the failure of empathy.

"I have learned over the years that when one's mind is made up, this diminishes fear; knowing what must be done does away with fear." —Rosa Parks

So what do we gain by facing these fears; by embracing them? We begin to create an environment within which men, women and families can understand what has happened to them. Understanding is the first step in healing. By tolerating our fears and the fears of others, we offer a model of hope, the possibility of trust, and an opportunity for growth.

"The cumulative affect of repeated disappointment and mistreatment resulted in the destruction of the basic capacity to trust."

—Dr. Barbara Romberg, "Facing Fear," from "Combat Stress: Understanding the Challenges, Preparing for the Return," Smith College of Social Work Symposium, June 26–28, 2008

39

AFRAID TO TRUST

The Story of Marine Corps Sergeants Kelly Meister and Cody Sepulvida

"After she was back, when we held hands I noticed that her right trigger finger would jerk like she was shooting off rounds."

"She was the love of my life," says Kelly Meister. "We were a military family in the truest sense." Yet nineteen years after they met Kelly lives alone in Tombstone, Arizona while her former partner, Cody Sepulvida, continues her struggle with PTSD from tours of duty in the Gulf War and Operation Iraqi Freedom. "My best hope is that I'll be sitting at the Six Gun City bar and she'll walk in."

In August 1989 Kelly was a Corporal in the Marine Corps stationed in Okinawa, Japan, but participating in a three-week joint exercise in South Korea. "Uichi Focus Lens '89" involved four branches of the service including Army and National Guard units from the states. "When I heard her voice I knew she was someone special," Kelly Meister remembers. "I was shining my boots in the hallway of the barracks, and two soldiers passed by. One asked, 'Are you a Marine?' Without looking up I said, 'Yup.' 'Well, why the Marines?' I heard the voice ask. Then I heard this second voice say, 'Because she's tough.' My heart started fluttering. I was sweating. I'd never felt that way in my life before. That one sentence changed my life."

The two women got to know each other during the exercise, but it was a casual flirtation since Cody had a partner waiting for her at home. Cody had teased Kelly about wanting a hat like the one she wore. When she left, she swiped Kelly's hat and left in its place, her name, address and phone number. They wouldn't see each other again for eight years.

Kelly was the oldest of six children from a blended military family in Hamilton, Ohio. Her father was a career Army man and her mother was a nurse. She went to the University of Miami, Ohio for a year but dropped out to join the Marines. Assigned to military intelligence, she quickly achieved a top secret security clearance and rose in rank to Sergeant. While her friends called her "Mouse" because she was so short, 4 feet 10 inches, Kelly was an extrovert with lots of energy and a rock solid commitment to the Corps, even though she had to hide her sexual preferences. "In the USMC they had this running haha joke: 'A female Marine is either looking for a husband or she's a dyke' and I would always say, 'well I'm not looking for husband.' That's as close as I could come to admitting who I really was except when I was around other gay Marines.

Cody Sepulvida was also petite and tough as nails, a horsewoman from Tucson, Arizona. She joined the Arizona National Guard at age 18 in 1983, two years before 19-year-old Kelly would join the Marines. At the start of the Gulf War in January 1991 she was deployed to Saudi Arabia to the port city of Dhahran, a staging point for many of the soldiers as they waited for their gear to come in by ship. She was a mechanic, "able to tear down an engine and build it back up in minutes."

They were barracked at the Khobar Towers, a sprawling high-rise apartment community that housed American, British and French military personnel assigned to the King Abdul Aziz Air Base, the main base used by American forces. Ordered to wear their NBC gear (Nuclear, Biological, Chemical protective clothing, including boots, gloves and mask) twenty-four hours a day, they sweltered, sweated and relieved themselves in their NBC suits for five days. As sirens screamed throughout the days warning of Scud missile attacks, Cody became increasingly anxious. Finally frustrated by the claustrophobic environment, the unit's sergeant ordered his soldiers out of the building and on to the dock to await their equipment. The next day, the section of Khobar Towers where they had been living was obliterated by a Scud. Later during the same deployment the convoy she was in became lost during a blackout. The string of vehicles found themselves at sunrise, to their surprise and dismay, at the front line behind a tank brigade engaged in fierce battle.

While Cody was serving in the Gulf War Kelly was transitioning out of the Marines due to injuries to her left knee suffered during her service. She would complete her education at the University of Maryland, double majoring in criminology/criminal justice in 1995. Then in 1997, after a year of losing contact with Cody, Kelly tracked her down. "At the time I was working Child Support Enforcement in Florida, suspending the drivers' licenses of people who couldn't pay. I located Cody through a colleague who found her address via her driver's license. We spoke at least once every day on the phone until I flew to Tucson to be with her for the holidays. We were totally head over heels about each other. Cody had just purchased a prefab house in Hereford outside of Tucson. It was pretty funny because all she had in it was two lawn chairs, a TV on an ice chest, and she was sleeping on a futon. In mid-December Cody flew back to Florida; I quit my job, and we loaded a U-haul with my furniture, drove back to Arizona and moved in together."

They built a life for themselves. "We had this great three-bedroom house on four acres with two horses, four dogs and four cars. We had everything we wanted. From December 1997 to February 1999 our world was perfect. It was great. My mom says, 'It was perfect; a Walt Disney thing.'" It was in February that Cody decided to join the Marine Corps. "Even though she'd experienced her 'share of demons' in the Gulf War, she was chomping at the bit to see action in Operation Iraqi Freedom. I was torn between worrying about her safety and understanding her desire to be a Marine, since I was one myself. But I loved Cody to death and we were very comfortable with me being her anchor, so to speak. I held down the home front while she took care of business."

On February 6, 2003, Cody was deployed to Iraq as a SNCO (Staff Non-commissioned Officer) liaison between the military and civilian contractors who were ordering parts for the mechanics. She was armed with a laptop, which meant that she would work in a safe zone behind the battle scenes. But it wasn't long before the need for truck drivers, particularly ones who were also trained as mechanics, overrode everything else, and Cody was reassigned to a Combat

Support Sustainment Battalion, or "CSSB" unit. She found herself driving a "Dragon Wagon," a flatbed truck assigned to haul ammunition for tanks. Twice when she was driving the convoy was ambushed by enemy fire.

The third time an ambush occurred the convoy retreated to a berm. With the boom of explosions shaking the earth around them, and after two previous ambushes, everyone was in a heightened state of alert. Without counting down from five to one before firing back, the gunnery sergeant screamed for everyone to take cover and fire their weapons. There was an exchange of heavy gunfire for several minutes before the radio burst forth with, "Cease fire! Cease fire! Friendly, friendly, friendly." Cody had been firing on fellow soldiers. She never found out if she was personally responsible for any of those who were injured.

The entire time Cody was in Iraq Kelly slept during the day and monitored the television at night. "I wrote her every day. I sent her care packages, photographs of the animals, anything and everything I could think of to keep her morale up." But Cody's PTSD worsened and eight months later she returned home a changed woman. "After she was back, when we held hands I noticed that her right trigger finger would jerk like she was shooting off rounds." When they went out for drinks at Six Gun City in Tombstone, "She'd tense up at the slightest noise. She hated having anyone standing or sitting anywhere. Every time they recreated Wild West gun fights (shooting blanks of course) she would freak out. She couldn't sleep, and when she did she had nightmares and night sweats. She was jumpy, irritable and easily frustrated."

While Kelly stayed in Hereford, Cody went back to Camp Pendleton where she'd been stationed before being deployed to Iraq for six months, then Okinawa for a year beginning in March 2004. Then in March of 2005 she went to Barstow, California. During all three deployments her PTSD kept getting worse, but she refused to tell anyone about her struggles. While stationed at Barstow, Cody became the second in command and the only female in the Marine Corps Mounted Color Guard. It was a dream assignment to the veteran horseback rider, and when her tour of duty was over in January 2007 Cody left the Marines rather than be deployed back to the war zone.

But that summer, while Kelly was recovering from a right knee replacement, which had taken place the 24th of May, Cody had a major breakdown. The 4th of July evening fireworks display brought back memories of both wars, the Gulf and Iraq. Worse, the next night their house took a direct hit from lightning while they were sleeping. Cody fell apart, screaming and "clutching on to me for dear life."

With the help of VA doctors, Kelly finally got Cody admitted to a three-week PTSD program at the Veterans Administration hospital in Tucson, but not before finances became a problem. During this time the Armed Forces Foundation stepped in and paid the mortgage on the house as well as some other past due bills. With only five in the session, the VA program promised to provide the intensive one-on-one therapy Cody needed. "The first week she must have called me 22 times a day. The second week she called to tell me about 'this nursing assistant who is taking me out for walks to calm me down.'"

By the third week Cody had stopped calling entirely. Unbeknownst to Kelly, the nursing assistant had befriended Cody and introduced her to drugs. "One time while she was in the program she called me and asked, 'What would you do if I was taking a street drug?' I said, 'What are you thinking? We would lose it all, the house, the animals, our cars.' And she said, 'I just thought I'd ask.'" Kelly would later discover that Cody became addicted even before she left the hospital. It was only weeks from her discovery that Kelly would start an investigation against the nursing assistant which ended with the woman being fired from the VA hospital for having an elicit relationship with a patient.

When Kelly returned to the hospital for her left knee replacement in September she thought everything was back on an even keel, but on the 26th of that month Cody appeared in her rehab hospital room distraught, verging on hysteria. "She said she was going to kill herself; that she was going to leave. She caught me totally off guard. I didn't have a clue." Kelly checked herself out of the rehab hospital two hours later, concerned that Cody might harm herself with one of the three guns they kept at the house. When Kelly got home she found that Cody and her father had driven from Tucson to the house to get some of her belongings. Cody left the next day.

After a number of heated arguments during the month of October, the two separated permanently. In fact, Cody took out a protection order against Kelly. Kelly was philosophical. "No matter how strong your love is for each other or how long you've been together, when one partner goes off to war they come home in their own 'mental world of hell.' There are no doctors, no medicines, and no programs that can make them the same person they were before they left for war. What I learned was that miracles will never happen."

But soon afterward Kelly became so depressed that she tried to kill herself by swallowing a handful of morphine pills. A neighbor got her to the hospital in time for them to pump her stomach. The next day she was given fifteen minutes to pack up her belongings and was then escorted out of Cody's house by two policemen. She went to a neighbor's house and tried to commit suicide a second time. "I was good friends with this older woman, Dorothy, who lived next door, so I went over there. While she was watching television I took a butcher knife and went out to my car. I wrote four notes: to my mother, my cousin, to Cody and one to Dorothy apologizing for taking her knife." When Cody drove up to their house, Kelly confronted her and threatened to slit her wrists. Cody called the police and soon the neighborhood was swarming with law enforcement officers including a Swat team.

Kelly ended up at a Veterans' hospital in Phoenix on the psychiatric ward. Meanwhile Cody was preparing to sell the house. "On Veterans Day, ironically enough, I heard she was going to have a moving sale. I called her from her sister's house and I said, 'Cody if you sell any of my stuff there's going to be hell to pay.' She sold all my stuff anyway, except for my camera." The next time Kelly saw Cody was in court on March 4, 2008. "We both had to appear in court because of a phone call I made. One stupid phone call got me six months probation and a $1,100 fine. When I saw her I couldn't believe how thin she was. She must have gone from 112 to 90 pounds. She was smoking nonstop. She'd never smoked before. She came up to me in the hallway and said, 'Hi, how are you? Do you want to step outside while I smoke?' She initiated the conversation. She acted like nothing was wrong. She smoked four cigarettes in that ten minute period."

Kelly saw Cody for the last time on May 5th. "I ran into her at the VA hospital. She looked even worse than she did in March, and Cody was always beautifully dressed, a real stickler for neat and clean. She wouldn't look at me; just hung her head in shame, so much so that she almost ran into a light pole." There was one more phone call. "On May 17th Cody called to tell me that she had to put one of our chocolate labs down. She said, 'I had to put Dakota down' and I said, 'Why are you calling me? I'm on probation. Now I have to call my probation officer.' Those were my last words to her."

Today, Kelly doesn't want to get back with Cody. She lives with one of the couple's dogs, a Blue Queensland Heeler named Durango Kid in Tombstone where she staffs the Desert Eagle Trading Post, a high-end jewelry store. "The reason I chose Tombstone is that Cody loved it here. She'll know where to find me if she ever needs me."

If Kelly had once piece of advice to give others it would be: "When you come home be brave enough to admit to your family, your command, but most of all to yourself that you need 'mental' help. There is nothing weak in asking for help. There is no shame in admitting that you saw ugly things and that you need to get them off your chest. Holding it in will not only destroy you, but will destroy everything and everyone around you that you have ever loved. You are an American fighting man or woman, and no one can beat you down. You will be in the fight of your life with PTSD and only you can win that fight. Fight those demons and fight them hard. In the end you and only you are in control of your life. Semper Fi and watch your sixes."

MEDALS

SSGT Cody L. Sepulvida, USMC:

US Army Citations: Army Achievement Medal, Army Good Conduct Medal (3 stars), Army Service Medal, South West Asia Service Medal, Army Overseas Service Ribbon, Kuwait Liberation Medal, Saudi Arabia Medal, 3 Certificates of Achievement.

Marine Corps Citations: Good Conduct Medal (2 stars), Navy Combat Action Ribbon, Sea Service Deployment Ribbon (2 stars), National Defense Services Medal, Global War on Terrorism Service Medal, Global War on Terrorism Expeditionary Medal, Presidential Unit Citation Ribbon, Golden Wrench Mechanic Award, Certificate of Commendation, 4 Rifle Expert Badges, Pistol Sharpshooter Badge.

SGT Kelly J. Meister, USMC:

Certificate of Appreciation, 3 Letters of Appreciation, Good Conduct Medal (2 stars), National Defense Service Medal, Sea Service Deployment Ribbon, Rifle Marksmanship Badge.

40

THE ROAD BACK TO SELF
It's the Journey, Not the Destination

By David Carroll, PhD

In 2003 the President's New Freedom Commission Report on Mental Health in America began with a bold vision: "A future when everyone with a mental illness will recover." Within our lifetime we are seeing the achievement of the promise of transforming mental health care in America. There has been a radical change in our understanding of mental illness and the outcomes of mental health services. I have seen this firsthand in my work with veterans who suffer from mental illnesses, including Post-Traumatic Stress Disorder (PTSD).

No more than sixty years ago, a serious mental illness was frequently regarded as a permanent disabling condition. Custodial care and stabilization were mainstream treatments. Veterans with serious mental illness were often admitted to long-term psychiatric hospitals. These hospitals were state-of-the-art and the care was compassionate. However, from today's vantage point, the scientific methods to treat mental illness at that time were limited, and the notions about mental illness in popular culture were often not helpful or respectful. Knowledge creates power. Our current knowledge about psychosocial rehabilitation and recovery in mental illness comes from science; and it comes from the lived experience of men and women—veterans and civilians—who have mental illness.

There is a range of severity in the experience of mental illness. Some individuals have a rough period, but with counseling or life changes, they bounce back and move ahead in life readily. For others, mental illness can be a profound and life-changing experience. At times, for those with serious mental health problems, it can seem like an outside force has taken control and it cannot be shaken. Nearly every aspect of life and even the sense of self can be affected. In addition, no one should assume that any person with a mental health diagnosis has "lost their mind" or that they cannot handle the everyday stresses and challenges of life. For those individuals who do have a tough time, mental health professionals are ready to help them find their way to a path of recovery and a meaningful life.

The onset of serious mental illness can come without warning. It occurs among service members, veterans and civilians. Serious mental illness is often defined by the presence of a psychiatric diagnosis such as schizophrenia, bipolar disorder (manic-depressive disorder), or major depression. However, the severity of any illness can only be determined by knowing about the experience of the person coping with it. Other mental health disorders, including PTSD, may lead to periods of severe impairment in everyday social, occupational and interpersonal functioning. Unlike many other health care problems, mental illness is often unseen or unnoticed by others. That may be due to the absence of any physical sign, or it may be due to a perceived need to hide mental illness based upon a sense of shame or guilt. Personal battles with mental illness are frequently hidden, occurring when home alone, perhaps late at night, or within a self-imposed isolation by persons and families trying to cope with something feared and misunderstood.

I think it is most unfortunate and mistaken that mental illness is sometimes seen as a sign of weakness, a defect, or a loss of positive expectation and future dreams. No one is at fault for having a mental illness; no one should ever be discouraged or ashamed. The hope and promise of psychosocial rehabilitation with mental health recovery is real, and it happens every day. All persons with mental illness can have meaningful, productive lives of their choice and in the community of their choice. Individuals and families coping with mental illness can speak openly and be respected and supported as friends and neighbors. Persons with mental illness can live, work and contribute alongside all others in the community. There is tremendous opportunity.

Individual, person-centered care is the core principle of psychosocial rehabilitation and recovery. The person, the veteran, must be a full and active partner in all aspects of care. This typically begins with identifying the life goals that the mental health problem has challenged or interrupted. No one knows about this better than the person trying to cope with it. That individual needs to be involved in every aspect of planning and decision-making about the mental health services that are provided. The best outcomes are born from collaboration between mental health service providers who have the latest and best scientific knowledge and the person who is the expert on life as they know it and wish it to be. This partnership is essential, and the partnership typically includes other health care professionals, family members, peers who are in recovery, and other individuals and agencies in the community. What Joe experienced is a good example.

Joe is in his late twenties. He was in the Army Reserves and his unit was activated for duty in Iraq. About a year after the unit returned home, life reached a critical point for Joe and he was discharged from the service. He blamed his commander for his discharge, but Joe's behavior in civilian life was unpredictable and unreliable as well. He could not keep a job or relationship. Reluctantly he agreed to meet with a psychiatrist for an evaluation. He was diagnosed with bipolar disorder (manic-depressive illness).

This was difficult for Joe to accept, and eventually he was admitted to a psychiatric unit at a VA hospital for several days for his safety. In what he felt to be his darkest moment, he told the hospital staff that his life was over. He saw the diagnosis of serious mental illness as a barrier to all he had hope for—things like a steady job, friends, and perhaps marriage someday. The treatment team told him about an approach called supported employment. Joe soon discovered that he could have a job even now, a job of his choice. He could receive follow-along support services from a vocational rehabilitation specialist as long as he needed them. The team asked Terry to see Joe while he was in the hospital. Terry is a veteran who struggled with serious mental illness for many years. Terry is in recovery now and is employed as a peer support technician by the VA.

Joe was encouraged by his conversation with Terry, but the next few months were rough. Joe started a new job, but he needed inpatient psychiatric care for another week. He chose to reveal his psychiatric illness to his employer, who worked with Joe and the vocational rehab specialist to adjust his schedule. The three of them together ensured his success. Several months later, he told the treatment team that having a job was a life-changing experience. It helped him focus on his life in spite of his psychiatric illness. In the process it had also helped him manage his illness more effectively.

Like Joe, Rachel found help when she needed it. Rachel was well on her way to a successful career in the military. She advanced quickly in her first six years of service, but then she experienced a sudden onset of schizophrenia. Her initial care was at the base hospital. After careful consideration Rachel was discharged from service. Her mental illness was determined to be service-connected, but Rachel struggled with everything. She found it very difficult to accept help from the local VA medical center other than repeated, brief psychiatric hospitalization following a crisis. She was developing a reputation as an unwelcome tenant in the community.

Rachel was referred to a program providing intensive case management and close support for managing her medications. These services were provided by a small team of VA mental health providers directly where she lived in the community. It took a few weeks for Rachel to accept the nearly daily contact by members of the team, but she gradually developed trust. Through their collaborative effort, she had only one hospitalization in the next fifteen months. She also reported that the landlord seemed to respect her and she began to work a few hours a week at a senior center that was a block away.

Like Joe and Rachel, Phil wrestled with his mental condition alone, but once he connected with the VA found the help he so badly needed. Phil suffered serious burns to his legs from an IED explosion. His wounds responded well to the medical care, and he completed the prescribed physical therapy and rehabilitation. Phil decided to leave the service.

He had been a good soldier, but he had problems with command. He questioned some decisions and sometimes felt uncertain about his role and contribution. A few months later he had a minor traffic accident, and was arrested for driving while intoxicated. He was assigned to treatment and was able to arrange it through the VA. He anticipated that this would be the easiest way to fulfill his obligation. Phil asked the therapist about the best way to fulfill the court's requirements. After an unexpected pause, the therapist suggested to Phil that he consider what was in his own best interest instead. The therapist noted that this might be quite different from what is easiest or shortest from the perspective of the court.

Phil was stunned, but he was also grateful for the therapist's invitation. Phil was drinking too much; that was the obvious problem. However, he was using alcohol to escape from the sadness he felt nearly all the time. He had little energy except to drink. He had thought it was best to keep that secret. In addition, Phil felt that his decorated combat service and successful rehabilitation did not mean much now that he was back at home. The VA therapist worked with Phil and engaged him with a team of mental health providers. They addressed his substance abuse, his depression, his employment and his relationships—all at the same time. His care was integrated and he was in the driver's seat. Members of his family were invited to participate.

Recovery from mental illness is not a status awarded after careful scrutiny by an independent panel or attained only after completion of measured steps over a long period of time. In line with the national consensus statement about recovery, it is in the present, it embraces the whole person, and it is guided by the individual. Recovery is based upon hope, respect, partnership, responsibility and strengths. The course of recovery is not linear, and challenges are new opportunities for learning, not failures or steps backward.

Psychosocial rehabilitation and recovery are the fundamental work of VA mental health providers such as myself. The care and safety of the veterans who seek our services are paramount to every action, and our commitment to the public trust and professional standards demands full attention. Providing comprehensive, evidenced-based psychosocial rehabilitation and recovery services promotes both the well being of veterans and our professional responsibility. These fit well together and support the highest quality care possible. The critical factors for simultaneously meeting the needs of veterans and professional obligations are partnership and open communication. Under this model, mental health providers work in close collaboration and have open communication with the veterans served and with fellow providers in the VA system, as well as veterans' family members, and community partners.

Having a mental health problem can be particularly challenging to service members and veterans. The men and women in the United States military are strong and faithful in their service, and they are rightfully honored as veterans. Pride in strength and faithfulness to duty are in no way diminished by mental illness. One's duty is fulfilled by engaging with the mental health service system. I have seen that strength comes in partnership with mental health providers, peers and family members. The journey of psychosocial rehabilitation and mental health recovery among those who have served in the military contributes to the good of all and of our society. It is a mission of strength and of hope. It is my duty and the privilege of VA mental health providers to offer the hand of partnership, evidenced-based mental health services, and a fully confident hope of recovery to all.

41

A FAMILY AFFAIR

The Story of Army Sergeant John Weinburgh
and Lindsey Weinburgh

"When I got home from Iraq, it was great but it was also uncomfortable. I couldn't sleep. We were living in the country where there were a lot of hunters, and every time I'd hear a gunshot, I'd pull down the shades and pull the kids down with me on the couch. I tried to make it a game but they knew there was something wrong with Daddy."

The day-to-day routines of John Weinburgh and his young family make the stress and anxiety of his year-long deployment in the heart of Baghdad pale by comparison. As a C5 quadriplegic with PTSD and TBI since February, 2007, John is confined to his bed and wheelchair at home in Belleview, Nebraska, and requires three shifts of nurses to care for him. Care includes cleaning, bringing his meals on a tray and changing his catheter. Meanwhile his wife Lindsey takes their three children off to work with her. She drops Mary Sue, age six, off at the local elementary school. Then she drives thirty minutes to Glenwood, Iowa, where she drops off James, age four, and Ashley, three, at the YMCA daycare center before going to her full-time job as a Medicare Fraud specialist for the state.

At around five o'clock, unless she has to stay late for an audit, she reverses the process, getting home in time to make dinner for the family. Once the children are in bed the Weinburghs tackle the mountains of paperwork associated with John's Veterans' benefits since he hasn't been formally discharged from the Army and there's still a lot to be negotiated. The dining room table holds the equivalent of a campaign map; the conversation is all about strategy. The outcome of these sessions will determine the quality of this family's life for decades. Yet despite the unrelenting stress, Lindsey, 27 and John, 31, remain energetic, resilient and surprisingly optimistic. For them life may not be fair but it certainly is full.

A high school dropout (he would later earn his GED), John joined the Army in 1996 at age 19 after his mother died of breast cancer. "Even though my parents were divorced, my father promised he'd be there for us when my mom got sick but he never appeared. I was mad at him and at the world, and the Army offered a way out." After basic training at Fort Benning, Georgia and a short stint at Fort Stewart, he deployed with Delta Company 29 as part of the 2nd Infantry Division at Camp Red Cloud in South Korea. "It may sound odd but Korea was a good fit for me. We were always training as if we were about to go to war. It was different being in a foreign country. And when I think back on it, I needed the structure, the sense of purpose. My buddies over there were like family." John has two younger brothers, Army Captain Joseph Weinburgh and Army Staff Sergeant William Weinburgh. Both deployed to Iraq in 2007.

By 2000 John had been promoted to E4 and was back at Fort Benning as part of the 3rd Infantry Division, but again feeling lost and lonely. "A buddy of mine who was dating a University of Nebraska student sent my photo to his girlfriend who taped it onto the bedroom door of her best friend, Lindsey James. It wasn't long before they sent us a video, and in it there was this gorgeous girl saying, 'John, you're cute.'" They talked on the phone every night for two months before finally meeting in person. "We were like two peas in a pod," John recalls. "She was the angel who came into my life." Lindsey agrees about their similarities. "We were so much alike, it was uncanny. We both wanted children right away. We both liked the Army life. Most important of all, we made each other laugh." In May 2001 they were married and moved to Barstow, California next to Fort Irwin and the Mojave Desert. Three years later, just after they found out Lindsey was pregnant with their third child, John was deployed to Iraq.

For a year, January 2005 to January 2006, Battalion 464 was tasked with securing the Green Zone. As part of Charlie Company, John was one of the soldiers manning the three main checkpoints into and out of the headquarters complex in central Baghdad. "We were shot at but it wasn't like combat. Our main problem was trying to determine who to allow in and who to keep out. A car would come toward me, and something would stand out or look funny and I'd say to myself, 'Is this going to be the guy who blows himself up? Is this going to be the car he does it in?'" The stray rounds could come from anywhere. "Someone would start shooting down the street and we'd ask each other, 'Is that guy going to keep walking and shooting straight for us or turn the corner?' We were always walking a thin line between not wanting to be a jerk but at the same time getting sort of mean about who we let pass and who we kept out."

Charlie Company first camped out on wood bunks on the first floor of a nearby palace where local contractors were already at work plastering up bombed-out walls and ceilings. For John the first winter was brutally cold, but when the seasons changed, adjusting to 130-degree heat wasn't so difficult after living on the Mojave Desert. Later on he would live in a trailer inside the Green Zone a few yards away from the Baghdad Highway. Besides manning checkpoints, John's unit was sent into the neighborhoods of Baghdad to search and clear houses. "We'd kick in the door never knowing what was on the other side. We had to swallow our fear. We were always jazzed, on edge. We were never alone or sitting still for very long."

When Charlie Company returned home, they were deployed back to Fort Stewart, where Lindsey had already moved with their two toddlers and new baby girl, Ashley. She'd gotten a job as a teaching assistant to bring in much needed extra income. Once he was out of the adrenaline rush of being deployed to the streets of Baghdad, John gradually became aware of his PTSD symptoms.

"When I got home from Iraq, it was great but it was also uncomfortable. I couldn't sleep. We were living in the country where there were a lot of hunters, and every time I'd hear a gunshot I'd pull down the shades and pull the kids down with me on the couch. I tried to make it a game but they knew there was something wrong with Daddy." In fact any loud noise made him jumpy. "My buddy and I were in town one day and a power transmitter blew. We immediately pulled the jeep over to the side of the street, jumped out and took cover. When we realized how stupid we must have looked, we started to laugh, but it's not always funny." He is terrified of closed doors. "Any closed door freaks me out. Even if I'm not in the room and I know the door is closed, I want it opened."

On February 28, 200,7 John was training with Charlie Company 464 for deployment back to Iraq. He was now staff sergeant, and as platoon leader was riding in the turret of a Bradley at the front of the convoy toward a mock village on a mission to search and clear houses. They were driving fast cross-country on new terrain. Suddenly his driver swerved to avoid a boulder in the road, lost control of the vehicle and hit a tree. As it fell it hit a second tree which split in half and landed on John, who was still in the open turret. It hit his back, crushing his spine and knocking him unconscious. For a short time he stopped breathing. Someone performed CPR. "My driver and gunner weren't hurt. I keep telling them, don't feel guilty, it was an accident."

He was medevac'd to Memorial University Medical Center in Savannah, Georgia under heavy sedation. For Lindsey it was the worst possible nightmare. "I didn't find out about what had happened from the chain of command. I found out from a neighbor. You can't imagine what it was like driving to the hospital. I was so scared." It wasn't long before doctors determined that John would be paralyzed from the neck down for the rest of his life. "It was pretty tough getting that piece of news. At first my mind was a blank."

There was one positive event out of what was a catastrophe of monumental proportions for the Weinburghs, and John is quick to describe it. "The Army flew my brothers back to see me, and for a couple days their visits overlapped. We took a lot of photographs of the three of us together because we so seldom are. I just wish it had been under different circumstances."

In April, John was transferred to the Veterans Spinal Cord Hospital in Augusta, where he would remain until mid-September. "I was supposed to be discharged in May, but then I began to get some feeling in my toes; I was able to move my hands and arms a little and I was able to kick my legs enough that they decided to keep me there. They wanted to find out what would happen next." The wait extended from weeks to months, but he had reached a plateau. During fire drills, when the fireproof door to his hospital room was shut tight, his fear of closed doors would kick in. "I panicked but I couldn't get up and get out. Part of me knew I was being irrational; another part was in fear or fight mode."

Meanwhile Lindsey had moved the family back to Nebraska, and with the help of America's First, a former military housing service that had been privatized, retrofitted a house for John's arrival. It was during this time that the Armed Forces Foundation paid for daycare for the children. Ramps replaced stairs. Doorways were widened and the knobs replaced with handles. The bathroom sink and shower were remodeled, and a lift was installed so John could get in and out of bed. By the time John arrived it was done. At first Lindsey stayed at home to care for him, but the toll it took on their relationship was obvious to both of them almost immediately. "When you're taking care of a member of your family, the intimacy can make it difficult," Lindsey explains. "I didn't want a thank you every time I brought him something, but I began to feel resentful."

"She never got out of the house. With three kids plus me to take care of, she was going crazy. I wasn't that easy either, not just because of my paralysis. It was hard to make peace with what had happened to me. On the other hand, what am I going to do? We have three little kids." They decided to take the Army up on the offer of nursing care. Nurses come three times a day, 7–9 a.m., 12–2 p.m. and 3–5 p.m. From 9 until 12 on Monday, Wednesday and Friday a van picks John up and takes him to physical therapy, and on Thursday mornings friends take him to his church to play cards.

On June 1, 2008, John was discharged from the Army. "Now that we're done we want to help other families who are going through the same thing," John says. "We've learned a lot about what you need in a house when you have someone in my condition and kids. Why not share that knowledge with other vets and their families?"

In August 2008 John and Lindsey moved into their new home.

MEDALS

5 Army Commendation Medals, 4 Army Achievement Medals, 3 Good Conduct Medals, Global War on Terror Sevice Award, Global War on Terror Expeditionary Award, National Defense Medal, Liberation of Iraq Ribbon, Overseas Ribbon, Non-Commissioned Officer Professional Developement with #2 Award.

"Every member of every community should be prepared to offer a hand, if asked, to a returning service member or his or her family. We all need to share the responsibility of understanding the roadblocks to reintegration faced by service members and their families. It's the least we can do considering the sacrifice they've made."

—From *After The War Zone, A Practical Guide for Returning Troops and their Families,* by Laurie B. Slone, PhD, and Matthew J. Friedman, MD, PhD

42

PREPARING OURSELVES TO HELP WITH THE JOURNEY HOME

By Barbara Tine

When the Iraq war started and I realized that there wasn't anything more I could do to stop it, I needed to channel my emotions and energies somewhere. What made sense to me was that if I couldn't do anything to stop our soldiers from being sent over, perhaps I could do something for them when they returned. At that time, I didn't even know anyone who was in the military; I'm not a health care professional, and I didn't know what I could do. I just knew I needed to do something.

Even though my father was in the Air Force and I was born on base, he served during peacetime and we never thought of ourselves as a military family. So when the war started, I really didn't know much about our military or the culture. And I didn't know what to say to someone in uniform other than the standard "thank you." That really troubled me. I was afraid to say the wrong thing, but I felt worse about not saying anything. I'm sure I'm not alone in this. Since historically, less than one percent of our population serves in the military, many of us don't need to pay attention, so there is a general lack of understanding of our people in uniform. We saw this in the citizen outrage over the lack of equipment for our troops, our shock at the conditions at Walter Reed, and the ongoing concern about medical care. Many of us just assumed that our soldiers were being taken care of.

This war is affecting all of us in ways we don't even understand, yet it will continue to have an impact on us for a long time. In an effort to lessen the negative impacts, civilians need to figure out what they can do to help make the veterans' transition home as smooth as possible. Most of us have members of the Reserves or National Guard living in our neighborhoods and we don't even realize it. The challenge for these families during times of deployment is that they don't have a military base where they can get support. And many feel that while they're dealing with all that comes with having a loved one deployed, those around them don't seem to realize there's a war going on.

I started to educate myself on the issues by searching online for stories or posts for and about soldiers/veterans. I did a lot of reading about PTSD and the other issues our returning troops face. And I followed the stories of local soldiers. One story in particular moved me to action. It's the heartbreaking story of Jeffrey Lucey, a 23-year-old Marine who committed suicide in 2004 after returning home from Iraq. Hearing his parents and sister tell his story at a local event was powerful, and getting to know them personalized the issues of the "return home" for me.

I went to "Welcome Home" celebrations for returning troops and other events where there were soldiers or veterans. Most importantly, I got involved with the Veterans Education Project (VEP), a local group that has been working with veterans for over 26 years to help them tell their stories in classrooms and in the community. Through my involvement with VEP, I came to appreciate the power of storytelling, both for the listener and the veteran. Many veterans say that telling their story is part of their healing process, and it gives the listener a firsthand, intimate understanding of war.

In many of the articles and books that I read I came to understand the need for shared responsibility for war and its importance in the healing process of many of our veterans. Our government makes the decision to send our soldiers to war, and as citizens of this country we must accept the responsibility, sharing the burden and the consequences for our military's effort, in more active ways than just paying our taxes. This can be very difficult, especially for those of us who work hard to stop war. However, I think that we learned from Vietnam the importance of separating the war from the warrior.

Everyone's military experience is different, and every soldier doesn't have PTSD, but war is a life-changing experience and everyone has a story. And the very least we can do is listen to these stories. If we start educating ourselves and creating places that are welcoming and supportive of our veterans and their families, we will be ready for them when they are ready to tell us their stories. For many, it will be years before they get to that point. They need to get home and readjust to family life and get back to their jobs before they can start processing their experiences. There is also a reluctance by many to seek help, especially early on.

Since the "return home" takes time, one of the biggest challenges right now is the difficulty in reaching the younger veterans. We've learned that it is important to support the family so that it can in turn support the soldier. And this outreach should be to all veterans. There are many veterans from past conflicts who are still on the "journey home" and in need of support and a chance to tell their story. There are also many veterans who have worked through their experiences and are a wonderful resource to other veterans as well as living history for the rest of us.

One way we've started the education process in western Massachusetts is through local faith communities. Two wonderful examples of what can be done are the efforts of Wesley United Methodist Church and Congregation B'Nai Israel. Each have members who felt called to do something for our troops but struggled with what to do and how to get started.

Wesley Church began by first reaching out to the veterans within their own congregation. It came as a surprise to some just how many of their members had served in the military. While they'd known each other for years, they didn't know about their military service. Many of the veterans were eager to help educate the congregation and to develop a project of outreach to the community.

The church hosted two workshops: one was targeted to interested laypeople and the other to clergy. The workshops included mental health professionals, a military chaplain and, most importantly, veterans and military families. The workshops were well received and started an important conversation and collaboration with others interested in doing this work within their own faith community. During Lent, the church held a series of discussions called "The Wounds of War." Veterans were invited to share their stories of preparing for war, combat and the return home. One Vietnam vet told those gathered that this was the first time (outside of therapy) that anyone asked him to share his story. The church also does ongoing outreach to the local VA hospital and military families, and has become a resource to other interested groups and individuals.

B'Nai Israel's response was to work with the town's Veterans Service Officer (VSO) to offer the professional services of members of their congregation for things like landscaping, carpentry, plumbing, electrical work and job hunting. The VSO is vital because he knows the folks who are in need of assistance. The congregation members also coordinated with the active duty soldiers and veterans group at the local university to collect items to send to area soldiers currently serving in Iraq and Afghanistan. And to help educate the congregation, they invited a veteran and a military family member to share experiences with them during a service.

No matter what kind of "community" you belong to or what your profession, you can do something. It might be to call your Senator or Congressman to advocate on issues that impact our veterans. Or you can support the efforts of a local veterans group. You might start by finding out what efforts and resources already exist in your community. Talk to your local veterans' agent to find out what the needs are. Talk to veterans you know. Wouldn't it be wonderful if every school, faith community, police station and town hall in this country had a list of the resources available in their area to offer our veterans and their family members?

And remember that while we might not be able to "fix" things for a veteran, we can be there to walk with and support him/her on the "journey home." While that might seem too simple, just showing that we care is often the most important thing we can do.

ACKNOWLEDGMENTS

By Celia Straus

Near the end of this project, the task of gathering together a few more photographs, a missing publicity release, or someone's medals and commendations—housekeeping, really—became an opportunity to circle back and speak with the service members profiled here to get an update on how they were doing. Sylvia Blackwood-Boutelle was redeploying to Iraq for a fourth time; Chris Harmon had been laid off from Norfolk Southern Railroad and was looking for work; Tyler Boudreau was pulling together a coast-to-coast bike trip for vets; the Weinburghs spent Christmas in their new home; Heather and Josh were planning a wedding; Rob Kislow was about to graduate from Northampton Community College while Nathan Toews was starting second semester of his freshman year at Dickinson College.

With the economy in a tailspin, some—Chris Harmon, Duval Diaz, Jon Campaz and William Berger among them—were facing yet another bout of unpaid bills, reordering of priorities and cutting back. For others, like "Bear," John Weinburgh and Richard Gutteridge, it wasn't the prospect of severe financial insecurity that haunted them; it was their own struggles with depression. Yet everyone was hopeful and certainly everyone was stronger—if generosity of the heart is any indication. Every conversation ended with the same questions: What else can I do? How else can I help?

This is no adequate way to thank the courageous and compassionate men and women who inspired *Hidden Battles*. Only through your unrelenting commitment to tell your story was this project possible. You allowed us into your lives and shared your innermost selves with clarity and candor while you coped with daunting emotional, physical and financial challenges. And through these stories you continue to wage battle on our behalf.

I am also deeply grateful to this book's contributors—experts in the field of mental health from psychologists, psychiatrists, scientists and surgeons, to social workers and volunteers. You crafted thoughtful and important work on the subject of how we help our veterans cope with TBI and PTSD far beyond anything I could have imagined when I asked for your participation. Moreover you honored my requests for rewrites and met the project's deadlines with equanimity and grace.

I am particularly indebted to my friend and colleague of many years, Patricia Driscoll, President of The Armed Forces Foundation, who believed in this book from its inception and made it possible with her generous support, enthusiasm and bold vision. It is because of Patricia and her leadership of the Foundation that thousands of military service members and their families have made it through their worst of times. To AFF staffers past and present, Matthew Berry, Ross Blankenship, Karna Sandler, Jim Dempsey, Wendy O'Neil, Bryan Lane, Lew Deal, "Judge Julie" Mogenis, "Uncle Joe" and Monika Finch and Tanya Finch, the Wasserman family, Alexandra Selekman, Kathleen Schumacher, Doug Stone, Anthony Guglielmi, Wyatt Smith and Meagan Vargas, I am so grateful for your support. A special recognition goes to Rebecca Woolson of the AFF who compiled and annotated the comprehensive and remarkably accessible resource section of this book.

Many contributors and others also acted as editors and advisers, making invaluable suggestions and introductions to both peers and veterans. Jim Mitchell, Alice Psirakis, Ivy Scricco, Barbara Tiner, Dennis Stone and Debra Ruh of TecAcess, Theresa Rankin, National Community Educator of Brainline/WETA, PBS, Jon Dodson of the WRAMC Wounded Warrior Mentor Program, Combat Stress Officer Lt. Colonel Cynthia Rasmussen and Dr. Barbara Romberg, President and Founder of Give an Hour, thank you.

Bill Yamanaka championed this project to Army Brigadier General Loree K. Sutton and her excellent staff at the Defense Centers for

Excellence in Psychological Health and Traumatic Brain Injury, and thanks to Bill, Colonel Chris Williams, David Egner, Crystal Colman, Captain Edward Simmer, Commander Anthony A. Arita and Mike Long. To General Sutton, I am humbled by your compassion and depth of understanding of this issue. Thank you for writing a stunning foreword.

I am also grateful to Bill Outlaw of the Department of Veterans Affairs, who gathered together the "best and the brightest" physicians and researchers as contributors, and navigated the book through a maze of clearances and approvals, all the while patiently and politely responding to my "nudging" emails and phone calls "to see how we are coming along." A special thanks also to authors Dr. Mathew J. Friedman and Dr. Laurie B. Slone, who generously offered content from their excellent guidebook, *After the War Zone: A Practical, Guide for Returning Troops and Their Families.*

From the get-go everyone agreed that the proceeds of *Hidden Battles* should go to wounded veterans with TBI and PTSD, but that would not have been possible without an extremely generous and caring publisher. Huge thanks to Casemate Publishing CEO David Farnsworth who took this project without a moment's hesitation, and to Jed Lyons, President of the National Book Network and his wife Blythe who were the conduits to Casemate. To managing editor Steven Smith, my heartfelt thanks for your wisdom, enthusiasm, patience, sense of humor and knowledge of writing and publishing, and for sharing the joys of launching not only books but also daughters. Thanks, also to Casemate marketing guru Tara Lichterman, and the public relations firm of Conway Associates where Paula Conway and Denise Mciver worked wonders to bring attention to this book.

I am as always indebted to my loving husband, Richard, and the lights of my life, my daughters Julia and Emily. I am also infinitely grateful to my father, USAF Colonel (Ret.) Ray Brim, who served his country with honor and valor during WWII as pilot of a B-17 Flying Fortress on 25 missions over Germany. You are and always will be my first patriot. And to my mother, Patricia, who was stricken with polio at age three and yet overcame her disabilities to live eighty-five extraordinarily courageous years, the last twelve of them as an amputee, you taught me resilience. Thank you.

ABOUT THE CONTRIBUTORS

FOREWORD

Army Brigadier General Loree K. Sutton is the highest ranking psychiatrist in the U.S. Army and has served as director of the Defense Centers of Excellence (DCoE) for Psychological Health and Traumatic Brain Injury since November 2007. She also serves as Special Assistant to the Assistant Secretary of Defense for Health Affairs. General Sutton has more than 20 years of leadership experience encompassing a diverse mix of domains: civilian and military; combat and peacekeeping; command and staff; clinical and academic; and policy and education. Before becoming the founding director of DCoE, Sutton was commander of the Carl R. Darnall Army Medical Center at Fort Hood, Texas. She is a graduate of the U.S. Army Command and General Staff College, and a distinguished graduate of the National War College. General Sutton has received numerous awards during her career, including the Legion of Merit, Bronze Star Medal, Defense Meritorious Service Medal, and the Order of Military Medical Merit.

2. DECIDING WHO IS SANE ENOUGH TO FIGHT

Alice Psirakis, LCSW, has worked for the United States Army Reserve from 1999 to 2008 as a Medical Service Corps Social Worker. She was mobilized for Operation Enduring Freedom from 2004 to 2007 to serve as Chief of Behavioral Health Services at Fort Dix, NJ. She currently serves as Director, Veterans and Families Initiative, Jewish Board of Family and Children's Services, developing a mental health program for OIF/OEF veterans and their families in the Bronx, NY. She is also an

Adjunct Instructor at St John's University, Queens, in the Department of Sociology.

4. AMERICA KEEPS ITS PROMISE

Colonel Christopher S. Williams is the Senior Executive Director for Traumatic Brain Injury at the Defense Centers of Excellence for Psychological Health and Traumatic Brain Injury. He is a 1976 graduate of Southwestern Oklahoma State University with a Bachelor of Science degree in Pharmacy. He received his Doctor of Osteopathic Medicine degree from the Oklahoma State University College of Osteopathic Medicine in 1980. Dr. Williams completed a Master of Public Health degree at Harvard University School of Public Health in 1993. He has completed residencies in Aerospace Medicine and Neurology, and a fellowship in Clinical Neurophysiology.

6. HEALING THE HUMAN SPIRIT, HOUR BY HOUR

Barbara Romberg, PhD, President and Founder of Give an Hour, is a licensed clinical psychologist practicing in the Washington, DC area for 16 years, specializing in the diagnosis and treatment of children. She served as an adjunct faculty member at George Washington University, where she participated in the training and supervision of developing clinicians. She received her PhD in clinical psychology from the University of Maryland in 1991, her MA in clinical psychology from the University of Maryland in 1987, and her BA, summa cum laude, in psychology from California State College in 1982.

8. THE VA'S SUICIDE PREVENTION HOTLINE

Janet Kemp, RN, PhD, has had over 20 years experience working with veterans. She currently is the Associate Director for Education and Training at the VISN 2 Center of Excellence (COE) in Canandaigua NY. She also serves as the VA National Suicide Prevention Coordinator. In her Center role she is responsible for provider and patient education in the areas of suicide awareness and prevention, current assessment and treatment strategies, and new findings in the area of suicide and assisting the Center Director in the implementation of Suicide Prevention Programs throughout the VA system. In the National Suicide Prevention Coordinator Lead position, Dr. Kemp directs and advises the suicide prevention coordinators at each local VA and is the national program manager for the VA Suicide Hotline.

10. THE EXPERT CONSULTANTS: OUR PATIENTS

Kelly Petska, PhD, is a licensed staff psychologist in the Polytrauma Transitional Rehabilitation Program (PTRP) on the Polytrauma Team at the Minneapolis VAMC. She works primarily with veterans and active duty servicemen/women who have experienced multiple injuries including Traumatic Brain Injury (TBI), physical injuries, cognitive impairments, and psychological/emotional stressors. Her primary duties at the VA include psychotherapy for groups, individuals, and couples, psychological evaluations, and psychological testing. Clinical areas of interest include posttraumatic stress disorder (PTSD), anger issues, Traumatic Brain Injury (TBI), and emotion regulation. Dr. Petska is also interested in treatment assessment and outcome measures.

Don MacLennan, MA, CCC, is a speech pathologist at the Minneapolis VA Medical Center. He helped establish the first traumatic brain injury team at that facility in 1984. Currently he works in the Polytrauma Transitional Rehabilitation Program (PTRP), a program designed to help people with brain injury regain independence within the community, including return to work or school. His primary duties include provision of group and individual therapies aimed at improving functional cognitive and communication skills. He works collaboratively with program participants and their families to develop cognitive strategies that will support everyday activities for participants with brain injury. He also provides a simulated college experience to prepare young men and women with brain injury for post-secondary education.

12. THE WEAPON OF CHOICE—PATIENCE

Dr. Charles "Chip" West, a psychologist by training, has for over twenty years worked with psychologically traumatized individuals in hospital and community treatment settings. After a three-year stint in Beijing, China as a psychologist consultant to the expatriate community there, he has for the past ten years broadened his background of working with people with psychiatric disabilities to include persons who have diverse cultural orientations and experience. Early in his career, he worked with veterans who served in Vietnam, and has more recently been directing a team that provides psychological support services to civilian contractors working in Iraq and Afghanistan. In his role with the disability-focused organization, TecAccess, Dr. West has designed behavioral health support services for veterans with disabilities who are re-entering the civilian work force.

14. I JUST WANT TO BE BACK IN IRAQ

Alice Psirakis, a licensed clinical social worker, is director of the Veterans and Families Initiative at the Center for Trauma Program Innovation of the Jewish Board of Family and Children's Services in New York City. She is also an adjunct instructor St. John's University. (See Chapter 2 for her further biography.)

16. WINNING HIDDEN BATTLES

Bill Yamanaka works in the communications office on the staff of the Deputy Assistant Secretary of Defense for Force Health Protection and Readiness. As such, he also supported the Defense Centers of Excellence in their communications office. He has a professional background of more than 25 years in the public affairs and strategic communications arena for multiple Defense organizations, the private sector, and as a career Public Affairs Officer in the US Navy. Prior to this health affairs contract work with the Wexford Group International, a CACI company, Bill was a US Army civilian in the Pentagon as the Team Chief for personnel issues in the Operational Planning Division of Army Public Affairs.

18. THE REAL STORY BEHIND YOUR STORY

Rick Levy, PhD, a licensed psychologist in private practice serving an international clientele, has been a pioneer in the field of mind-body medicine since 1976. His groundbreaking work has been featured in various media, including Prime Time Live, FOX News, ABC Radio & Washingtonian Magazine. As a respected clinician and proponent of state-of-the-art mind-body medicine, Dr. Levy has consulted with numerous health organizations, universities, government agencies, the US Congress, and international peacekeeping organizations. Dr. Levy has also served as Chair of the Greater Washington Association for the Advancement of Psychology, Legislative Affairs Chairman of the District of Columbia Psychological Association, and as a member of the American Psychological Association's (APA) Joint Hospital Privileges Task Force. Dr. Levy was awarded a PhD in Clinical Psychology from Duquesne University in 1976.

20. A VETERANS' GUIDE TO MENTAL HEALTH SERVICES IN THE VHA

Dr. Ira Katz is currently Deputy Chief Patient Care Services Officer for

Mental Health. He comes to his VA position after serving as Professor of Psychiatry and Director of Geriatric Psychiatry at the University of Pennsylvania Medical Center, as well as Director of the Mental Illness Research Education and Clinical Center of the Philadelphia VA Medical Center. He was principal investigator of a NIMH-supported Advanced Center for Interventions and Services Research that investigated depression in late life and psychiatric-medical comorbidity. Over the past several years, his research has focused on the integration of mental health services with primary care, and area of major importance to the VA. He has served on numerous professional and scientific societies including the Aging Committee of the Group for the Advancement of Psychiatry, the Public Policy Committee of the Gerontology Society of America, the History Committee of the American College of Neuropsychopharmacology, the Committee of Long Term Care and Treatment for the Elderly, and the Board of Directors of the American Geriatrics Society. He is past President of the American Association of Geriatric Psychiatry, and an associate editor for the American Journal of Geriatric Psychiatry.

Dr. Bradley E. Karlin is Director of Psychotherapy and Psychogeriatrics for the Department of Veterans Affairs, in the VA's Central Office in Washington, DC. He has national responsibility for implementing, overseeing, and evaluating national mental health programs in evidence-based psychotherapy and geriatric mental health care. Dr. Karlin has been actively involved in transforming mental health care in the Veterans Health Administration, and is also Adjunct Associate Professor at the Erickson School of Aging Studies at the University of Maryland, Baltimore County. Dr. Karlin serves as the Secretary of the Society of Clinical Geropsychology of the American Psychological Association. He is also Past Convener of the Mental Health Practice and Aging Formal Interest Group of the Gerontological Society of America and Past Chair of the Public Policy Committee of Psychologists In Long Term Care. Dr. Karlin received his BA in political science and sociology from the University of Michigan, graduating with highest distinction and Phi Beta Kappa. He received his MS and PhD in clinical psychology, from Texas A&M University, where he also completed proficiency in clinical gero-

psychology. Dr. Karlin completed a clinical internship and postdoctoral fellowship in clinical geropsychology at the Veterans Affairs Palo Alto Health Care System. He is a licensed clinical psychologist with special clinical interests in depression, grief and loss, general anxiety, and geropsychology. Dr. Karlin has numerous publications, presentations, and government briefings related to geriatric mental health care access, utilization, and policy.

22. WHY ARE YOU SO ANGRY, MOMMY?
Michael Genhart, PhD, is a clinical psychologist in private practice in San Francisco and Mill Valley, CA. He sees children, adolescents, adults, and couples in his clinical work and provides supervision in local training institutions. Previously, he was Director of Training, Child and Family Therapy at California Pacific Medical Center in San Francisco and worked as a psychologist at the Adolescent Day Treatment Center and the Ann Martin Children's Center.

24. THE MENTAL TRANSCEIVER
Norman McCormack retired in 2006 after 25 years with the Department of Veterans Affairs' (VA) Vet Center program. Norm holds a Masters Degree in Guidance Counseling and a Master of Public Administration degree both through the University of Nebraska at Omaha. Since 1988 Norm has been adjunct faculty at Metropolitan Community College in Omaha, where he teaches courses in the behavioral sciences and in management. He is a veteran of the United States Marine Corps, having served on active duty from April of 1969 through April of 1972.

26. THE FACES BEHIND THE FILES
Barbara Sigford, MD, PhD, is the VHA National Program Director for Physical and Medicine Rehabilitation (PM&R). She is field based in Minneapolis where she also serves as the Director of Physical Medicine and Rehabilitation for the Minneapolis VA Medical Center. In her role as National Director of PM&R, she provides national leadership in the VA for Polytrauma and Traumatic Brain Injury (TBI) rehabilitation programs and services. In her role as Director of PM&R at the Minneapolis VAMC she has taken a leadership role in the establishment of the Minneapolis Polytrauma Rehabilitation Center; the Polytrauma Network Site; the Transitional Rehabilitation Unit; and development of community extended care services for veterans with polytrauma and TBI. She serves as the Clinical Co-Coordinator for the newly established Polytrauma/Blast Related Injury QUERI. From 1999 until 2005, she served as the Director of the CARF accredited Traumatic Brain Injury Program and Compre-

hensive Inpatient Rehabilitation Program at the Minneapolis VAMC. Dr. Sigford is a Clinical Assistant Professor in PM&R at the University of Minnesota. Her primary clinical and research interests are in the area of traumatic brain injury rehabilitation.

28. FAMILIES OF HONOR

Mary Car-Blanchard, OTD, OTR/L, is an independent medical writer, presenter, and consultant with extensive experience in the field of Traumatic Brain Injury and a broad knowledge of medical topics, having worked in the health care field for over 20 years. She is the Former Administrator of Information and Resources for the Brain Injury Association of America and served as an occupational therapist on a TBI neurorehabilitation team. Dr. Car-Blanchard's written work has been published in peer-reviewed journals, national health awareness campaigns, website content, and medical brochures. She previously worked as an occupational therapist on a brain injury rehabilitation team and as a patient education provider for reconstructive and cosmetic surgery team. Dr. Car-Blanchard graduated Summa Cum Laude from Creighton University Medical Center where she earned a Clinical Doctorate and Bachelor's Degree in Occupational Therapy. Creighton University awarded her their prestigious Young Alumni Award in 2004.

30. REALIZING THE PROMISE OF EVIDENCE-BASED PSYCHOTHERAPIES IN THE VHA

Dr. Bradley E. Karlin is Director of Psychotherapy and Psychogeriatrics for the Department of Veterans Affairs at the VA's Central Office in Washington, DC. (See Chapter 20 for his further biography.)

Josef I. Ruzek, PhD, is Director of the Dissemination and Training Division of the National Center for PTSD at the VA Palo Alto Health Care System. Dr. Ruzek is a past member of the (VHA) Undersecretary's Special Committee on PTSD and currently serves on the Board of Directors of the International Society for Traumatic Stress Studies. He is an editor of two editions of Cognitive-Behavioral Therapies for Trauma, and his major current interests are dissemination of evidence-based cognitive-behavioral treatments for PTSD and Internet-based interventions for trauma survivors.

Dr. Kathleen Chard is the Director of the PTSD and Anxiety Disorders Division at the Cincinnati VA Medical Center and Associate Professor of Clinical Psychiatry at the University of Cincinnati. Dr. Chard is a co-author of the Cognitive Procession Therapy: Veteran Military treatment manual and she has conducted extensive funded research on the assessment and treatment of PTSD.

32. FALLING THROUGH THE CRACKS

Lieutenant Colonel Cynthia Rasmussen has served as a mental health nurse in the Army Reserves for 20 years. She is currently serving her third year of mobilization to support the Global War on Terror. An Adult Nurse Practitioner on leave from the Veterans Administration she now works as a Combat Stress officer and Sexual Assault Response coordinator for the 88th RRC. LTC Rasmussen recently spoke at the Veterans Affairs National Polytrauma Conference and has testified before the Senate Committee on Veterans Affairs as well as at Veterans Hospitals and Centers across the country. She received the MOPH Honorary Service Award from the Military Order of the Purple Heart National Service Officer Training. She earned both her Bachelor's and Master's Degrees in Nursing from Marquette University.

34. TENDING, ATTENDING AND HEALING

Dr. Joseph Bobrow, Roshi, MD, PhD, is the founder and director of Deep Streams Zen Institute. A Zen master in the Diamond Sangha tradition, he is also a clinical psychologist and a relational psychoanalyst. Joseph writes on Zen, psychotherapy, and the interplay of Buddhism and psychology. He is also the founder of the Coming Home Project.

36. THE BATTLE FOR LOVE

Mitchell Tepper, PhD, MPH, is Assistant Project Director at The Center of Excellence for Sexual Health, and Research Assistant Professor of Pediatrics, Series II at Morehouse School of Medicine, under the Satcher Health Leadership Institute. He is also the Founder and President of The Sexual Health Network, Inc. and SexualHealth.com. He is a pioneer in the delivery of sexual health information online, an American Association of Sexuality Educators, Counselors and Therapists (AASECT) Certified Sexuality Educator and Counselor, and a nationally recognized researcher, author, and advocate dedicated to ending the silence around issues of sexuality and disability. His years of research at Yale, Rutgers and the University of Pennsylvania have served as the basis for numerous professional, academic and public presentations. He currently serves on the editorial boards of the journals *Sexuality and Disability* and the

American Journal of Sexuality Education and on the board of directors of the Institute for the Study of Disadvantage and Disability and The Women's Sexual Health Foundation. Dr. Tepper has a Master of Public Health from Yale University and a PhD in Human Sexuality Education from the University of Pennsylvania.

38. FACING OUR FEARS

Barbara Romberg, MD, President and Founder Give an Hour, is a licensed clinical psychologist, practicing in the Washington, DC., area for 16 years, specializing in the diagnosis and treatment of children. Dr. Romberg served as an adjunct faculty member at George Washington University, where she participated in the training and supervision of developing clinicians. She received her Ph.D. in clinical psychology from the University of Maryland in 1991, her MA in clinical psychology from the University of Maryland in 1987, and her BA, summa cum laude, in psychology from California State College in 1982.

40. THE ROAD BACK TO SELF

Dr. David Carroll is the Director of Recovery Services in the Office of Mental Health Services in the VA's Central Office. He is responsible for the national network of local recovery coordinators who guide the transformation of VA mental health services into a recovery-based system of care. Dr. Carroll began his career at the VA Medical Center in Milwaukee where he served in various roles including program manager for the mental health rehabilitation treatment program and Lead Psychologist. He earned his PhD in clinical psychology from Ohio University and is a graduate of the VHA Executive Career Field Development Program.

42. PREPARING OURSELVES TO HELP WITH THE JOURNEY HOME

Barbara J. Tiner lives in western Massachusetts with her husband, three children and assorted animals. In addition to running an environmental education and training company, she is on the board of the Veterans Education Project (VEP), a 26-year-old group who trains veterans to share their stories and life lessons in western New England classrooms and communities. Through VEP she helped start a support group for military families and is working with faith communities to provide ongoing support to veterans and their families, as well as to educate others on the issues our troops face on their journey home.

REFERENCES FOR CHAPTER 30

Butler, A.C., Chapman, J.E., Forman, E.M., & Beck, A.T. "The empirical status of cognitive-behavioral therapy: A review of meta-analyses." *Clinical Psychology Review*, 26 (2006), 17–31.

Chard, K.M. "An evaluation of cognitive processing therapy for the treatment of posttraumatic stress disorder related to childhood sexual abuse." *Journal of Consulting and Clinical Psychology*, 73 (2005), 965–971.

Edwards, D. "Transforming the VA." *Behavioral Healthcare*, 28 (2008), 15–17.

Foa, E.B., Hembree, E.A. & Rothbaum, B.O. *Prolonged Exposure Therapy for PTSD: Emotional Processing of Traumatic Experiences.* New York: Oxford University Press, 2007.

Goisman, R.M., Warshaw, M.G., & Keller, M.B. "Psychosocial treatment prescriptions for Generalized Anxiety Disorder, Panic Disorder, and Social Phobia, 1991–1996." *American Journal of Psychiatry*, 156 (1999), 1819–1821.

Institute of Medicine. *Treatment of Posttraumatic Stress Disorder: An Assessment of the Evidence.* Washington, DC: National Academies Press, 2007.

Monson, C.M., Schnurr, P.P., Resick, P.A., Friedman, M.J., Young-Xu, Y., & Stevens, S.P. "Cognitive processing therapy for veterans with military-related posttraumatic stress disorder." *Journal of Consulting and Clinical Psychology*, 74 (2006), 898–907.

Resick, P.A., Monson, C.M., & Chard, K.M. *Cognitive processing therapy: Veteran/military version.* Washington, DC: Department of Veterans Affairs, 2007.

Resick, P.A., Nishith, P., Weaver, T.L., Astin, M.C., & Feurer, C.A. "A comparison of cognitive-processing therapy with prolonged exposure and a waiting condition for the treatment of chronic posttraumatic stress disorder in female rape victims." *Journal of Consulting and Clinical Psychology*, 70 (2002), 867–879.

Rosen, C.S., Chow, H.C., Finney, J.F, Greenbaum, M.A., Moos, R.H., Sheikh, J.I., & Yesavage, J.A. "VA practice patterns and practice guidelines for treating Posttraumatic Stress Disorder." *Journal of Traumatic Stress*, 17 (2004), 213–222.

Schnurr, P.P., Friedman, M.J., Engel, C.C, Foa, E.B., Shea, M.T., Chow, B.K., Resick, P.A., Thurston, V., Orsillo, S.M., Haug, R., Turner, C.,

& Bernardy, N. "Cognitive-behavioral therapy for posttraumatic stress disorder in women: A randomized controlled trial." *Journal of the American Medical Association*, 297 (2007), 820–830.

Willenbring, M. L., Kivlahan, D., Kenny, M., Grillo, M., Hagedorn, H., & Postier, A. "Beliefs about evidence-based practices in addiction treatment: A survey of Veterans Administration program leaders." *Journal of Substance Abuse Treatment*, 26 (2004), 79–85.

RESOURCES FOR MILITARY SERVICE MEMBERS AND FAMILIES

CONTENTS

EMPLOYMENT AND CAREER SUPPORT/ TRANSITION TO CIVILIAN WORKFORCE

DoD TransPortal—Transition Assistance Program
Website designed specifically to assist service members leaving active duty by providing information and resources to help in the transition period.
www.dodtransportal.dod.mil

Vet Centers
Vet Centers provide readjustment counseling and a wide range of services for veterans transitioning from military to civilian life. The counseling is provided at community-based "Vet Centers" located near vet-

erans and their families. Find locations on the website or in your local blue pages.
East Coast: 1-800-905-4675
West Coast: 1-866-496-8838
http://www.vetcenter.va.gov/

Career Center for the Military Severely Injured Center
This website provides a search engine of veteran-friendly employers.
www.military.com/support

Employer Support of the Guard and Reserves (ESGR)
ESGR promotes cooperation and understanding between the Reserves and their civilian employers and helps to resolve conflicts between a Reservist's military commitments.
(800) 336-4590
USERRA@osd.mil
www.esgr.org

Department of Labor Veteran's Employment and Training Service (VETS)
VETS provides transitioning service members and veterans resources and services that will help them succeed in the workforce.
1-866-4-USA-DOL (1-866-487-2365)
www.dol.gov/vets

HireVetsFirst
HireVetsFirst works to connect veterans, human resource specialists and managers to match employment opportunities.
202-693-4700
www.hirevetsfirst.gov

National Partnership for Workplace Mental Health
The Center for the Study of Traumatic Stress provides information and training to prepare for and respond to the psychological effects and health consequences of traumatic events.
www.usuhs.mil/csts

Operation Healthy Reunions
This website offers tips for service members returning home to their pre-

deployment jobs. The transition can be difficult for the individual and workplace.
(703) 684-7722
www.mentalhealthamerica.net/reunions/infoReturnWork.cfm

Transition Assistance
Transition Assistance Online is a database with transition assistance information and tools for service members going from their military to civilian careers.
www.taonline.com

Turbo Tap
Website offers transition support for Active Duty, Guard and Reserves; also offers to help build a "Transition Plan."
www.transitionassistanceprogram.com/register.tpp

VA's Compensated Work Therapy Program
The CWT works with business and industry to promote employment opportunities for veterans with physical and mental disabilities. There are CWT locations across the country. Specific contact information for different locations can be found on the website below.
www.va.gov/Vetind

Vet Success
This website provides information on the services of the Vocational Rehabilitation and Employment program and vocational counseling for active duty and veterans.
http://vetsuccess.symplicity.com

FINANCIAL ASSISTANCE (Housing, Essential Needs, Food, etc.)

Armed Forces Relief Trust
AFR Trust distributes interest-free loans and grants to service members and their families that are in need.
www.afrtrust.org

Army Emergency Relief
AER is financial assistance organization for soldiers, active and retired,

and their dependents when there is a valid need.
703-428-0000
www.aerhq.org

Navy-Marine Corps Relief Society
NMCRS provides financial, educational and other assistance to members of the Naval Services of the U.S., family members, and survivors that are in need.
(877) 272-7337
www.nmcrs.org

Air Force Aid Society
AFAS provides aid to Air Force members and their families and assists with the finance of education.
1-800-769-8951
www.afas.org

Coast Guard Mutual Assistance
CGMA provides financial assistance to the Coast Guard community.
(800) 881-2462
www.cgmahq.org

American Red Cross
The Red Cross works to provide emergency communications between military members and their families, access to financial assistance, and assistance to veterans.
800-733-2767
www.redcross.org — Follow link "Military Members and Families"

Food Allowance
Basic Allowance for Subsistence (BAS) is meant to offset the cost of meals for a service member. Most enlisted members get a full BAS: $326.87/month; Officers receive $223.04/month.
www.military.com/benefits/military-pay/basic-allowance-for-subsistence

Housing Allowance
Basic Allowance for Housing (BAH) is to provide uniformed service members housing compensation based on costs in civilian housing mar-

kets and is due when government housing is not provided.
http://perdiem.hqda.pentagon.mil/perdiem

The Fisher House program
Fisher House provides homes for families of patients receiving medical care at military and VA medical centers.
(301) 294-8560   (888) 294-8560
www.fisherhouse.org
info@fisherhouse.org

Defense Finance and Accounting Service (DFAS)
DFAS provides accounting and finance services for the military departments and defense agencies.
www.dod.mil/dfas

FAQs on Debt
The website below offers answers to frequently asked questions on debt and bankruptcy.
www.dfas.mil/militarypay/debt/frequentlyaskedquestions.html

Personal Finance Assistance for Vets
The website below offers advice on personal finances.
www.transitionassistanceprogram.com/portal/transition/lifestyles/Personal_Finances

VA Guaranteed Home Loan
The website below has information on the VA's guaranteed home loan and also offers advice on buying a home.
www.military.com/Finance/HomeBuying

Homeless Veterans
Information on the VA's program of treatment and services for homeless veterans.
1-800-827-1000   www1.va.gov/homeless

myPay
myPay allows service members to manage pay information, leave, earning statements, W-2s, and more.
https://mypay.dfas.mil/mypay.aspx

FINDING HELP AND INFORMATION

Outreach Center for Psychological Health and Traumatic Brain Injury
The Outreach Center is open 24-hours to provide information and referrals to service members, veterans, their families and others with questions about TBI and psychological health.
1-866-966-1020
resources@dcoeoutreach.org
www.dcoe.health.mil

National Center for Post Traumatic Stress Disorder
The National Center for PTSD is a center of excellence for research and information on the prevention, understanding and treatment of PTSD.
PTSD Information Line: (802) 296-6300
Email: ncptsd@va.gov
www.ncptsd.va.gov

Veterans for America
Veterans for America compiled *The American Veterans and Servicemembers Survival Guide* to help guide through bureaucracy and find the help one needs and deserves. The Guide can be viewed online:
http://www.veteransforamerica.org/wp-content/uploads/2007/12/survivalguide1.pdf

Walter Reed Army Medical Center Behavioral Health Clinic
The Behavioral Health Clinic is an adult mental health service with providers in psychiatry, psychology and social work.
(202) 782-6061
www.wramc.army.mil

Operation Comfort
Operation Comfort is a nationwide network of mental health professionals and agencies that provide their services free of charge to the family members of those serving in the Middle East.
1-866-632-7868
http://operationcomfort.com/

National Alliance on Mental Illness (NAMI)
NAMI works at local, state and national levels to provide support,

information, referral and advocacy resources on mental health issues. There is a section specifically for Veterans resources.
Main: 703-524-7600
Help Line: 800-950-NAMI (6264)
www.nami.org
Email: info@nami.org

Military OneSource
Military OneSource offers short-term, nonmedical counseling services to active-duty, Guard, and Reserve members and their families.

The types of counseling are face-to-face, telephone and online consultations.
1-800-342-9647
www.militaryonesource.com
Click on "counseling" link

SAMSHA's National Mental Health Information Center
SAMSHA's National Mental Health Information Center was developed to provide information about mental health services. Staff can quickly direct calls to Federal, State and local organizations that work to treat and prevent mental illness.
1-800-789-2647
http://mentalhealth.samhsa.gov/
Mental Health Services Locator
http://mentalhealth.samhsa.gov/databases/

American Veterans with Brain Injuries (AVBI)
AVBI is dedicated to supporting the families of American service members and veterans who have a brain injury. AVBI is a web-based peer support network.
www.avbi.org

The Anxiety Disorders Association of America (ADAA)
ADAA provides information and resources on anxiety disorders. ADAA also provides a tool to find local therapists.
240-485-1001
Website: www.adaa.org
Find therapists: www.adaa.org/GettingHelp/FindATherapist.asp
Find a support group: www.adaa.org/GettingHelp/SupportGroups.asp

The Association for Behavioral and Cognitive Therapies (ABCT)
ABCT provides a "Find-a-Therapist" service that gives access to therapists practicing cognitive and behavioral techniques.
(212) 647-1890
http://www.abct.org/members/Directory/Find_A_Therapist.cfm

Deployment Health Clinical Center (DHCC)
DHCC is a comprehensive source of deployment-related health information for service members, veterans and their families and healthcare providers.
1-800-796-9699
www.pdhealth.mil

Give an Hour
Give an Hour is an organization that provides free mental health services to OEF and OIF veterans and their families.
www.giveanhour.org
email: info@giveanhour.org

The National Institute of Mental Health (NIMH)
NIMH researches to better understand, treat, and prevent mental disorders and to promote mental health.
301-443-4513   1-866-615-6464
www.nimh.nih.gov

Homecoming: Resilience after Wartime
The American Psychological Association offers a brochure on "10 Tips for Resilience in a Time of War."
www.apahelpcenter.org/featuredtopics/feature.php?id=43

Controlling Anger Before It Controls You
Below is an American Psychological Association website on anger and anger management.
800-374-2721
www.apa.org/topics/controlanger.html

Department of Defense Deployment Health Clinical Center
The website serves as an introduction to traumatic brain injury and the

military's policies and directives in regard to TBI.
www.pdhealth.mil/TBI.asp

Defense and Veterans Brain Injury Center (DVBIC)
The DVBIC serves active duty military, their dependents and veterans with TBI through medical care, clinical research initiatives and educational programs.
1-800-870-9244
Email: info@dvbic.org
www.dvbic.org

National Brain Injury Information Center
The number below connects callers to local brain injury services in Minnesota, Michigan and Mississippi.
1-800-444-6443
http://www.biausa.org/BIAUSA.ORG/word.files.to.pdf/good.pdfs/NBBI
Cannouncement2.pdf

DoD Transition Assistance Program
This website provides comprehensive information on the DoD Transition Assistance Program.
www.dodtransportal.dod.mil/dav/lsnmedia/LSN/dodtransportal/op.htm

The Rape, Abuse, and Incest National Network
RAINN is an anti-sexual assault organization with free and confidential services, and works to educate people about sexual assault and its prevention.
1-800-656-HOPE
www.rainn.org

Sleepnet
Sleepnet provides information on sleep disorders.
www.sleepnet.com

Alcohol and Drug Treatment Center Referral
The number below connects the caller to a provider of referrals to local facilities where adolescents and adults can seek help.
1-800-821-4357

National Institute of Drug Abuse (NIDA)
The website provides educational materials on drug abuse.
Treatment Referral: 1-800-662-HELP
www.nida.nih.gov

The Partnership for a Drug-Free America
The Partnership works to motivate and equip parents to prevent their children from using drugs and alcohol, and to help find treatment for those in trouble.
(212) 922-1560
www.drugfree.org/Intervention

National Suicide Prevention Lifeline
The number below was founded by the Department of Veterans Affairs to ensure that veterans have free 24/7 access to trained counselors.
1-800-273-TALK (8255), and press "1" to be routed to the Veterans Hotline.
http://www.suicidepreventionlifeline.org/Veterans/Default.aspx

VA Military Sexual Trauma Coordinator
VA Medical centers have healthcare professionals that can help veterans cope with and work through a sexual trauma experience.
1-800-827-1000
http://www1.va.gov/wvhp/page.cfm?pg=20

Military Sexual Trauma on Miltary.com
The website below offers information on sexual trauma and its effects.
www.military.com/benefits/veterans-health-care/sexual-trauma

Dare to Know
The website below is an introduction to Dr. Rick Levy's work on mind-body medicine. His book and TV show, *Miraculous Health*, provide steps for the reader to use to heal themselves from body and mind ailments.
http://drr-daretoknow.com/

The Coming Home Project
The Coming Home Project is a nonprofit organization led by veterans, psychotherapists and interfaith leaders committed to providing care,

support and stress management tools for OEF/OIF veterans.
415-353-5363
http://www.cominghomeproject.net/ComingHome/

Army Wounded Soldier and Family Hotline
The Army started the hotline to offer wounded soldiers and family members a way to seek help and to resolve medical issues. The hotline also serves as an avenue for soldiers to voice their experiences with the medical care system.
1-800-984-8523

Wounded Warrior Project (WWP)
WWP works to honor and empower wounded warriors by: raising awareness about the needs of severely injured service men and women; growing a sense of community among the severely injured; and providing programs that meet their needs.
1-877-832-6997
www.woundedwarriorproject.org/index.php

HEALTH/MEDICAL BENEFITS AND INSURANCE

Military.com
The website offers wide-reaching resources for service members, their families and veterans, including benefits, scholarships, networking, discounts, financial advice, news, etc.
www.military.com
The website below provides comprehensive information on Veteran disability compensation.
1-800-827-1000
www.military.com/benefits/military-pay/va-disability-compensation

Deployment LINK
This website provides information about the health care of service members and their families.
http://deploymentlink.osd.mil

Department of Labor Employee Benefits Security Administration
The website below provides answers to frequently asked questions for

reservists being called to active duty.
www.dol.gov/ebsa/faqs/faq_911_2.html

Family Service Members' Group Life Insurance (FSGLI)
FSGLI is a program that extends to the spouses and dependent children of members insured by SGLI.
1-800-419-1473
www.insurance.va.gov/sgliSite/FSGLI/sglifam.htm
osgli.osgli@prudential.com

Service Members' Group Life Insurance (SGLI)
SGLI is life insurance for service members and veterans who may not be able to get private or commercial insurance because of the extra risks of military service.
1-800-419-1473
www.insurance.va.gov/index.htm

Traumatic Injury Protection Under Service Members' Group Life Insurance (TSGLI)
TSGLI is for service members who are severely injured (on or off duty) as the result of a traumatic event and suffer a loss that qualifies for payment under TSGLI.
www.insurance.va.gov/sgliSite/TSGLI/TSGLI.htm

MORALE, WELFARE AND RECREATION (MWR)

Army MWR
Army MWR is a comprehensive network of support and leisure activities to enhance morale and the lives of service members and their families.
www.armymwr.com

Air Force MWR
The Air Force MWR has service programs that provide essential food, fitness, lodging, recreation and services for military members.
www.afsv.af.mil

Coast Guard MWR
The Coast Guard MWR website has information on activities, sports, recreation lodging, travel and other services.
www.uscg.mil/mwr

Navy MWR
The Navy MWR website has information on fleet and family recreation, fleet readiness, MWR food and beverages, cabins and RV parks, child and youth programs, etc.
www.mwr.navy.mil

Marine Corps Community Services
MCCS provides information on family life, retiree life, recreation/fitness, shopping, etc.
www.usmc-mccs.org

Armed Forces Vacation Club (AFVC)
AFVC is a program that offers DoD affiliated personnel affordable condominium vacations around the world.
1-800-724-9988
www.afvclub.com

Space-Available and Space-Required Travel
Space-available travel allows authorized personnel DoD aircraft seats that are not occupied after "space-required" travelers have been accommodated.
www.militarypay.com/SpaceAvailableTravel.html

Operation Hero Miles and The Fisher House
Operation Hero Miles and The Fisher House partnered for a program that allows troops stationed in Iraq and Afghanistan to fly home for free. The program also allows family members of wounded servicemembers to fly for free to visit their loved one recovering in VA hospitals across the country.
(888) 294-8560
www.heromiles.org
http://www.fisherhouse.org/programs/heroMiles.shtml

SUPPORT FOR LOVED ONES

Battlemind
The website offers informational tools and guidance to the different stages that service members and their families face.
https://www.battlemind.army.mil/
Email: Battlemind@amedd.army.mil

Operation Comfort
Operation Comfort is a nationwide network of mental health professionals and agencies that provide their services free of charge to the family members of those serving in the Middle East.
Phone: 1-866-632-7868
http://operationcomfort.com/

Tragedy Assistance Program for Survivors (TAPS)
TAPS is a resource providing support, comfort and information for those grieving the death of a loved one that occurred in the line of duty.
1-800-959-TAPS (8277)
www.taps.org
Email: info@taps.org

Military Child Education Coalition (MCEC)
MCEC is works to ensure quality education for all military children affected by mobility, family separation and transition.
(254) 953-1923
www.militarychild.org

National Association of Child Care Resource and Referral Agencies (NACCRRA)
NACCRRA and the DoD are partnered to help service members find and afford child care that is suited to their unique needs.
703-341-4100
1-800-424-2246
http://www.naccrra.org/MilitaryPrograms/

Talk, Listen, Connect DVD
Sesame Workshop created "Talk, Listen, Connect," a DVD, as a bilingual educational outreach initiavite to help young military children

deal with deployments, homecoming and changes.
To order the free kit, visit Military OneSource:
www.militaryonesource.com
DVD Website: www.sesameworkshop.org/tlc

Family Readiness
The DoD has created integrated family readiness and support programs to provide information to all service members and their families to ensure they are prepared for short- and long-term deployments. The website below offers resources for families facing a deployment.
www.defenselink.mil/ra/html/familyreadiness.html

Military Homefront
The official DoD website for "Military Community and Family Policy" program information, policy and guidance for the troops and their families.
www.militaryhomefront.dod.mil

Military Spouse Career Center
A website that provides job search support for military spouses and the unique challenges they face.
www.military.com/spouse

Military Spouses' Career Network
MSCN is a website that promotes the education, employment and career development of military spouses and offers information to achieve its end.
www.mscn.org

National Toll-free Domestic Violence Hotline
NDVH provides crisis intervention, information and referral to victims of domestic violence, perpetrators, friends and families.
1-800-799-SAFE (7233)
www.ndvh.org

Military Impacted Schools Association
MISA is an organization of school superintendents that wish to help educators provide resources and guidance for the unique needs of the children of military families.

(800) 291-6472
www.militaryimpactedschoolsassociation.org

Army One Source

Army One Source is an integrated family support network for Army families and soldiers that provides a vast array of advice and information.
www.myarmylifetoo.com

Lifelines—Answers for Sailors, Marines & their families

Lifelines offers advice and information on the different stages of military life with a focus on Navy personnel and their families.
www.lifelines.navy.mil

Marine Corps Community Services

The MCCS family life site offers support for the spouses and families of Marines and offers a variety of programs that help build strong famlies.
www.usmc-mccs.org/family/

Air Force Crossroads

The official community website of the U.S. Air Force offers forums, information and advice for Air Force families.
www.afcrossroads.com

Department of Defense Deployment Health and Family Readiness Library

The library provides information and resources on deployment health and family readiness.
http://deploymenthealthlibrary.fhp.osd.mil/home.jsp

Family Matters

The website below has resources and guidebooks for the family members of deployed service members.
www.hooah4health.com/deployment/familymatters

Fleet and Family Support Division

The Fleet and Family Support programs offer commands, sailors and family members access to programs focused on adaptation to the special demands of military life.

www.npc.navy.mil/CommandSupport/CommunitySupportProgramPoli
cies/fleet.htm

Military and Family Life Consultants (MFLC)
MFLC provides consultations to individuals, couples, families, and
groups for support and assistance.
(254) 288-0400
www.hoodmwr.com/ACS/sfrb_mflc.html

National Guard Bureau Family Program
A resource for National Guard families which provides information on
programs, benefits, resources and more.
703-607-5414
www.guardfamily.org

Veterans and Families Coming Home
This non-profit organization serves to help families of returning veterans in their transition and to ensure that families stay together and stay
strong.
www.veteransandfamilies.org/home.html

Virtual Family Readiness Program
Army FRRG is a direct connection to Command information for a soldier's unit. Online tools include forums, video email, telephone tree, and
photo gallery.
www.armyfrg.org

Military Spouse Center
Military Spouse Center is a resource library for spouse employment,
education, and relocation information.
www.milspouse.org

VETERANS SERVICE ORGANIZATIONS

America Supports You
The website below has an extensive list of organizations sorted by the
type of aid they give to veterans.
www.americasupportsyou.mil/americasupportsyou/help.html

Directory of Veterans Service Organizations
An extensive list of VSOs developed by the Department of Veterans Affairs.
www1.va.gov/vso/index.cfm

American Legion
The American Legion is a war-time veterans organization with a variety of programs and benefits for its members.
(317) 630-1200
www.legion.org

AMVETS
AMVETS provide fellow veterans with support, professional advice, legislative efforts on Capitol Hill and other services.
www.amvets.org

Disabled American Veterans (DAV)
DAV is dedicated to building better lives for disabled veterans and their families through services and advocacy.
877-I Am A Vet *(877-426-2838)*
www.dav.org

Iraq and Afghanistan Veterans of America (IAVA)
IAVA works to improve the lives and advocate on behalf of Iraq and Afghanistan veterans and their families.
212-982-9699
202-544-7692
www.iava.org

Paralyzed Veterans of America (PVA)
PVA works to improve the quality of life of its members and is a leading advocate for health care, spinal cord injury/disease research and education, veterans' benefits and rights, and disability rights.
1-800-555-9140
www.pva.org

Veterans of Foreign Wars (VFW)
The VFW is a war veterans organization that lobbies Congress for better health care and benefits. VFW has a variety of programs that extend

beyond veterans helping veterans.
(816) 756-3390
www.vfw.org

Vietnam Veterans of America (VVA)

VVA works to promote and support issues specifically important to veterans of the Vietnam War and to change public perception of Vietnam veterans.
800-VVA-1316
www.vva.org

GENERAL RESOURCES

Military OneSource

Military OneSource has a wide range of resources for service members and their families.
1-800-342-9647
www.militaryonesource.com

State Guard

The home page of the State Guard with links to individual states.
www.sgaus.org/States.htm

U.S. Air Force

The website of the United States Air Force.
www.af.mil

U.S. Air Force Reserve Command

The website of the United States Air Force Reserve Command.
www.afrc.af.mil

U.S. Air National Guard

The website of the United States Air National Guard.
www.ang.af.mil

U.S. Army

The website of the United States Army.
www.army.mil

U.S. Army National Guard
The website of the United States Army National Guard.
www.arng.army.mil

U.S. Army Reserve
The website of the United States Army Reserve.
www.armyreserve.army.mil

U.S. Coast Guard
The website of the United States Coast Guard.
www.uscg.mil

U.S. Coast Guard Reserve
The website of the United States Coast Guard Reserve.
www.uscg.mil/reserve

U.S. Marines
The website of the United States Marine Corps.
www.usmc.mil

U.S. Navy
The website of the United States Navy.
www.navy.mil

U.S. Navy Reserve
The website of the United States Navy Reserve.
www.marforres.usmc.mil

VA Services
The website of the United States Department of Veterans Affairs.
www.va.gov

VHA: Veterans Health Administration
The website of the United States Veterans Health Administration.
www1.va.gov/health

VBA: Veterans Benefits Administration
The website of the Veterans Benefits Administration.
www.vba.va.gov